Intelligent Automation with VMware

Apply machine learning techniques to VMware virtualization and networking

Ajit Pratap Kundan

BIRMINGHAM - MUMBAI

Intelligent Automation with VMware

Commissioning Editor: Amey Varangaonkar
Acquisition Editor: Reshma Raman
Content Development Editor: Kirk Dsouza
Technical Editor: Jovita Alva
Copy Editor: Safis Editing
Project Coordinator: Namrata Swetta
Proofreader: Safis Editing
Indexer: Pratik Shirodkar
Graphics: Alishon Mendonsa
Production Coordinator: Aparna Bhagat

First published: March 2019

Production reference: 1290319

Published by Packt Publishing Ltd.
Livery Place
35 Livery Street
Birmingham
B3 2PB, UK.

ISBN 978-1-78980-216-0

www.packtpub.com

`mapt.io`

Mapt is an online digital library that gives you full access to over 5,000 books and videos, as well as industry leading tools to help you plan your personal development and advance your career. For more information, please visit our website.

Why subscribe?

- Spend less time learning and more time coding with practical eBooks and Videos from over 4,000 industry professionals

- Improve your learning with Skill Plans built especially for you

- Get a free eBook or video every month

- Mapt is fully searchable

- Copy and paste, print, and bookmark content

Packt.com

Did you know that Packt offers eBook versions of every book published, with PDF and ePub files available? You can upgrade to the eBook version at `www.packt.com` and as a print book customer, you are entitled to a discount on the eBook copy. Get in touch with us at `customercare@packtpub.com` for more details.

At `www.packt.com`, you can also read a collection of free technical articles, sign up for a range of free newsletters, and receive exclusive discounts and offers on Packt books and eBooks.

Contributors

About the author

Ajit Pratap Kundan stands at the leading edge of the most innovative cloud technology in the world. He has helped position VMware as a leader in the private cloud area in relation to his federal government customers through an SDDC approach. An innovative techy with 18+ years of industry experience, he has promoted technologies to his government and defense customers.

Ajit is a valued writer on cloud technologies and has authored one book, *VMware Cross-Cloud Architecture*, published by Packt. He currently resides in Delhi, India, with his wife, Archana, and their two sons, Aaradhya and Akshansh.

I would like to give deep thanks and gratitude to my VMware and partner colleagues, along with their customers, for their guidance and suggestions.

About the reviewers

James Bowling is a cloud infrastructure architect/engineer, VCIX-DCV/CMA, VCP-DTM, VMware vExpert (x7), Cisco Champion – Datacenter(x3), EMC Elect(x2), DFW VMUG Leader, and virtualization enthusiast located in Dallas, Texas, with over 18 years' experience. His experience ranges from designing, deploying, and maintaining virtualized infrastructures, while utilizing different types of technology, to automation and scaling resources.

He also maintains a personal blog focusing on virtualization, *vSential (dot) com*.

He has spoken at the following events:

- Veeam User Group
- Veeam Whiteboard Friday
- VMware User Group (VMUG)
- VMworld (US/EMEA)
- Interop – Las Vegas (Virtualization and Data Center Architecture Track Chair)

Martin Gavanda has more than 10 years' experience, mainly in connection with service providers offering IaaS solutions based on VMware vSphere products. He was responsible for the design and implementation of IaaS solutions in the Central Europe region.

Currently, he is working as an independent cloud architect, focusing on large infrastructure projects and practicing as a VMware instructor. For the past year, he has led more than a dozen on-site VMware workshops. He has created several virtual classes focusing on the VMware vSphere platform, with thousands of students subscribed, and he runs his own blog regarding virtualization and the cloud.

Packt is searching for authors like you

If you're interested in becoming an author for Packt, please visit `authors.packtpub.com` and apply today. We have worked with thousands of developers and tech professionals, just like you, to help them share their insight with the global tech community. You can make a general application, apply for a specific hot topic that we are recruiting an author for, or submit your own idea.

Table of Contents

Preface   1

Section 1: VMware Approach with ML Technology

Chapter 1: Machine Learning Capabilities with vSphere 6.7   9
  Technical requirements   10
  ML and VMware   10
    ML-based data analysis   10
      Using virtualized GPUs with ML   11
  Modes of GPU usage   13
    Comparing ML workloads to GPU configurations   13
      DirectPath I/O   14
      Scalability of GPU in a virtual environment   15
      Containerized ML applications inside a VM   16
      vGPU scheduling and vGPU profile selection   17
        Power user and designer profiles   18
        Knowledge and task user profiles   18
        Adding vGPU hosts to a cluster with vGPU Manager   18
  ML with NVIDIA GPUs   19
    Pool and farm settings in Horizon   19
    Configuring hardware-accelerated graphics   22
      Virtual shared graphics acceleration   23
      Configuring vSGA settings in a virtual machine   24
      Virtual machine settings for vGPU   24
        GRID vPC and GRID vApps capabilities   27
        GRID vWS to Quadro vDWS   28
  Summary   31
  Further reading   32

Chapter 2: Proactive Measures with vSAN Advanced Analytics   33
  Technical requirements   33
  Application scalability on vSAN   34
    Storage and network assessment   34
      Storage design policy   35
        VMware best practices recommendations   35
      Network design policy   37
        VMware best practices recommendations   38
        VMware's Customer Experience Improvement Program/vSAN ReadyCare   39
  Intelligent monitoring   40
    General monitoring practices   41
      vSAN Health Check plugin   41
      vSAN Observer   42
      vRealize Operations Manager monitoring   42

Challenges affecting business outcomes   43
Business benefits   43
Technical Issues   44
Technical solution   44
Log Intelligence advantages   44

HA configuration in stretched clusters   45
Two-node clusters   46
Witness appliance for the vSAN cluster   46
Configuring the vSAN cluster   47

vSAN policy design with SPBM   50
Defining a policy based on business objectives   50
FTT policy with RAID configurations   52

Summary   53
Further reading   53

Chapter 3: Security with Workspace ONE Intelligence   55
Technical requirements   56
Workspace ONE Intelligence   56
Business objectives of Workspace ONE Intelligence   57
Integrated deep insights   58
App analytics for smart planning   59
Intelligent automation driven by decision engines   60
Design requirements   61
Conceptual designs   62
Top ten use cases of Workspace ONE Intelligence   68
Identifying and mitigating mobile OS vulnerabilities   68
Insights into Windows 10 OS updates and patches   69
Predicting Windows 10 Dell battery failures and automating replacement   69
Identifying unsupported OS versions and platforms   69
Tracking OS upgrade progress   70
Monitoring device utilization or usage   70
Increasing compliance across Windows 10 devices   71
Comprehensive mobile app deployment visibility   71
Tracking migration and adoption of productivity applications   72
Adopting internal mobile applications   72

Workspace ONE Trust Network   73
Workspace ONE AirLift   74
Workspace ONE platform updates   74
Expanded Win32 app delivery   75
Simplified macOS adoption   75
Extended security for Microsoft Office 365 (O365) applications   75
VMware Boxer with Intelligent Workflows   75
Extended management for rugged devices   76

Summary   76

Chapter 4: Proactive Operations with VMware vRealize Suite   77
Technical requirements   78
Unified end-to-end monitoring   78
Intelligent operational analytics   78

The vRealize Operations Manager architecture 79
Application architecture overview 80
Capacity planning 80
Critical success factors 81
Kubernetes solution from VMware 82
Pivotal Container Service and VMware Kubernetes Engine 82
SDDC journey stages 83
VMware container-based services 84
Deploying NSX-T for network virtualization on ESXi and deploying PKS for use in a private cloud 84
Deploying the NSX-T foundation 85
Deploying and running containerized workloads 85
VMware Cloud on AWS 86
VMware Cloud on AWS differs from on-premises vSphere 87
VMware Cloud on the AWS implementation plan 88
Implementation plan for VMware Cloud on AWS 89
Detailed initial steps to configure VMC on AWS 90
Installation, configuration, and operating procedures 90
Hybrid-linked-mode testing functionality 95
Support and troubleshooting 97
Summary 98
Further reading 99

Chapter 5: Intent-Based Manifest with AppDefense 101
Technical requirements 102
VMware innovation for application security 102
Digital governance and compliance 103
Intelligent government workflows with automation 104
Transforming networking and security 105
Business outcomes of the VMware approach 105
Expanding globally with AppDefense 108
Application-centric alerting for the SOC 109
Transforming application security readiness 110
Innovating IT security with developers, security, and the Ops team 110
Least-privilege security for containerized applications 111
Enhanced security with AppDefense 112
AppDefense and NSX 113
Detailed implementation and configuration plan 116
Environment preparation for AppDefense deployment 117
Summary 121

Section 2: ML Use Cases with VMware Solutions

Chapter 6: ML-Based Intelligent Log Management 125
Technical requirements 125
Intelligent log management with vRealize Log Insight 126
Log Intelligence value propositions 126
Log Intelligence key benefits for service providers 129
Audit log examples 130

Cloud operations stages 131
  Standardize 131
  Service Broker 132
  Strategic partner 132
The Log Insight user interface 133
  Indexing performance, storage, and report export 134
    The user experience 135
      Events 137
VMware vRealize Network Insight 139
  Supported data sources 140
Summary 142

Chapter 7: ML as a Service in the Cloud 145
Technical requirements 145
MLaaS in a private cloud 146
  VMware approach for MLaaS 146
    MLaaS using vRealize Automation and vGPU 146
      NVIDIA vGPU configuration on vSphere ESXi 147
      Customizing the vRealize Automation blueprint 147
LBaaS overview 151
  LBaaS design use cases 151
Challenges with network and security services 155
  The NaaS operating model 156
    LBaaS network design using NSX 159
    BIG-IP DNS high-level design 160
      Customizing the BIG-IP DNS component 160
    The BIG-IP DNS load-balancing algorithm 161
      Global availability 161
      Ratio 161
      Round robin 162
    The LBaaS LTM design 162
      Configuring BIG-IP LTM objects 162
      Designing the LTM load-balancing method 163
      Designing the LTM virtual server 164
Summary 164

Chapter 8: ML-Based Rule Engine with Skyline 165
Technical requirements 165
Proactive support technology – VMware Skyline 166
  Collector, viewer, and advisor 167
    Release strategy 168
Overview of Skyline Collector 170
  The requirements for Skyline Collector 170
    Networking requirements 171
    Skyline Collector user permissions 172
    VMware Skyline Collector admin interface 174
    Linking with My VMware account 176
    Managing endpoints 176

Configuring VMware Skyline Collector admin interface	177
Auto-upgrade	178
CEIP	179
Types of information that are collected	179
Product usage data utilization	180
Summary	182
Chapter 9: DevOps with vRealize Code Stream	183
Technical requirements	184
Application development life cycles	184
CD pipeline	185
CI pipeline	185
Planning	186
SDLC	186
SCM	186
CI	187
AR	187
Release pipeline automation (CD)	187
CM	187
HC	188
COM	188
Feedback	188
Request fulfillment	189
Change management	189
Release management	190
Compliance management	190
Incident management	191
Event management	191
Capacity management	191
Wavefront dashboard	193
Getting insights by monitoring how people work	194
Automation with vRealize	195
Deploying Infrastructure as Code	197
vRealize Code Stream	198
Pipeline automation model – the release process for any kind of software	201
vRCS deployment architecture	201
System architecture	202
Integrating vRCS with an external, standalone vRA	205
Summary	206
Further reading	207
Chapter 10: Transforming VMware IT Operations Using ML	209
Overview on business and operations challenges	210
The challenges of not having services owners for the operations team	211
A solution with service owners	212
Responsibilities of the service owner	212
Transforming VMware technical support operations	213
SDDC services	215
Service catalog management	215
Service design, development, and release	215

Cloud business management operations   215
Service definition and automation   216
NSX for vSphere   216
Recommendations with priority   219
Recommendations with priority 1   219
Recommendations with priority 2   221
Recommendations with priority 3   223
Virtual data centers   224
IaaS solution using vRealize Suite   226
Business-level administration and organizational grouping   227
vRA deployment   230
vRA appliance communication   230
Services running as part of the identity service   231
A complete solution with the desired result   233
Summary   234

Section 3: Dealing with Big Data, HPC , IoT, and Coud Application Scalability through ML

Chapter 11: Network Transformation with IoT   237
Technical requirements   238
IoT   238
VMware Pulse   239
The queries that arise related to VMware Pulse   239
Pulse IoT Center infrastructure management blueprint   241
Deploying and configuring the OVA   241
Configuring IoT support   245
Virtual machines in the OVA   245
IoT use cases with VMware Pulse   253
Powering the connected car (automotive industry)   254
Entertainment, parks, and resorts   254
Smart hospitals (medical)   254
Smart surveillance (higher education)   255
Smart warehouse (retail industry)   255
The internet of trains (transportation and logistics)   256
The financial industry   256
Smart weather forecasting   256
IoT data center network security   257
NSX distributed firewall   258
Prerequisites to any automation   258
Hybrid cloud for scale and distribution   260
Summary   260

Chapter 12: Virtualizing Big Data on vSphere   263
Technical requirements   263
Big data infrastructure   264
Hadoop as a service   264
Deploying the BDE appliance   266
Configuring the VMware BDE   267
The BDE plugin   268

Configuring distributions on BDE   270
The Hadoop plugin in vRO   271
Open source software   276
Considering solutions with CapEx and OpEx   277
Benefits of virtualizing Hadoop   278
Use case – security and configuration isolation   279
Case study – automating application delivery for a major media provider   279
Summary   280
Further reading   281

Chapter 13: Cloud Application Scaling   283
Technical requirements   283
Cloud-native applications   284
Automation with containers   285
Container use cases   286
Challenges with containers   286
PKS on vSphere   287
PKS availability zone   289
PKS/NSX-T logical topologies   293
Use cases with different configurations   293
PKS and NSX-T Edge Nodes and Edge Cluster   294
PKS and NSX-T communications   295
Storage for K8s cluster node VMs   296
Datastores   297
Summary   298

Chapter 14: High-Performance Computing   299
Technical requirements   299
Virtualizing HPC applications   300
Multi-tenancy with guaranteed resources   301
Critical use case – unification   303
High-performance computing cluster performances   305
A standard Hadoop architecture   308
Standard tests   309
Intel tested a variety of HPC benchmarks   311
Summary   312

Other Books You May Enjoy   315

Index   319

Preface

This book presents an introductory perspective on how **machine learning** (**ML**) plays an important role in the VMware environment. It offers a basic understanding of how to leverage ML primitives, along with a deeper look into integration with VMware tools that are used for automation purposes today.

Who this book is for

This book is intended for those planning, designing, and implementing the virtualization/cloud components of the Software-Defined Data Center foundational infrastructure. It helps users to put intelligence in their automation tasks to get self driving data center. It is assumed that the reader has knowledge of, and some familiarity with, virtualization concepts and related topics, including storage, security, and networking.

What this book covers

Chapter 1, *Machine Learning Capabilities with vSphere 6.7*, covers performance benchmarking on ML-based applications using GPUs in vSphere environment to support different customer business objectives.

Chapter 2, *Proactive Measures with vSAN Advanced Analytics*, explains how to improve the support experience for HCI environments, which will help customers maintain performance by rapidly resolving issues and minimizing downtime by means of proactive telemetry capabilities from vSAN Support Insight advanced analytics.

Chapter 3, *Security with Workspace ONE Intelligence*, describes an innovative approach to enterprise security for employees, apps, endpoints, and networks with access management, device, and app management, and for trusted analytics frameworks.

Chapter 4, *Proactive Operations with VMware vRealize Suite*, explains how to automate data centers and public clouds running on vSphere by injecting advanced analytics into its VMware vRealize Suite.

Chapter 5, *Intent-Based Manifest with AppDefense*, explains how to learn to use ML to create an intent-based manifest for an app running in a VM so as to secure the app against malicious behavior with an algorithm, which measures the run state against the intended state.

Chapter 6, *ML-based Intelligent Log Management*, covers how to innovative indexing and ML-based intelligent grouping in order to facilitate high-performance searching for faster troubleshooting across physical, virtual, and cloud environments by aiding fast troubleshooting through root cause analysis.

Chapter 7, *Machine Learning as a Service in the Cloud*, explains how to build and maintain each ML process with customization of the hardware and software and eliminate this complexity by automating the deployment of hardware resources, configuring them with the required operating system and application stack, and making them available to data scientists.

Chapter 8, *ML-Based Rule Engine with Skyline*, describes how to collect information from a customer and use ML as an intelligent rule engine to monitor whether anything deviates beyond normal behavior and then raise a red flag to offer proactive support.

Chapter 9, *DevOps with vRealize Code Stream*, looks into the highest priority processes to transform and apply techniques to compare and contrast the key differences between legacy operating models, processes, and team structures with the strategic operating model required for DevOps.

Chapter 10, *Transforming VMware IT Operations Using ML*, covers the operational challenges facing IT teams in this changing environment, and how they are resolving them to meet customer demands with the agility and scalability necessary to support rapid business innovation and growth.

Chatpter 11, *Network Transformation with IoT*, describes how to deliver data applications across regional boundaries, from heart monitors in hospitals to connected cars in cities, and wind turbines in rural regions, by embedding security into the architecture and managing data distribution from the data center to the cloud to the edge.

Chapter 12, *Virtualizing Big Data on vSphere*, explains how to leverage shared storage in modern big data platforms by evaluating first current in-memory big data platforms and how this fits in with virtualization with in-memory features of these platforms.

Chapter 13, *Cloud Application Scaling*, describes how to support cloud app development by providing developers access to traditional, cloud-native, and modern application development frameworks and resources, including container services and open APIs on a common virtualized environment.

Chapter 14, *High-Performance Computing*, goes into the learning capabilities provided by VMware vSphere to improve scientific productivity through features such as SR-IOV, RDMA, and vGPU to architect and meet the requirements for research computing, academic, scientific, and engineering workloads.

To get the most out of this book

It is important to focus on identifying the benefits, complexities, risks, and related costs associated with building a complete automation engine, from the data center to the end user device, along with the applications.

To achieve this we will cover a diverse range of topics, beginning with advanced GPU configuration and their performance comparison to HPC and big data workloads running on the ever reliable vSphere platform which will help you to get the most out of this book.

Download the color images

We also provide a PDF file that has color images of the screenshots/diagrams used in this book. You can download it here: https://www.packtpub.com/sites/default/files/downloads/9781789802160_ColorImages.pdf.

Conventions used

There are a number of text conventions used throughout this book.

CodeInText: Indicates code words in text, database table names, folder names, filenames, file extensions, pathnames, dummy URLs, user input, and Twitter handles. Here is an example: "If we can't connect using wget, download the .rpm."

Any command-line input or output is written as follows:

```
# cd /opt/serengeti/www/yum/repos/centos/6/base/RPMS/
wget
http://mirror.centos.org/centos/6/os/x86_64/Packages/mailx-12.4-7.e
l6.x86_64.rpm
```

Bold: Indicates a new term, an important word, or words that you see on screen. For example, words in menus or dialog boxes appear in the text like this. Here is an example: "We have to select the **Install** radial button and fill out the form with vCenter information and click **Submit**."

Warnings or important notes appear like this.

Tips and tricks appear like this.

Get in touch

Feedback from our readers is always welcome.

General feedback: If you have questions about any aspect of this book, mention the book title in the subject of your message and email us at customercare@packtpub.com.

Errata: Although we have taken every care to ensure the accuracy of our content, mistakes do happen. If you have found a mistake in this book, we would be grateful if you would report this to us. Please visit www.packt.com/submit-errata, selecting your book, clicking on the Errata Submission Form link, and entering the details.

Piracy: If you come across any illegal copies of our works in any form on the internet, we would be grateful if you would provide us with the location address or website name. Please contact us at copyright@packt.com with a link to the material.

If you are interested in becoming an author: If there is a topic that you have expertise in, and you are interested in either writing or contributing to a book, please visit authors.packtpub.com.

Reviews

Please leave a review. Once you have read and used this book, why not leave a review on the site that you purchased it from? Potential readers can then see and use your unbiased opinion to make purchase decisions, we at Packt can understand what you think about our products, and our authors can see your feedback on their book. Thank you!

For more information about Packt, please visit packt.com.

Section 1: VMware Approach with ML Technology

In this section, we will see how VMware is addressing the business issues related to its workforce, customers, and partners by means of emerging technology, such as machine learning, in order to create new, intelligence-driven end user experiences that accelerate productivity and responsiveness to achieve real business value with digital transformation. Readers will learn how to apply machine learning techniques incorporated in VMware solutions to their data center operations.

This section contains the following chapters:

- Chapter 1, *ML Capabilities with vSphere 6.7*
- Chapter 2, *Proactive Measures with vSAN Advanced Analytics*
- Chapter 3, *Security with Workspace One Intelligence*
- Chapter 4, *Proactive Operations with VMware vRealize Suite*
- Chapter 5, *Intent-Based Manifest with AppDefense*

1

Machine Learning Capabilities with vSphere 6.7

This book will brief you about how different VMware tools will help customers to reap the benefits of intelligent automatic detection and prediction. This offering will enable them to detect, visualize, and troubleshoot anomalies, future needs, and potential modern applications and infrastructure issues—all this without any additional skillset for statistical or algorithm expertise from the user's side. VMware provides customers unified visibility into the health and typical behavior of metrics across all services without user assistance, and therefore reduces troubleshooting time. These tools will also help in forecasting to understand future capacity needs and to maximize application and infrastructure efficiency cost-effectively.

This chapter briefs you on how to virtualize GPU in a vSphere environment by using different modes, creating profiles for specific groups of users, and information about different **NVIDIA graphics cards** and their usage. We will also learn about configuring NVIDIA GPU in vSphere for **machine learning** (**ML**)-based workloads with different use cases to achieve specific business objectives while reducing cost.

The topics that we we will cover in this chapter are as follows:

- ML and VMware
- Different modes of using GPUs
- ML with NVIDIA GPUs

Technical requirements

You can download the following:

- VMware vSphere 6.7 from `https://my.vmware.com/en/web/vmware/info/slug/datacenter_cloud_infrastructure/vmware_vsphere/6_7`
- VMware vCenter Server 6.5 U1 `https://my.vmware.com/web/vmware/details?downloadGroup=VC65U1productId=676rPId=28154`
- VMware Horizon 7 `https://my.vmware.com/en/web/vmware/evalcenter?p=horizon-7src=WWW_HrzOld_TopNav_DownloadFreeTrail`

ML and VMware

VMware is extensively leveraging AI and ML techniques in most of its products. We can see this with the new version of vSphere 6.7 features and also with products such as **AppDefense** and **Workspace**. This is one intelligence that will help in achieving the future vision of self-driving data centers. VMware has already done the performance benchmarking regarding how it can help its customers to run their own ML workloads on vSphere with improved support from NVIDIA GPUs.

ML is important for VMware mixed cloud vision, as ML has the ability to absorb a huge amount of data to utilize it for precise learning and with end users.

ML-based data analysis

ML is helping customers to fetch better granular-level information from large datasets. This will give a huge competitive advantage in business, as the customer is able to integrate their data from different sources, which will help the management to take major decisions ahead of their competitors. As we get this result with the relevant reasons behind it, we can help customers with accurate and productive data. The potential of AI in our daily life is immense.

We have a new development in ML every day, and ML will be extended even further. All the biggest public cloud vendors use ML-based techniques in their daily operations. Apple, GE, and Bosch are also gathering massive amounts of data and applying machine learning techniques to filter out only useful data. GE is accumulating data analytics through its industrial internet, and Apple has a huge amount of consumer and health data from its millions of end users, which helps them to emerge as major players in AI.

Embedding AI within present cloud technologies is helping businesses and consumers to grow and also creating new opportunities with all the relevant information to plan for the future. We are moving toward intelligent infrastructure where AI uses machines to adopt human intelligence. AI is based on rules-based logic, decision trees, and methodology to enable it to behave like a human. ML analyzes data and enhances the performance of repetitive tasks. DL will help machines learn by locating and checking various options against one another in order to get the best result or solution.

Customers have adopted the cloud and are now embedding ML techniques and its capabilities to extend its dynamics and delivering values to customers. Customers get a safe and secure environment with the scale up and out capabilities. The cloud provider receives loyal long-term customers in return. Every cloud provider is better than others in specific fields, from a business and an AI perspective. This will give customers diverse offerings with specialized intelligence for their unique requirements.

VMware will help customers with intelligent infrastructure that can deliver a comparable and secure solution across mixed clouds to choose the right cloud provider for their unique business requirements, such as security, backup, disaster recovery, networking, storage, graphics, and management with basic compute resources.

A good example of intelligent technology is Google Maps. When we leave our office for a meeting, with Google Map's guidance, we are able to identify alternative routes via AI, saving us valuable time.

Using virtualized GPUs with ML

ML is being extensively used in research and development these days, and the computing power enhancement of accelerators such as GPUs has enabled a rapid adoption of ML applications.

Designers, engineers, and architects are the extensive end users who frequently use 3D graphics for a wide-range of use cases and expect their IT teams to assist them in this. They use high-end graphics workstations handling 3D models of automobiles, manufacturing components, and buildings in real time. They are part of manufacturing, architecture, engineering and construction, higher education, public sector, oil and gas, and so on. They have to view and control this rich, visual 2D and 3D data in real time. Power-user groups such as clinicians, engineers, and office professionals represent millions of users who rely on rich 2D and 3D graphics for their deliverables.

Organizations are evolving today as their footprint increasing with the global workforce who are geographically distributed teams using virtual desktop with graphics from anywhere, anytime and on any workstation. As these power users are working in the field and need application access from anywhere using their end-point devices such as laptops, tablets, and mobile devices, they need to collaborate with their team members in real time without the risk of data loss and with full compliance. We have to redefine the workflow for designers and engineers with a **Virtual Desktop Infrastructure (VDI)** solution:

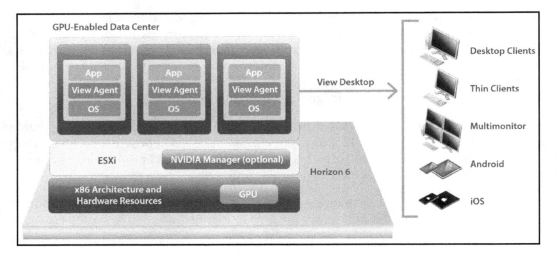

VMware Horizon VDI with NVIDIA GPU

A VMware VDI solution is certified with all leading 3D apps workstations—world-class graphics from endpoint to data center are accessible on any device while lowering the operating expenses. VMware Horizon with protocol Blast ensures a tremendous user experience based on NVIDIA GRID vGPU technology by providing secure, native, 3D graphics from the cloud and delivered across any endpoint devices and from any locations with lower OpEx. Graphics commands executed on each virtual machine are directly passed to the physical GPU without any overheads at the hypervisor layer with NVIDIA GRID vGPU technology.

It helps with application compatibility as the applications have access to the same graphics card as earlier on their workstations. NVIDIA GRID vGPU makes it possible for the GPU hardware to be time-sliced to provide the best in shared virtualized graphics performance.

VMware, vSphere, and VMware Horizon ensure power users, designers, and engineers can get a fabulous graphics experience that is equivalent to native hardware and certified by NVIDIA and VMware for most of the important business applications.

Modes of GPU usage

Applications running in virtual machines hosted on vSphere can make use of GPU processing power in two ways.

vSphere DirectPath I/O is a vSphere inherent feature that leverages **virtualization technology** (**VT**)-enabled processors configured to the hosts to enhance the performance of virtual machines. **General purpose Input Output** (**GPIO**) is a processor feature of Intel/AMD CPUs known as an I/O memory management unit that assigns direct memory access transfers and device interrupts. This way, virtual machines are able to bypass the VMkernel and get direct access to the underlying physical hardware. vMotion is supported with DPIO-enabled server hardware.

Hardware-assisted I/O MMU virtualization is called **Intel Virtualization Technology for Directed I/O** (**VT-d**) in Intel processors and **AMD I/O Virtualization** (**AMD-Vi** or **IOMMU**) in AMD processors. It is a function of the chipset that assists virtual machines to get direct access to hardware I/O devices such as network cards, storage controllers, and GPUs.

NVIDIA GRID GPUs support vGPU, which is the capability for multiple users to share a single physical GPU in a virtualized environment. There are three types of hardware-based graphics acceleration configurations possible for Horizon View virtual desktops. vGPU offers the best performance and compatibility options.

Comparing ML workloads to GPU configurations

We can compare the same ML workload by testing it with three different GPU configurations; these are as follows:

- GPU using DirectPath I/O on vSphere
- GRID vGPU on vSphere
- Native GPU on bare metal host

We have tested and found that the virtualization layer (DirectPath I/O and GRID vGPU) introduced only a 4% overhead for the tested ML application. Learning times can be compared to the specific model by using two virtual machines with different configurations.

VM resources along with OS of two VMs with and without GPU:

- **NVIDIA GRID Configuration**: 1 vGPU, 12 vCPUs, 60 GB memory, 96 GB of SSD storage, CentOS 7.2
- **No GPU configuration**: No GPU, 12 vCPUs, 60 GB memory, 96 GB of SSD storage, CentOS 7.2

Let's look at the following table:

MNIST workload	1 vGPU (sec)	No GPU (sec)
Normalized learning time	1.1	10.01
CPU utilization	9%	45%

vGPU reduces the training time by 10 times and CPU utilization also goes down 5 times as shown in the preceding table. ML can be referenced with two components; these are as follows:

- The convolutional neural network model derived from the TensorFlow library.
- The **Canadian Institute For Advanced Research (CIFAR)**-10 dataset has defined images datasets, which we utilize in ML and IT vision algorithms.

DirectPath I/O

First, we focus on **DirectPath I/O (DPIO)** passthrough mode as we scale from one GPU to four GPUs:

CIFAR-10	1 GPU	2 GPUs	4 GPUs
Normalized images/sec in thousands (w.r.t. 1 GPU)	1.1	2.01	3.77
CPU utilization	23%	41%	73%

Images processed per second get better with the increased number of GPUs on the server. One GPU almost used to normalized data at 1,000 images/second and will grow further with the increase of GPUs. DPIO and GRID vGPU mode performance can be compared by configuring with one vGPU/VM in both modes:

MNIST Workload (lower is better)	DPIO	GRID vGPU
Normalized training times	1.1	1.03
CIFAR-10 Workload (Higher is better)	**DPIO**	**GRID vGPU**
Normalized images/second	1.1	0.83

DPIO and GRID mode vGPU have more-or-less the same performance as one vGPU/VM. We can configure a VM with all the available GPUs on the host in DPIO, but a VM can configure a maximum of one GPU in GRID vGPU mode. We can differentiate between four VMs running the same job and a VM using four GPUs/hosts in DPIO mode:

CIFAR-10 Workload	DPIO	DPiO (four VMs)	GRID vGPU (four VMs)
Normalized images/second (higher is better)	1.1	0.96	0.94
CPU utilization	73%	69%	67%

We should configure virtual machines with low latency or require a shorter training time in multi-GPU DPIO mode. As they are dedicated to specific virtual machines, the rest of the virtual machines will not be able to access the GPUs on the host during this time. We can leverage virtual machines with longer latencies or learning times by configuring 1-GPU in GRID vGPU mode and enjoy the virtualization benefits.

Scalability of GPU in a virtual environment

Horizon and vSphere support vGPU, and vGPU brings the benefit of broad API support and native NVIDIA drivers with maximum scalability. NVIDIA GRID GPUs are based on the NVIDIA Kepler GPU architecture. NVIDIA GRID GPUs support vGPU capability for multiple users to share a single physical GPU in a virtualized environment. Horizon will automatically load-balance vGPU-enabled virtual desktops across compute and storage resource pools with the required GPUs, even with different pools using various user profiles. If we create two linked-clone pools, one with a K120Q profile and another with K220Q, Horizon will put the first profile on hosts with K1 cards and the latter on K2 without any effort. vGPU profiles entitle dedicated graphics memory. The GPU manager allocates memory size to meet the specific asks of each user.

The ESXi host can go up to a maximum 16 physical GPU-based graphics to be shared among different virtual machines/users.

Horizon have three kinds of graphics acceleration:

- Virtual shared graphics
- Virtual shared passthrough graphics
- Virtual dedicated graphics
- Total memory (including volatile and non-volatile memory) can't exceed the maximum memory limit (6,128 GB) per virtual machine

Containerized ML applications inside a VM

The **vSphere Integrated Containers** architecture gives two container deployment models:

1. **Virtual container hosts**: vSphere Integrated Containers leverages the native constructs of vSphere to provision containers. It extends the availability and performance capabilities (DRS, HA, vMotion) of vSphere to containerized workloads. A container image can be used as a virtual machine, and developers can also consume it as a Docker API.
2. **Docker container hosts**: Developers can self-provision Docker container hosts on demand and use them as a development sandbox to repackage apps. This architecture complements agile development practices and DevOps methodologies such as **continuous integration** (**CI**) and **continuous deployment** (**CD**).

It will be costly and time consuming to re-architect an in-house application that is tightly coupled to its data and other application components/logic, so it cuts costs to repackage the application in a container without changing the application's design. The learning curve for repackaging an application is small.

vSphere Integrated Containers gives an option to instantiate a Docker image by using the Docker command-line interface and then deploying the container image as a VM instead of as a container on top of a Docker host, so we can get the benefits of packaging the application as a container without re-architecting it. This way, we keep the isolation of VMs. vSphere Integrated Containers is the ideal solution for application repackaging without any new infrastructure/dedicated hardware or the need to implement new tools.

The repackaged containerized application can run alongside other virtual machines running traditional or containerized applications. vSphere Integrated Containers have high availability at the infrastructure level without developer intervention to support the repackaged container. We can also utilize core vSphere features such as **vSphere high availability** and **vSphere vMotion**.

vGPU scheduling and vGPU profile selection

GPUs support by default an equal share and have to configure a fixed share as per a customer's requirement.

We can configure GPU with the following two options:

- **Equal share scheduler**: A physical GPU is shared among all the virtual desktops as vGPUs running on the same host. The share of processing cycles changes as vGPUs are added/removed to a GPU and the performance of a vGPU depends on whether other vGPUs are running or stopping.
- **Fixed share scheduler**: Each vGPU is allocated a fixed share of the physical GPU's processing cycles in spite of whether vGPUs are added to or removed from a GPU. It will be constant, even if other vGPUs are running or stopping.

NVIDIA GRID vGPU on vSphere can be configured with various options for the vGPU profile that defines the GPU memory each VM can use with the maximum number of VMs that can share a single GPU.

vGPU profiles provides a line up of virtual GPUs with different buffer memory frame sizes and numbers of heads. The number of users will be defined by the division of a frame buffer per GPU attached to a specific profile, and the number of heads denotes the supported number of displays, while the maximum resolution will be consistent across all the profiles. vGPU profiles ending in Q have to follow an application certification process the same as the NVIDIA Quadro cards for professional graphics applications. We can get 100% compatibility and performance with these applications. You can refer to this link for a list of certified applications: https://www.nvidia.com/en-us/design-visualization/solutions/virtualization/.

Power user and designer profiles

We can move our most demanding end users into the data center with **NVIDIA Grid** and **Horizon**. We can help these users with mobility, easy management, centralized data and security, disaster recovery protection, and other benefits of virtualization. We can bind these users with their workstation by subsequentially chaining them to a desk. Although **Virtual Dedicated Graphics Acceleration** (**vDGA**) passthrough allows remote workstation access with a 1:1 ratio with a higher cost and without any optimization of resources, now, we can have mixed workstation users along with task/knowledge users for better resource optimization. We are getting lots of options for designing a solution with the desired compatibility and performance. We can get high-quality experience with a design application on certified software and hardware by utilizing the NVIDIA platform. Profile selection depends on the primary application's requirements, and based on these requirements we can choose the suitable Quadro-certified vGPU profile to achieve the end user's requirements.

Knowledge and task user profiles

Task workers mostly need **Soft 3D**, a software-based 3D renderer good for less graphics-intensive applications. They do not require, or get a noticeable advantage from, hardware-based 3D acceleration. Soft 3D is a standard component of Horizon.

Office workers and executives come into this profile, mostly using applications such as Microsoft Office, Adobe Photoshop, and other non-specialized end-user applications. A **Virtual Shared Graphics Acceleration** (**vSGA**) solution can optimize performance for this use case by providing high levels of consolidation of users across GPUs. vSGA does not provide a broad range of graphics API support, as it is always better to consider a vGPU-based solution for knowledge workers.

Adding vGPU hosts to a cluster with vGPU Manager

We have to install the NVIDIA GPU manager **vSphere Installation Bundle** (**VIB**), as NVIDIA VIB has drivers that are a must for the host to identify the GPU. This will give you **vGPU Manager**. ESXi host's BIOS power and performance settings should be set to the high performance policy before installing the supported version of vCenter and ESXi. ESXi hosts are managed through vCenter and configured with NTP and DNS.

 vGPU Manager VIB is loaded the same as a driver in the hypervisor. vGPU Manager can provision up to eight users to share each physical GPU. M60 can be set up to 32 users per card. This cluster must have hosts that have NVIDIA Tesla M60 vGPU. This is to optimize the distribution of resources for the GPU.

ML with NVIDIA GPUs

ML helps computers to work without being explicitly programmed in a user-friendly way so anyone can learn and utilize it in their daily life such as health, research, science, finance, and intelligent system:

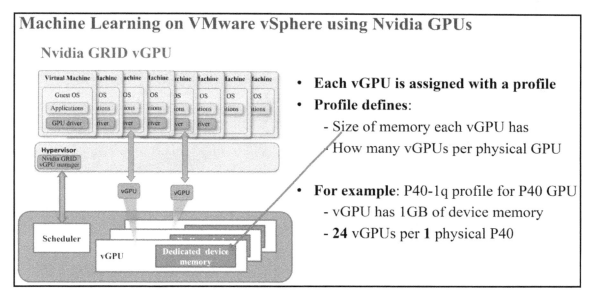

Assigning a GPU in NVIDIA GRID vGPU

Pool and farm settings in Horizon

We have to configure a 3D farm like a normal farm in Horizon:

1. Configure this pool in the same way as we used to configure the pool in Horizon, until we reach the **Desktop Pool Settings** section.
2. Scroll to the **Remote Display Protocol** section in the **Add Desktop Pool** window.
3. We have to choose between two of the following options in the **3D Renderer** option:
   1. Choose either **Hardware** or **Automatic** for vSGA
   2. Choose **Hardware** for vDGA or MxGPU

4. Set the default display protocol to **PCoIP** in the **Desktop Pool** settings and allow users to decide to choose **No** in the dropdown with **3D Renderer** to NVIDIA GRID VGPU.

5. To enable the **NVIDIA vGPU**, enable vGPU support for a virtual machine:

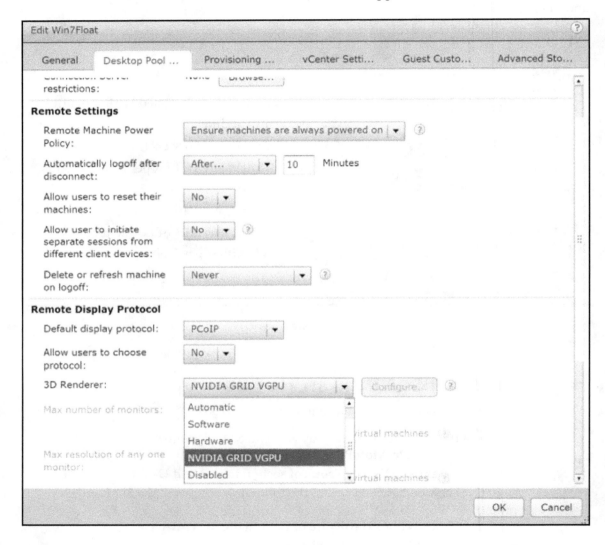

6. Power down the virtual machine.
7. Click on **VM** in the **Navigator** window. Select the **Manage** tab and **Settings**. Click on the **Edit** button:

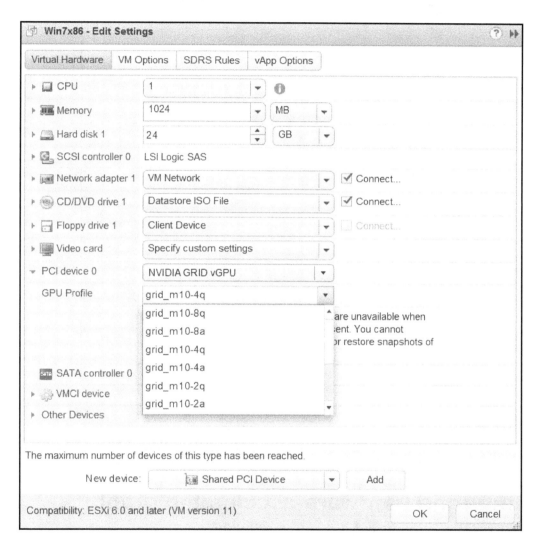

8. Click the **New PCI Device** bar and choose **Shared PCI Device** and then **Add** to continue:

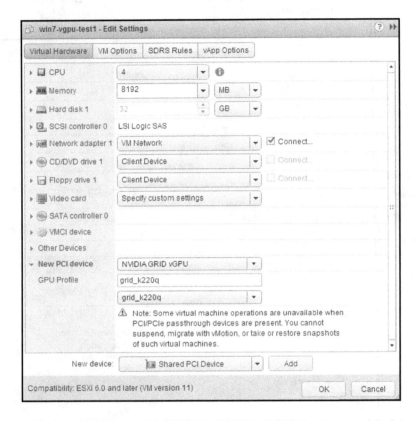

9. Now it's showing that the **NVIDIA GRID vGPU** device is added.
10. Configure the GPU with the **GPU Profile Selection** bar and then click **OK** to finish the configuration.

Configuring hardware-accelerated graphics

We can configure acceleration in three ways with VMware Horizon:

- Virtual shared graphics
- Virtual dedicated graphics
- Virtual shared passthrough graphics

Virtual shared graphics acceleration

vSGA is the driver that supports DirectX and OpenGL. vDGA configurations do use the native graphics card driver. SVGA or VMware SVGA 3D is the VMware Windows Display Driver Model-compliant driver included with VMware Tools on Windows virtual desktops. This 3D graphics driver can be installed on Windows for 2D/3D and can also can be utilized for both 3D and vSGA software.

VMware SVGA 3D can be configured for both 2D/3D software and vSGA deployments, and a virtual desktop can be rapidly switched between either with software or hardware acceleration, without any change to the existing configuration. vSGA supports vMotion with hardware-accelerated graphics configuration. Universal driver will work across platform without any further configuration:

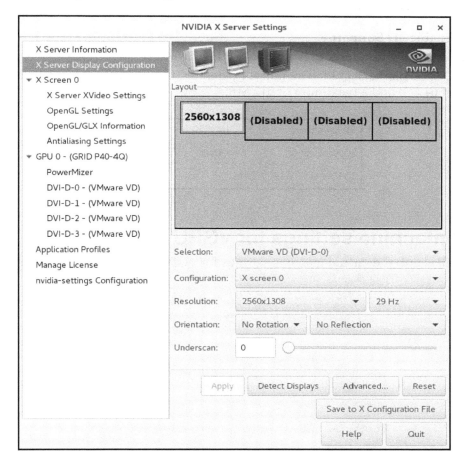

The server's physical GPUs are virtualized and shared with the number of guest virtual machines residing on the same host server with vSGA techniques. We have to integrate a specific driver in the hypervisor and all guest virtual machines will leverage the VMware vSGA 3D driver. vSGA has performance limitations with few applications which don't have needed API support and also have limited support for OpenGL and DirectX.

Configuring vSGA settings in a virtual machine

There are three existing 3D settings in vSphere and View Pool settings. We can enable or disable 3D to set the 3D setting to automatic through vSphere. If we change the 3D configuration, then it will revert back the amount of video memory to the default value of 96 MB, so be sure before changing the video memory. These configurations have the following: **Automatic** (by default), **Software**, and **Hardware**:

1. **Enable 3D Support**.
2. Set the **3D Renderer** to **Automatic** or **Hardware**.
3. Decide on the 3D video memory. By default, it is 96 MB, but it can be a minimum of 64 MB and a maximum of 512 MB:

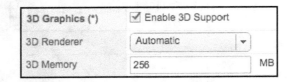

Virtual machine settings for vGPU

Now we will set up the virtual machine settings for vGPU with following screenshot:

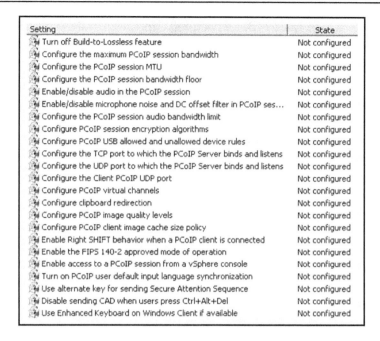

The preceding image will give us multiple configuration options as per application requirement with all security measures.

1. Select the virtual machine to be configured and click **Edit Settings**. First, add a **Shared PCI Device** and then choose the **NVIDIA GRID vGPU** to enable GPU passthrough on the virtual machine:

2. Choose the required profile from **GPU Profile** drop-down menu:

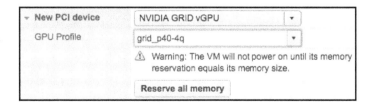

GPU profile string 4q notifies the size of the frame buffer (VRAM) in GB and the needed GRID license.

VRAM 0,1 notifies 512 MB, 1,024 MB, respectively, and so on. GRID license types are as follows:

- GRID virtual PC vGPUs for business desktop computing notifies with *b*
- GRID virtual application vGPUs for remote desktop session hosts notifies with *a*
- Quadro **Virtual Data Center Workstation (vDWS)** for workstation-specific graphics features and accelerations, such as up to four 4K monitors and certified drivers for professional applications notifies with *q*:

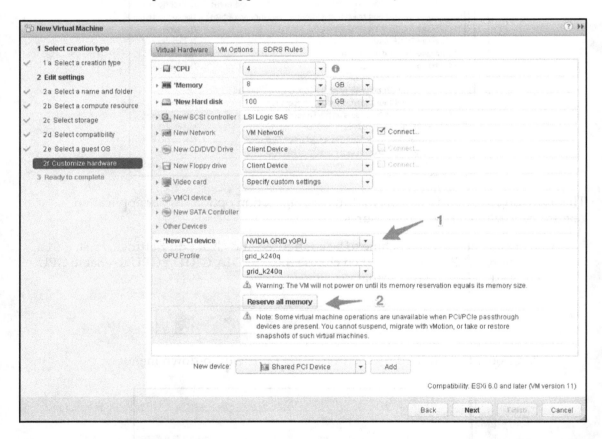

Click **Reserve all memory** when creating a virtual machine. We can manage end-to-end NVIDIA virtual GPU solutions such as Quadro vDWS and **NVIDIA GRID Virtual PC (vPC)** with complete vGPU visibility into their entire infrastructure at the host, guest, or application level. This helps us to become more responsive and agile for a better end-user VDI experience.

We can deliver a far better user experience from high-end virtual workstations to enterprise virtual workspaces, which are cost effective to purchase, easy to deploy, and efficient to operate.

Users such as engineers, designers, content creators, and architects using the Pascal-based GPU with the Quadro vDWS software are able to get the best experience of running both accelerated graphics and compute (CUDA and OpenCL) workloads on any virtual workstation or laptop.

Knowledge workers use programs such as Windows 10, Office 365, and YouTube, which need graphics acceleration to achieve a better virtual desktop user experience using the NVIDIA Pascal™-based GPU with NVIDIA GRID™ virtual PC. NVIDIA NVENC delivers better performance and user density by off-loading H.264 video encoding from CPU to Linux virtual workstation users, which is a heavy compute task. Horizon provides customers with a single platform to publish all kinds of desktops (Windows and Linux) and applications, as per the user's graphics requirement.

GRID vPC and GRID vApps capabilities

NVIDIA GRID has software editions based on specific use cases:

- **NVIDIA GRID Virtual Applications (vApp)**: We can use it for app virtualization or RDSH-based app publishing.
- **vPC**: It will be suitable for a virtual desktop providing standard desktop applications, browser, and multimedia.
- **NVIDIA GRID Virtual Workstation (vWS):** This will be worthwhile for scientists and designers who work on powerful 3D-content creation applications such as CATIA, S, 3DExcite, Schlumberger Petrel, or Autodesk Maya, and so on. vWS only has this NVIDIA Quadro driver.

NVIDIA GRID software editions can be purchased in both annual subscription, perpetual license, and in combination with support. A high-availability license server ensures users get uninterrupted work even in situations where a primary license server goes offline; then, a secondary license server will provide the license services to clients.

NVIDIA virtual GPU solutions and Maxwell-powered GPUs (NVIDIA® Tesla® M60, M6, and M10) are supported in this Pascal-based launch. NVIDIA virtual GPU solutions will be supported on all Pascal GPUs with the Tesla P40 and always-recommended P6 (blade) with the appropriate software licenses.

Even if you have Maxwell-powered GPUs with a NVIDIA GRID solution, we require Pascal GPUs to benefit from the performance improvements, increased frame buffer, larger and more granular profile sizes, bigger system memory, the ability to run both virtualized graphics and compute workloads to scale on the same GPU, and utilize the new task scheduler.

Features such as streamlining management and monitoring that help in application-level monitoring and integrations work on both Maxwell and Pascal cards with the NVIDIA GRID software release and GRID Management SDK 2.0. We have to choose the recommended Pascal/Maxwell boards for specific workloads.

We can recommend P40 or M60 for commercial customers. The P40 provides the highest performance, larger memory, and easier management, and enables the virtualization of graphics and compute (CUDA and OpenCL). The P40 is recommended when upgrading from M60 or K2 or the Skylake-based server. The M60 will continue to be offered and provides heterogeneous profiles and larger OEM server support.

M10 is suggested for customers with density-driven deployments, and for knowledge workers running everyday graphics-accelerated applications, the M10 is recommended. For high-density blade-server deployments, the P6 is a recommended to follow on to the M6.

GRID vWS to Quadro vDWS

We can leverage Quadro/GRID capabilities and compare it with VMware virtual workstation/PC/virtual apps solutions. NVIDIA GRID vWS is now **NVIDIA Quadro Virtual Data Center Workstation** or **Quadro vDWS**. The GRID brand will be used to describe a PC experience and will have two editions: NVIDIA GRID vPC and NVIDIA GRID vApps. While these 2 software editions were once called the NVIDIA GRID software platform, they will now be referred to as **NVIDIA virtual GPU solutions**.

MxGPU is a GPU virtualization technique with a built-in hardware engine responsible for VM scheduling and management. It leverages the underlying SR-IOV protocol as per the application's requirement. GPUs that are in passthrough mode can't be virtualized, so first run the script to disable passthrough mode. If MxGPU is enabled and vCenter is accessible, then use the plugin to configure instead of the script. vDGA can help a user with unrestricted and dedicated access to a single vGPU by providing direct passthrough to a physical GPU. The steps for installing the driver on a VM using an MxGPU device are the same for a regular passthrough device under vDGA.

Configure the virtual machine while using MxGPU and vDGA:

1. For devices with a large BAR size, such as Tesla P40, we have to set the configuration parameters on the VM:

    - `firmware="efi"`

    - `pciPassthru.use64bitMMIO="TRUE"`

    - `pciPassthru.64bitMMIOSizeGB="64"`

2. Add a **PCI Device** to the specific virtual machine and choose the required **PCI Device** to enable GPU passthrough:

3. Log into vSphere Web Client via the Administrator account on the **Home** page and click **Radeon Pro Settings**. Go to the **Data Center** and manage all MxGPU hosts in a specific data center.

4. We can install **Radeon Pro Settings** on the **vSphere Client** plugin with MxGPU:

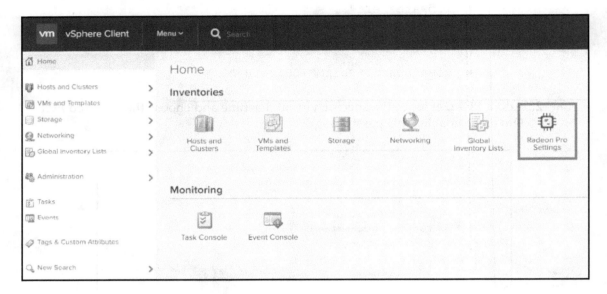

VMware supports both AMD and NVIDIA graphics cards. We can download the appropriate VMware graphics driver from the vendor website to use the graphics card or GPU hardware. We can add **PCI Device** to a single virtual machine as well as to multiple virtual machines.

5. To add a **PCI Device** for a number of virtual machines in one go with commands, do the following:
    1. Browse to the AMD FirePro VIB driver and install AMD VIB utility: `cd /<path_to_vib from ssh`.
    2. Edit `vms.cfg: vi vms.cfg`.

6. Press *I* and change the instances of `.*` to match the names of the VMs that require a GPU like to match `*MxGPU*` to VM names that include MxGPU: `.MxGPU`.

7. Save and quit by pressing *Esc*, type `:wq`, and press *Enter*.

8. Assign the virtual functions to the VMs:

```
sh mxgpu-install.sh -a assign
Eligible VMs:
WIN10-MxGPU-001
WIN10-MxGPU-002
WIN8.1-MxGPU-001
WIN8.1-MxGPU-002
These VMs will be assigned a VF, is it OK?[Y/N]y
```

9. Press *Enter* and choose **Reserve all guest memory (All locked)**.
10. Reboot the system to automatically assign **Virtual Function** (VF) by using the MxGPU script.

We should then verify that all VFs are populated in the device list. This way, we can automatically assign VF by using the script.

Summary

Remote computing solutions for applications such as CAD/CAM, diagnostic imaging, molecular design, and space exploration proved elusive. NVIDIA GRID vGPU technology and VMware, vSphere, and Horizon virtualization software offer cost-effective solutions for design engineers, scientific investigators, and data explorers.

Horizon offers software-based graphics acceleration, which is sufficient for basic use, but hardware-based graphics acceleration have different combinations of GRID graphics cards with server configurations and can be used to address a wide range of advanced user requirements and fulfil them within a budget. We can configure the GPU in two modes:

- DirectPath I/O passthrough mode
- GRID vGPU mode

Shared access to the virtualized GPU makes immersive 3D graphics applications accessible from remote devices. This solution eliminates the need for dedicated graphics workstations, improving security and freeing the users from their offices.

The next chapter is about strategies for hosting applications in such ways as to provide freedom to end users as well as full control to administrator/service providers with policy-based operations based on ML algorithms, which will also help in improving the end-user experience.

Further reading

- *VMware Documentation* at `https://www.vmware.com/support/pubs/`
- *VMware Compatibility Guide* at `https://www.vmware.com/resources/compatibility/search.php`
- *vSphere 6.0 Configuration Maximums* guide at `https://www.vmware.com/pdf/vsphere6/r60/vsphere-60-configuration-maximums.pdf`
- *VMware vCenter Server* datasheet at `http://www.vmware.com/files/pdf/products/vCenter/VMware-vCenter-Server-Datasheet.pdf`
- *VMware vSphere* datasheet at `http://www.vmware.com/files/pdf/vsphere/VMW-vSPHR-Datasheet-6-0.pdf`
- *VMware Horizon 7* datasheet at `http://www.vmware.com/files/pdf/products/horizon/vmware-horizon-7-datasheet.pdf`
- *Multisite deployment best practices for each solution component* at `https://www.vmware.com/content/dam/digitalmarketing/vmware/en/pdf/techpaper/vmware-horizon-7-enterprise-edition-reference-architecture-multi-site.pdf`
- *NVIDIA vGPU deployment guide for VMware Horizon 7.x* at `https://images.nvidia.com/content/pdf/vgpu/guides/vmware-horizon-vsphere-deployment_guide.pdf`
- *Preparing for NVIDIA GRID vGPU capabilities—VMware docs* at `https://docs.vmware.com/en/VMware-Horizon-7/7.6/horizon-virtual-desktops/GUID-AB1B6311-DB31-4982-ACDF-0E1A5ED3B17D.html`
- *Configuring desktop pools in Horizon Administrator* and for complete information and a detailed procedure at `https://www.vmware.com/content/dam/digitalmarketing/vmware/en/pdf/products/horizon/grid-vgpu-deployment-guide.pdf`

Proactive Measures with vSAN Advanced Analytics

2

This chapter will brief you on **virtual storage area network** (**vSAN**) design recommendations, as well as all of the monitoring options through which your customers can assess, recommend, and design their environment. This will help them achieve different business objectives by automating their operations with smart policies.

We will learn to configure policy-based operations as per ML algorithms and we'll learn how the end user experience is improved by the proactive resolving of customer issues. We'll also learn to optimize a **hyperconverged infrastructure** (**HCI**) to achieve customer business objectives.

The following topics will be covered in this chapter:

- Application scalability on vSAN
- Intelligent monitoring
- **High availability** (**HA**) configuration in stretched clusters
- vSAN policy design with **Storage Policy-Based Management** (**SPBM**)

Technical requirements

You can download VMware vCenter Server 6.5 U1 from the site at `https://my.vmware.com/web/vmware/details?downloadGroup=VC65U1amp;productId=676amp;rPId=28154`.

Application scalability on vSAN

VMware vSAN can support containers and a next-generation application based on an updated vSphere Docker volume driver with native support directly through Docker APIs. This allows Docker to be built on top of vSAN and take advantage of the proven, persistent storage capabilities of vSAN. This driver update has new features, including support for multi-tenancy, SPBM, cloning, and snapshots. VMware has a principle of *APIs first*, and all management features are available through APIs, which are extensions of the vSphere APIs that tens of thousands of enterprise customers use to automate their operations.

The following parameters should be taken into consideration to detain the storage tier where application data should be stored:

- **I/O operations per second (IOPS)** requirements
- MBps requirements
- Capacity requirements
- Availability requirements
- Latency requirements
- Consider any existing SLAs
- Consider whether data might move between storage tiers during the information life cycle

These details can be used to move applications and services to the storage tier that's been designed with matching characteristics.

Storage and network assessment

A holistic approach to vSAN management can have a significantly positive impact on the infrastructure. It integrates with vRealize Operation and complements it by providing more in-depth information about resources. The following VMware recommendations view the business challenges from three different perspectives:

- **Organizational recommendations**: Develop a virtualization policy with a service-centered approach such as a menu of offerings and service levels.

- **Operational recommendations**: Focus on process definition and improvement, specifically in the areas of provisioning, systems monitoring, and problem management. Research and evaluate virtual infrastructure monitoring tools.
- **Technical recommendations**: Implement consistent configurations across similar systems, perform minor network adjustments to greatly improve network performance during contention and backup windows, and configure virtual machines to exploit the benefits of virtualization.

Storage design policy

The assessment summaries are based on the **VMware Health Analyzer** (**vHA**) checkpoints and documented vSAN best practices. We will take a look at some of the recommendations in the next section.

VMware best practices recommendations

The following are VMware's best practices, along with recommendations for the storage design policies:

- Verify that we have set up storage policies correctly in vCenter console:
    - Default rule settings should be modified by default. The policy should be applied as per your requirements.
    - **Policy settings**: **Force provisioning** should be set to true during configuration.
    - **Object space reservation (%)** should be set to 100%.

Justification: The VM storage policies in vSAN can affect the performance of VMs running on the vSAN datastore. These include the **Number of disk stripes per object, Flash read cache reservation (%)**, **Number of failures to tolerate**, and **Object space reservation (%)** parameters.

VMware recommends that you go with the default policy of one failure to tolerate and one disk stripe. We can change the policy as per customer requirements and also change the configuration. We have to update the policy for each additional failure to tolerate. *2n+1* hosts are required to fulfill the policy, where *n* is number of failure to tolerate.

- Verify that VMs are distributed evenly across vSAN nodes. Just as disk resources should generally be distributed evenly across vSAN hosts, for the best performance, virtual machines should also be distributed relatively evenly across those hosts.

Justification: This reduces the chances of performance being impacted due to an imbalance of virtual machines on a single host, which could saturate the vSAN network. vSphere's **Distributed Resource Scheduler** (**DRS**) can help with disk resource distribution by monitoring and balancing the virtual machines as needed.

- The storage controller's settings should be configured correctly for best performance.

Justification: The VM storage policies in vSAN can affect the performance of VMs running on the vSAN datastore. A low controller queue depth may impact the availability of production VMs during rebuild/resync, so a minimum queue depth of 256 is required in vSAN. The VMware Compatibility Guide for vSAN has been updated to include only adapters with this requirement. However, certain adapters with older firmware might still have the queue depth artificially limited. The controller should have caching disabled. If this is not possible, set read caching to 100%. If the controller is not set to pass-through, present each disk as its own device. Do not configure drives as one large RAID volume.

- Avoid using the flash read cache policy reservations unless absolutely necessary.

Justification: vSAN allows for the customization of policies for use with virtual machines. One of the policy options, **Flash read cache reservation (%)**, allows for the reservation of read cache. Do not set this policy option unless absolutely necessary. These reservations reserve a portion of the read cache for objects based on the percentage of capacity disk size (10% of a 250 GB disk is 25 GB.) If they are not used sparingly, cache reservations quickly reduce the available cache and the effectiveness of vSAN.

- We should upgrade the on-disk file format to 3.0.

Justification: To use the full set of vSAN capabilities in vSphere, be sure to upgrade the on-disk file format. During the vSAN upgrade from version 5.5 to version 6.7, it is possible to keep the on-disk format version, that is, 1.0, but you cannot use many of the new features. vSAN supports both on-disk formats.

- vSAN should be using optimal **non-volatile memory express** (**NVMe**) CLASS E disks. Verify that you are using supported and high-performing **solid state drives** (**SSDs**) for best performance.

  Justification: All writes hit SSDs in vSAN first. vSAN read cache hits come from SSDs, so the performance of the SSDs is a critical factor in the overall performance of vSAN.

  We can use SSDs instead of magnetic disks for the capacity tier as well. The VMware Compatibility Guide helps customers in selecting the right SSDs by segregating them into different groups based on their performance, as follows:

- **Class A**: 2,500–5,000 writes per second
- **Class B**: 5,000–10,000 writes per second
- **Class C**: 10,000–20,000 writes per second
- **Class D**: 20,000–30,000 writes per second
- **Class E**: 30,000+ writes per second

VMware always recommends using flash drives that meet application performance needs for optimal performance. As per best practices, we have to consider 10 percent of projected used **hard disk drive** (**HDD**) capacity before the failures-to-tolerate policy is applied for a minimum flash drive.

Network design policy

vSAN requires a VMkernel network configuration for synchronization and replication activities. This port group should generally be dedicated and isolated to vSAN traffic. However, if a 10 gigabits network interface is being used, it can be shared. 1 gigabit networks require a dedicated **network interface card** (**NIC**) to be assigned to the port group.

The following are the major decision points regarding vSAN network configuration:

- **Network speed requirements**: All-flash vSAN configurations (with Advanced and Enterprise Edition) will only work with 10 gigabits Ethernet network uplinks. A 10 gigabits network is required to achieve the highest performance (IOPS). VMware recommends a 10 gigabits Ethernet connection (MTU 9000) for use with vSAN in all configurations.

- **Type of virtual switch to be used**: vSAN supports both vSphere standard virtual switch configurations and distributed switch configurations. A distributed switch allows network I/O control to be used for the prioritization of bandwidth. It allows the interface to be shared and prioritizes performance levels in contention scenarios. VMware recommends using a **vSphere Distributed Switch (VDS)** for the vSAN port group.
- **Jumbo frame**: vSAN supports using jumbo frames for vSAN network transmissions. VMware recommends using jumbo frames for vSAN, but only if the underlying physical environment is already configured to support them.
- **Business continuity and disaster recovery (BC/DR) and teaming considerations**: BC/DR is critical in any environment in case of a network failure. vSAN supports teaming configurations for network cards to enhance the availability and redundancy of the network. VMware recommends that configurations use an active/active redundancy with a route based on physical adapter load for the teaming in the environment. Idle network cards do not wait for a failure to occur and aggregate bandwidth in this configuration.

VMware best practices recommendations

The following are VMware's best practices with recommendations for the network design policies:

- We should distribute VMNICs for a port group across various **Peripheral Component Interconnect (PCI)** buses for enhancing availability

  Justification: Distributing VMNICs for a port group across different PCI buses provides protection from failures related to a specific PCI bus. You need to team VMNICs from different PCI buses to improve fault resiliency from component failures.

- Configure NICs, physical switch speed, and duplex settings consistently

  Justification: Incorrect network speed and duplex settings can impact performance. The network adapter (VMNIC) and physical switch settings must be checked and set correctly. If your physical switch is configured for a specific speed and duplex setting, we must force the network driver to use the same speed and duplex setting. Network settings should be set to auto-negotiate and not forced for gigabits links. We can set network adapter speed and duplex settings from the vSphere client, but a reboot is required for the changes to take effect.

- It is always recommended to use 10 gigabits or faster networks with vSAN

  Justification: Small vSAN deployments can perform well with 1 gigabit Ethernet links between the ESXi hosts in the vSAN cluster, but most deployments will require 10 gigabits or faster links. VMware recommends using a minimum of 10 gigabits links for best datastore performance.

- **Network I/O control** (**NIOC**) shares are configured to ensure at least 8 gigabits are available for vSAN traffic to avoid contention. We will use vSAN reservations while using NIOC.

  Justification: VMware suggests reservations with vSAN for specific use cases but primarily for environmental conditions in the physical network, thus reducing the actual bandwidth. This can be scheduled between the physical NIC and the physical network. Reservations ensure that the vSAN network traffic is not consumed by other traffic types. NIOC can redistribute reserved bandwidth to other system traffic types (management, **internet small computer system interface** (**iSCSI**), **fault tolerance** (**FT**), vMotion, and so on), but not to VM traffic. VM traffic is limited without any congestion even with minimal management traffic.

- Multicast networking is enabled for efficient operation as one multicast group contains no network partitions

  Justification: Multicast networking using **internet group management protocol** (**IGMP**) snooping is required for vSAN. We should validate that the networking infrastructure supports this requirement by running network discovery commands. The infrastructure will require either a snooper carrier configured for the vSAN network, or IGMP snooping to be disabled explicitly on the VLAN or ports which are used by default in many environments. All of the physical switches and routers handling vSAN traffic, along with the layer 2 path and the layer 3 (optional) path, should be enabled with multicast. VMware recommends using layer 2 multicast for the simplicity of configuration and operations.

VMware's Customer Experience Improvement Program/vSAN ReadyCare

We have enhancements that have been added to and developed by an engineering team based on customer feedback from the past 6 – 12 months. VMware retrieves technical data regarding VMware solutions that are deployed in the customer's environment and other services that are integrated with the customer's VMware license keys.

Depending on the nature of the VMware product or service and the level of participation the customer selects, the technical data that's accumulated is comprised of all or some of the following data:

- Configuration data providing information about the configuration of VMware solutions, along with associated products that are deployed in the customer's environment, like the version of VMware products, configuration details, and applications/hardware configuration with VMware products/services
- Product feature-specific data, which provides information about how VMware tools are utilized in a customer's data center, including user interface activity and integration with third-party tools
- Performance data helps with the different metrics to measure the performance of various VMware product features, like availability/scalability/security, along with response times for user interfaces and API integrations
- Product log data that's fostered from the initial deployment to the production stage by VMware products, such as the logs of past system events and different system states for a specific time period, without having a customer's application data/content

VMware updates all of this information at regular intervals to reflect changes in its products/services through the **Customer Experience Improvement Program** (**CEIP**), and we always suggest that our customers browse this web page (CEIP) regularly so that they're always updated: `https://www.vmware.com/in/solutions/trustvmware/ceip.html`.

We will now see how we can use machine learning techniques to collect logs and for monitoring purposes.

Intelligent monitoring

vSAN environment monitoring is critical for a successful deployment. We have to follow the following monitoring practices:

- General monitoring practices
- vSAN Health Check plugin
- vSAN Observer
- VMware vRealize Operations Manager Monitoring
- Monitoring design

General monitoring practices

vSAN supports monitoring datastores through the VMware vSphere Web Client, the HTML 5 client, and the vSAN Management API. The vSphere Web Client monitors different objects, like clusters and datastores.

Without effective control over the infrastructure, a VM or ESXi host sprawl can quickly diminish the return of investment from virtualization. Areas for improvement include assessing workloads to determine performance metrics that can then be used to create VM-specific vSAN policies to better suit the workload. A stripe policy of two nodes for write-intensive workloads that are bigger than the cache disk size may lead to performance improvements. We can minimize the troubleshooting time that is spent by the operations teams on VMs that have performance-related issues.

vSAN Health Check plugin

The vSAN Health Check plugin is a simple way to check the health of the vSAN cluster. It is included by default in the installation. The health check technical recommendations are as follows:

Priority	Component	Recommended action item
P1	vSAN	Verify vSAN firmware and driver versions.
P2	vSAN network	Distribute VMNICs for a port group across different PCI buses for greater redundancy.
P3	vSAN network	Configure NICs, physical switch speed, and duplex settings consistently. Set to auto negotiation for 1 gigabit NICs.
P3	vSAN	Verify that you have set up the storage policies correctly.
P3	vSAN	Verify that the VMs are distributed evenly across vSAN nodes.

VMware recommends using the Health Check plugin to allow for easy monitoring of the vSAN clusters.

vSAN Observer

vSAN Observer does in-depth monitoring of disk groups, shows an aggregate view for the group and disk layers, and also monitors vSAN physical disk layer latencies. It reads cache hit rate, evictions and performance, and other parameters, such as size, disk type, manufacturers, model, local/non-local, and so on. vSAN Observer is part of the **Ruby vSphere Console (RVC)**, which supports the use of the vCenter Server certificate on Windows platforms and provides network, a **Content-Based Read Cache (CRBC)**, and vSANSparse statistics. The following tools/data can help your customers troubleshoot vSAN-related issues:

- vSAN configuration
- vSAN health monitoring
- vSAN disks statistics
- vSAN performance statistics
- Observer

vSAN Observer recommends that you deploy a vCenter Server appliance and run the observer session on the newly deployed or remote vCenter Server appliance to increase the data gathering time beyond the default (2 hours).

The vSAN Observer user interface displays the following performance details:

- Statistics of the physical disk layer
- Extensive physical disk group details
- CPU usage statistics
- Consumption of vSAN memory pools
- Physical and in-memory object distribution across vSAN clusters

vRealize Operations Manager monitoring

A business can be heavily impacted when service interruptions continue to rise and IT teams become more eager to find interruption issues in a small time period. Logs have become a critical source of information and are required to troubleshoot IT operations issues. However, the amount and size of logs have grown due to increasingly complex IT environments.

As customers become more cost-sensitive, Log Intelligence, one of the VMware Cloud services, helps customers overcome these challenges by providing valuable insights into public and private cloud infrastructure. Log Intelligence offers rapid IT troubleshooting, deep operational visibility across multiple clouds, including VMware Cloud on AWS, and centralized log management. VMware recommends installing and monitoring vSAN with vRealize Operations Manager, which helps in the comprehensive monitoring of vSAN in the environment.

Challenges affecting business outcomes

The following are the challenges that affect business outcomes:

- **Lack of visibility**: IT teams that don't have system-wide visibility through a single pane of glass spend an ample amount of time manually reviewing logs, preventing them from spending time on more strategic tasks
- **Reactive troubleshooting**: IT teams spend too much time identifying and solving issues due to isolated metrics that trigger alarms, increasing time spent, cost, and downtime

Business benefits

Log Intelligence is a service that offers rapid IT troubleshooting, deep operational visibility across public and private cloud environments, and centralized log management, making it easier for IT teams to decipher and solve issues more efficiently.

Following are the benefits:

- **Minimize costs**: Help customers improve performance and create a faster problem resolution that raises savings at a company's top and bottom line
- **Prevent downtime**: Move away from a reactive mechanism to spot potential problems and track infrastructure whose log values were out of normal operation, preventing future downtime
- **Saving time**: Use a centralized log management tool to automatically collect and organize information

Technical Issues

The technical issues such as monitoring and proactive support to reduce resolution time are as follows:

- **Lack of insight into the SDDC environment**: IT administrators generally don't have good visibility into their organization's cloud environment, especially the workloads that are deployed by their application teams in public clouds.
- **Reactive performance troubleshooting**: Traditional log management tools rely on raw performance metrics and typically do not go beyond alerting administrators when performance thresholds are exceeded. In addition, they do not provide additional insights from log files for troubleshooting and root cause analysis.

Technical solution

Log Intelligence, a SaaS offering, is easy to onboard and use. IT administrators can use it to collect and analyze various types of machine-generated log data. Log Intelligence can be connected to infrastructure and applications for enterprise-wide visibility via log analytics.

Log Intelligence offers an intuitive GUI-based interface, making it easy for IT administrators to run simple interactive searches, as well as deep analytical queries for quick insights that provide immediate value and improved IT efficiency.

Log Intelligence advantages

Let's take a look at some of the advantages of Log Intelligence:

- **Immediate time to value**: Log Intelligence provides automated data collection from public and private cloud environments and provides immediate time to value by helping customers ingest universal log collection and analytics efficiently, while delivering intuitive, interesting events
- **Cost savings**: It helps customers in reducing the resolution time of escalated support requests with its innovative approach of indexing and grouping in rapid troubleshooting across virtual and cloud deployments
- **Increased productivity**: It has a single log management console with all of the relevant information, which helps users to innovate new things in the organization

We will now learn about the different configuration parameters that you can use during a stretched clusters deployment.

HA configuration in stretched clusters

VMware vSAN has the option to deploy two ESXi hosts in a cluster with a remote witness appliance. We can define specific vSphere HA behaviors for vSAN to validate the VM's individual state. vSphere HA can dictate a particular VM failover action if the virtual machine's components are accessible from a defined partition.

The following is a screenshot of the cluster settings:

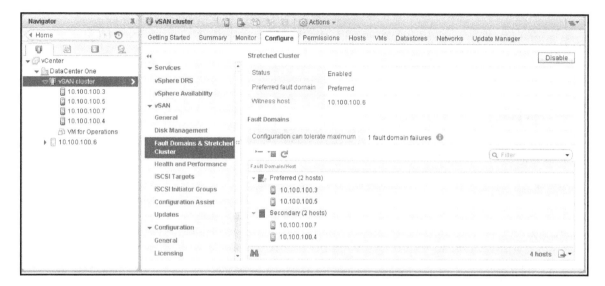

vSAN stretched cluster-enabled HA has the following configurations in the cluster's settings:

vSphere HA	Configuration **parameters**
Host Monitoring	Yes
Host Hardware Monitoring —VM Component Protection: Protect against Storage Connectivity Loss	No, default
Virtual Machine Monitoring	No, default
Admission Control	Enabled
Datastore Heartbeats	Datastore Heartbeat will be disabled by using datastores from the defined list, but without choosing any datastores from this list

To configure the policy to enable HA, follow these steps:

1. Go to the HA Settings (HA enabled) and configure the static routes on the host servers and witness host
2. Add static routes to the witness VM's vSAN VLAN to the vSAN network of the ESXi hosts in the data centers
3. The traffic for the vSAN is enabled for the VMkernel port groups
4. Static routes are added by executing the `esxcfg-route -a` command on all the ESXi hosts in the cluster across data sites and the witness host
5. The `esxcli` command is used to add a static route, as follows:

```
esxcli network ip route ipv4 add -n <remote network> -g <gateway to use>
```

Two-node clusters

Two-node clusters aren't possible with vSAN as a minimum of three hosts are required to make sure that all of the components are protected.

A two-node cluster can be configured from the configuration wizard with a witness. This is good for smaller environments. VMware introduced **witness traffic separation** (**WTS**) for two-node configurations and also supports this feature for stretched clusters. Most of the stretched vSAN customers leverage this feature by configuring (witness) through the CLI (`esxcli`). All we have to do is tag a **VMKernel NIC** (**vmknic**) for witness traffic with the following command:

```
esxcli vsan network ip set -i vmk<X> -T=witness
```

Witness appliance for the vSAN cluster

VMware has a vSAN witness appliance, which is basically an ESXi instance running in a VM to act as a witness. A witness host needs less capacity, bandwidth, and performance compared to hosts in normal vSAN clusters, or hosts in data center parts of the vSAN stretched cluster. A witness appliance stores the VM's witness components and is responsible for object quorums in the case of failure or a split-brain situation to make the required VM available.

The configuration of the witness appliance for a tiny environment are as follows:

- Tiny (10 VMs or less: application/domain controller/file and print server)
- Two vCPUs, 8 GB vRAM
- 8 GB ESXi Boot Disk, one 10 GB SSD, one 15 GB HDD
- Supports a maximum of 750 witness components

Configuring the vSAN cluster

All VMware vSAN certified servers that are mentioned in the VMware HCL can be considered to be a part of the vSAN cluster, which utilizes both magnetic disks and flash disks for capacity and cache tiers. 70% of the available cache is allocated for storing frequently read disk blocks by reducing accesses to the slower magnetic disks, while the remaining 30% of the available cache is allocated to writes. Multiple writes should be coalesced and written sequentially to enhance magnetic disk performance:

1. Choose the cluster that the host servers are added on.
2. Click the **Configure...** option on the right-hand side to manage all the datastores powered by vSAN:

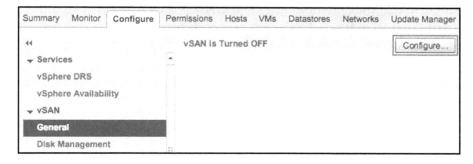

3. Find the option to configure the vSAN under **Virtual SAN**.
4. Go to the configuration page.

5. Then, go to **Claim disks** from datastore, and then choose **Manual**:

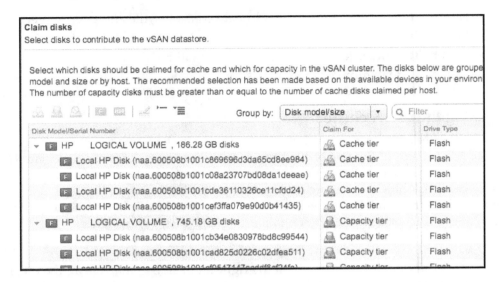

6. **Fault Domains & Stretched Cluster**: Configure two host vSAN clusters.
7. Confirm that the networking is valid on the vSAN VMkernel adapters.
8. Verify that all of the disks show up for each server.
9. Collapse the disks to their logical drives. Then, set the SSDs to the **Cache tier** and the HDDs to the **Capacity tier.**
10. Choose the fault domains and the **Preferred fault domain** and **Secondary fault domain.**
11. Click **Next** and continue.
12. Select the option to choose the witness VM.

13. Map the capacity and the **Cache tier** for the witness VM host. Then, deploy the witness VM to monitor the vSAN cluster:

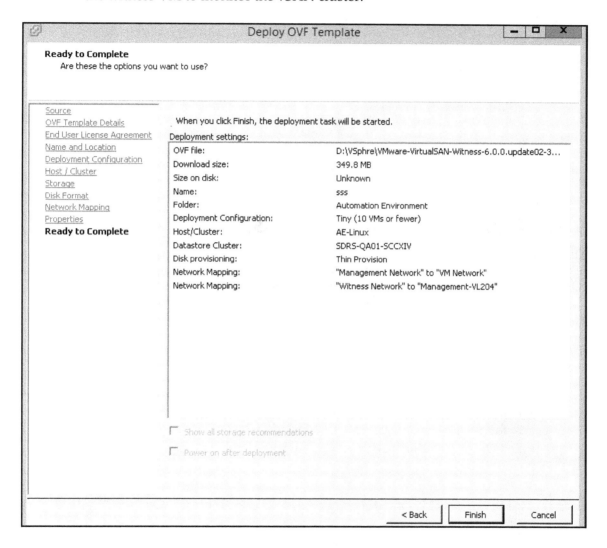

14. Click on **Finish** to complete the vSAN configuration. The disks should now be visible.

15. Log on to a host server and type the following command:

```
localcli vsan cluster get
```

16. Verify that the cluster shows up as healthy.

17. Under **Cluster** | **Monitor** | **VSAN** |, run the health check to confirm that the configuration is correct.

We have gone through how to configure a vSAN cluster, as well as how to perform health check monitoring. Now, we will learn about the various policies that we can configure through SPBM.

vSAN policy design with SPBM

The storage class definition in vSphere maps to policies that are defined through vSAN SPBM to achieve different levels of **service level agreements (SLAs)** and **quality of service (QoS)**, and can leverage these benefits from advanced vSAN data service functionalities such as de-duplication, compression, and checksums. Using general policies is advisable if no specific use cases exist.

Start by assessing the following different application requirements:

- I/O performance and the profile of your workloads on a per-virtual-disk basis
- Working sets of your workloads
- Hot-add (feature of vSphere) of additional cache requires re-population of the cache
- Specific application best practices, such as block size

Defining a policy based on business objectives

vSAN integrates storage parameters into vCenter Server by using vSphere APIs for storage awareness. SPBM further helps in defining VM-centric policies, which are basically constructs that store VM storage provisioning needs based on the available storage features with various policies (with configuration parameters).

These are given here:

- **Number of disk stripes per object** (performance): Default value = 01, maximum value = 12

  Remarks: VM disk performance gets enhanced with RAID 0 stripe configuration by defining the HDD's number.

- **Flash read cache reservation (%)** (performance): Default % = 0, maximum % = 100

  Remarks: We can leverage this configuration exclusively for VMs, which must have read IOPS issues. This needs to be sorted out, but reservations should be not recommended as per VMware best practices.

- **Number of failures to tolerate**, FTT (redundancy): Default value= 01, maximum value = 03

  Remarks: The FTT number decides the number of host, disk, or network failures a storage object can tolerate. We can tolerate n (0, 1, 2, 3) failures when $n+1$ copies of the disk are created and $2n+1$ hosts or fault domains need to contribute to the storage alongside mirroring. We can tolerate one failure, with minimum four nodes or fault domains and subsequent can tolerate two failures with minimum six hosts or fault domains along with erasure coding. The maximum value is 1 if the disk size is greater than 16 TB.

  These parameters are configured in the **Configure** interface:

- **Failure tolerance method (Performance/Capacity)**: Default = **RAID 1 (Mirroring)-Performance**

  Remarks: RAID 1 can tackle failure tolerance using mirrors with good performance, while RAID 5/6 helps with failure tolerance by using parity blocks with great space efficiency. RAID 5/6 is only available on all-flash vSAN clusters, and when the **Number of failures to tolerate (FTT)** is set to 1 or 2. A value of 1 FTT implies a RAID 5 configuration, and a value of 2 FTT implies a RAID 6 configuration.

- **IOPS limit for object** (performance): Default = 0

  Remarks: The IOPS limit for a disk IOPS is calculated as the number of I/Os using a defined size. It uses a base size of 32 KB by default, so a 64 KB I/O will represent 2 I/O. No limit policy is defined by setting the limit equal to 0.

- **Disable object checksum** (override policy): Default = No

  Remarks: This setting determines whether checksums will be calculated for the data being written to the volume or not. Checksum calculation and error-correction are executed in the background.

- **Force provisioning** (override policy): Default = No

  Remarks: Force provisioning overrides the current policy if it won't comply with the available resources.

- **Object space reservation** (thick provisioning %): Default value = 0, maximum = 100

  Remarks: It will help with a percentage of thick-provisioned storage objects upon VM creation, while the rest of the storage objects are thin-provisioned. When the expected amount of storage is already filled with objects, then it will help in reducing repeatable disk growth operation tasks.

FTT policy with RAID configurations

Policies are configured based on application requirements and are applied based on the objects that are available. The following table lists the FTT policy options that are applied in different scenarios:

NumberOfFailuresToTolerate	Fault Tolerance Method	Implemented Configuration	Number of hosts required
0	RAID-1	RAID-0	1
1	RAID-1	RAID-1	2
1	RAID5/6	RAID-5	4
2	RAID-1	RAID-1	5
2	RAID5/6	RAID-6	6
3	RAID-1	RAID-1	7

RAID-1 will be used for the **Fault Tolerance Method** on the host servers. If we are not using the HBA mode for the hosts, then we will have to RAID the individual disks as RAID 0. Sometimes, RAID 5 and RAID 6 over the network are also referred to as erasure coding. This is done inline so that no post-processing is needed. Erasure coding distributes the **RAID5/6** stripe across multiple hosts without any overhead or need of data locality. **RAID-5** needs a minimum of **4** host clusters, with 3+1 logic, and has to sustain one node failure without data loss. This reduces disk capacity consumption. Erasure coding can guarantee capacity reduction. This policy can be executed on a per **virtual machine disk (VMDK)** file/disk using the SPDM system.

Summary

The vSAN performance and health service helps with updated health checks for known issues and provides visibility to the end user. It will not help users collect the logs from a customer's site and send them in for support so that the development team will get the incident after the end user has logged a support ticket with issues. Instead, it helps with data that assists the engineering team in enhancing VMware products and related services, resolving issues, and recommend best practices to follow while implementing VMware solutions.

In the next chapter, `Chapter 3`, *Security with Workspace One Intelligence*, we will learn about how customers are becoming increasingly pressured to provide more intelligent insights about their organizations and user behavior to deliver the best IT service possible. Having different tools and systems that house this insightful data across **mobile device management** (**MDM**), PC, and other third-party systems causes fragmentation of this data and inconsistency in the process of training, as well as the end user experience.

Further reading

- *VMware Virtual SAN Design and Sizing Guide,* at `https://www.vmware.com/files/pdf/products/vsan/VSAN_Design_and_Sizing_Guide.pdf`
- *VMware Virtual SAN Health Check Plugin Guide,* at `http://www.vmware.com/files/pdf/products/vsan/VMW-GDL-VSAN-Health-Check.pdf`
- *vSphere 6.0 Configuration Maximums guide,* at `https://www.vmware.com/pdf/vsphere6/r60/vsphere-60-configuration-maximums.pdf`
- *Virtual SAN documentation from the vSphere Storage guide in the VMware vSphere Documentation,* at `https://www.vmware.com/support/pubs/vsphere-esxi-vcenter-server-pubs.html`
- *VMware Virtual SAN section of Performance Best Practices for VMware vSphere 6.0,* at `http://www.vmware.com/files/pdf/techpaper/VMware-PerfBest-Practices-vSphere6-0.pdf`
- *Solutions for Poor Network Performance section of vSphere Monitoring and Performance vSphere 6.0,* at `https://pubs.vmware.com/vsphere-60/topic/com.vmware.ICbase/PDF/vsphere-esxi-vcenter-server-60-monitoring-performance-guide.pdf`

Security with Workspace ONE Intelligence

3

This chapter will focus on VMware Workspace ONE in detail and its innovative ways to secure applications, data, endpoints, and networks. It can manage access of both applications and devices with its intelligent analytics engine and by integrating third-party tools to provide end-to-end security for end users.

We will learn how to protect customer's digital workspaces through advanced analytics and how to create smart policies to detect, protect, and re-mediate their applications from threats. We will also learn how to design a solution to be compliant as per the customers' policies and use cases of Workspace ONE Intelligence.

The topics that we will cover in this chapter are as follows:

- Overview on Workspace Intelligence and its business objectives
- Integrated deep insights, smart planning, and intelligent automation
- Conceptual and logical design requirements
- Use cases of Workspace Intelligence
- Overview on Workspace ONE Intelligence Trust Network and Workspace ONE AirLift

Technical requirements

You can download VMware Workspace ONE Intelligent Hub `https://my.workspaceone.com/products/VMware-Workspace-ONE-Intelligent-Hub`

Workspace ONE Intelligence

Workspace ONE Intelligence has capabilities to better leverage the Workspace ONE platform with data-based actions and resolution from a single repository. Users want to access their corporate data and applications from anywhere on any device. Security tools are not able to take care of end user requirements and security risks in a proactive way in the current environment. Customers can't get complete insight into device, application, and user data due to the always-changing perimeter (Location of End User's Device) which creates big cybersecurity threats and complicates the management task.

Every organization has to take care of their employees as well as not compromise security. Employee productivity is affected by application execution issues and irregular services. It will be affected by frequent changes in application access by reducing privileges. We have to find a way around security and user's productivity and avoid a complicated management process by using intelligent data analysis and automation. We also need a solution for frequently-changing threat areas, which can integrate with all relevant services and provide assurance on security aspects in the current digital workspace system.

Workspace ONE Intelligence is a cloud service built on the Workspace ONE platform, which helps customers with great graphics, user interface tools, and an intelligent process, to take data-driven decisions from a single source of truth. Workspace ONE Intelligence helps to filter and find **key performance indicators** (**KPIs**) on demand by collecting, examining, and connecting device, application, and user data. As it gets the required data information, it then can leverage the built-in rule engine to automate policies that can make moves based on broad metrics. Customers can define rules that can make intelligent remediation moves as per context. AI and ML techniques can be utilized for suggested actions and future-planning for an entire digital workspace system that customers can manage without compromising the end user's productivity.

Cybersecurity in the mobile cloud era needs a comprehensive enterprise security strategy and approach. The Workspace ONE Intelligence compliance engine continuously monitors devices and performs escalating actions to prevent noncompliance.

Business objectives of Workspace ONE Intelligence

Workspace ONE Intelligence will help customers to handle the following business objectives:

- It helps administrators to get end-to-end visibility during different phases of app deployment starting from app engagement with great end user response on the ground to rapidly troubleshoot issues, minimize support calls, and improve user productivity.
  The end-to-end visibility from a single console is shown in the following screenshot:

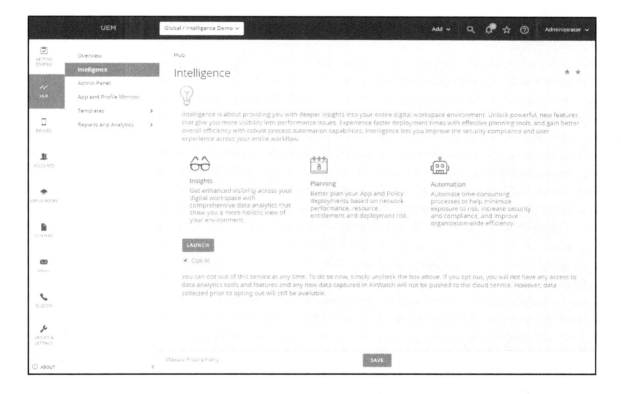

- It assists in better utilizing resources in organizations by providing users what they need and lowering capex on hardware and software, which are less consumed with insights visibility into resource utilization.
- It can find and fix all kinds of vulnerabilities rapidly by recognizing non-compliant systems and then patching with current security patches by automating access control rules based on end user behavior.

Workspace ONE Intelligence helps in three important domains by leveraging the Workspace ONE platform.

Integrated deep insights

Integrated insights means having full visibility of a customer's digital workspace and having granular insights that assist in data-driven business strategies:

- Workspace ONE Intelligence combines and connects all hardware (system), application, and end user data with each other at a single platform to get full visibility of the digital workspace system.
- Customers can make their decisions in real time, resolve end user problems, and avoid all security risks.
- Customers can run or define tailored reports to have authenticate data based on past data and use these insights in other decisions that are correlated with each other.
- Customers have to keep their investments on the data that is critical to them as per their business requirements. They can think proactively about all upcoming security loopholes, application roadmaps, hardware enrollment, application life cycles, and their future patch timelines.

Customers can get visibility of complete digital workspace systems from one console, including the capability to search and query the system to analyze data, identify patterns, and detect abnormal behaviors. They can make accurate data-based decisions for their complete systems with predefined dashboards and past data.

We will get critical information related to the following attributes/parameters:

- Application life cycle
- Application consumption
- Application commitment
- User commitment
- Kind of devices

- OS deployment
- Application description
- Application subscription

Customers can run reports to find systems with patch vulnerabilities, monitor critical Windows security statuses across the entire system including monitor installation stages for application release, or fetch software and device inventories on Workspace ONE Intelligence platform.

App analytics for smart planning

Customers can better utilize the software development life cycle across the environment, and end users to rapidly solve incidents, minimize support calls and enhance end user ease of use.

Smart business analytics for maximum productivity:

- Customers can see real-time application actions that help them to make immediate decisions on issues that are creating problems for end users. They can sort out all critical issues first, then define application upgrade timelines based on end users' requirement. We can get a 360-degree view of application process with 24/7 monitoring of application utilization at the ground level across systems, geographical boundaries, connection state, or application version. Customers can get detailed analysis with all relevant data regarding application consumption by various user groups.

- Customers can quantify application consumption and usage in their system and identify the applications that are most utilized and easily calculate the return on investment (ROI). It will assist decision-makers to have a better understanding of how mobility helps their end users with end-to-end visibility from each phase of application deployment.

- Customers can find their critical flows or actions in their applications and correlate them with important business parameters.

- Workspace ONE Intelligence customers can get the benefits of automation for their homegrown applications.

Workspace ONE Intelligence assists in policy-based app deployments. Policy is defined with recommended contexts as parameters to monitor application performance by detecting the root cause of problems and enhance the application delivery with required and tested patches.

Value propositions of Workspace ONE Intelligence are as follows:

- Accurate plan for asset life cycle refresh
- Application license updates and upgrades
- Day-one support for operating system
- Customized devices and application configurations
- Define security policy baselines based on work domains

Intelligent automation driven by decision engines

Customers can automate defined workflows to leverage decision engines to improve utilization across the organization:

- Customers can configure predefined automations to assist in managing digital workspaces in a smart way.
- Customers can automate operations and security processes by creating policies that fire based on the parameters configured in these policies. Context-based policies improve the automation process by avoiding manual work.
- Customers can build rules that help in automation with remediation processes related to context, which improves end user productivity and ease of use.
- Customers can create context-based rules, which are related to the customer environment, and by automating workflows, which can integrate with third-party applications such as ServiceNow and Slack through the REST API.

Workspace ONE Intelligence has rules engines with intelligent tasks across the system by creating rules for automated moves based on number of metrics. It will help to build contextual workflows for intelligent remediation moves based on security policies and be compliant. Workspace ONE Intelligence can integrate with the third-party API layer to create workflows that can utilize customer's specific requirements, as follows:

- Detect actions with a high security threat and get desired access control without any manual intervention
- An intelligent application release cycle can detect issues before deployment

- Define the desired system state by automating data discovery
- Integrate third-party applications to automate business tasks

Automated workflow utilizes third-party services to avoid application installation failure.

Design requirements

A customer has to implement an enterprise initiative to provide flexible and robust access to enterprise systems through mobile devices to their users, such as the following:

- Provide employees secure access to mobile email from any device, anywhere
- Deliver secure content to specific employees to increase efficiency in the field
- Provide a layer of security and oversight for central IT and confirm that access to enterprise systems is occurring in an expected and trusted fashion

When determining the appropriate design solution, multiple options might be possible for a design element. In such instances, the following design qualities in prioritized order are used to determine the best design solution for the customer:

Design quality prioritization (Highest to lowest consideration)	Description
Availability	Ability to achieve highly-available operation
Manageability	Flexibility, scalability, and ease of operations
Performance	Performance of the environment
Recoverability	The ability to recover from an unexpected incident that affects the availability
Security	Overall infrastructure security and compliance with regulatory policies

Conceptual designs

The VMware platform for customers is composed of multiple interconnected tiers, each of which provides functionality to deliver against the business requirements. We will go through each layer in detail as shown in the following diagram:

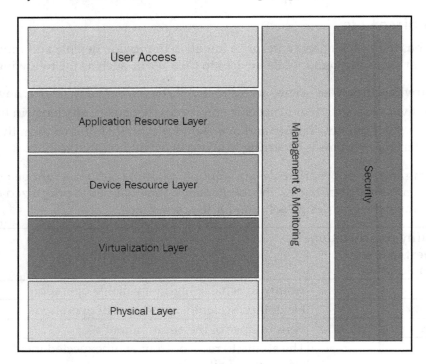

Each of the individual layers provides a specific functionality to deliver the overall end user computing solution:

- **User Access**: This is the single interface for all mobile applications and resources
- **Application Resource Layer**: These are the components necessary to provide application resources to users
- **Desktop Resource Layer**: These are the components necessary to provide device resources to users

- **Virtualization Layer**: Applications are hosted in virtual machines on a hypervisor
- **Physical Layer**: This is the physical infrastructure used to run the workloads

In addition to the horizontal tiers, there are two vertical tiers that interact with each of the five horizontal tiers:

- **Management**: The components necessary to manage the provisioned infrastructure
- **Security**: The components used to confirm provisioned workloads and infrastructure are compliant with customer-defined policies

The following items were identified as key business drivers for the workspace environment:

Business driver	Description
Security	Confirm that unmanaged devices do not access enterprise systems
Employee efficiency	Provide mobile access to enterprise systems for employees
Cost savings	Drive cost savings through reduction in mobility-based IT hardware spending

We will now discuss the horizontal layers:

- **User Access**: The user portal provides the consistent interface users start from. The portal core functions are as follows:
  - **Single Point of Access to Enterprise Applications**: This is the ability for users to select items from a catalog and have them rapidly deployed, modified, or decommissioned as required
  - **Adaptive Enrolment**: This is the device enrolment that takes place based on the security posture of the application being requested

The following diagram describes various business drivers in detail with their use cases:

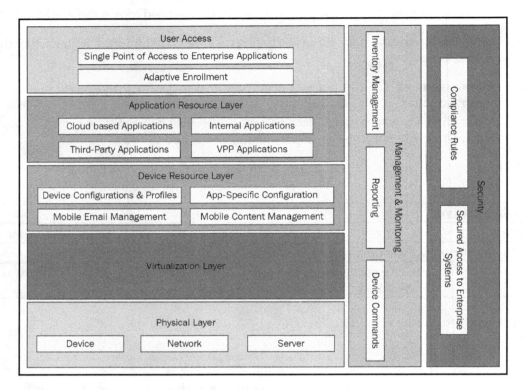

- **Application Resource Layer**: The **Application Resource Layer** provides application resources to the user. These resources consist of the following:
  - **Cloud based Applications**
  - **Third-Party Applications**
  - **Internal Applications**
  - **VPP Applications**

- **Device Resource Layer**: The **Device Resource Layer** provides the following:
    - **Device Configurations & Profiles**
    - **Mobile Email Management**
    - **App-Specific Configuration**
    - **Mobile Content Management**
- **Virtualization Layer and Physical Layer**: The **Virtualization Layer** hosts all applications in virtual machines. The **Physical Layer** provides the physical components utilized by the AirWatch **Enterprise Mobility Management (EMM)** platform. These include the following:
    - **Device**: The physical device presented to the user
    - **Servers**: The physical servers that host the virtualized workloads
    - **Network**: The physical network infrastructure including switches, routers, and WAN links required for interconnectivity of the various components
- **Management & Monitoring**: Management is a critical component due to the dynamic nature of the end user platform. The management vertical interacts with all five layers of the platform to enable management to be efficient and proactive across the whole stack. The vertical management provides the following components:
    - **Inventory Management**: The ability to manage and view devices from a single administrative interface
    - **Reporting**: The ability to report on sets of devices or configurations
    - **Device Commands**: The ability to push commands to user devices as required
- **Security**: The security vertical has interactions with all layers to enable security requirements to be met. The security vertical provides the following:
    - **Compliance Rules**: The ability to confirm devices are behaving as expected
    - **Secured Access to Enterprise Systems**: The ability to secure access to enterprise systems (email, content, and data servers)

This section builds upon the conceptual design by adding the logical components that serve as the core of the solution. The logical design is reflected in the following diagram, and the following subsections discuss each component:

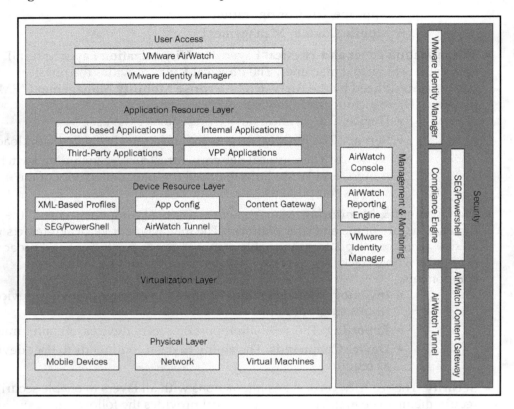

This section discusses, from a high level, the logical components that make up the design of the preceding diagram:

- **User Access**
    - **VMware AirWatch** provides the enrollment and data processes required to provide a unified user-access posture.
    - **VMware Identity Manager** provides authentication policies, and queries existing authentication sources for authorization. Customers utilize **VMware Identity Manager** to enforce multifactor authentication based on the network origination of the user. Once authentication is successful, **VMware Identity Manager** provides the user with their catalog of accessible resources.

- **Application Resource Layer**
    - **Cloud-based Applications (Software as a Service (SaaS) model)** are configured and presented as catalog items on the **VMware Identity Manager** portal. Users that access the customer's portal select the application from their catalog.
    - **Third-Party Applications** are those available in OS-specific application stores, such as iOS App Store and Google Play Store.
    - **Internal Applications** are those developed internally by the customer. **VMware AirWatch** allows administrators to push these applications directly to devices.
    - **VPP Applications** are those purchased through the Apple Volume Purchase Program.
- **Device Resource Layer**
    - **XML-Based Profiles**: **VMware AirWatch** utilizes XML-based configuration profiles to enforce restrictions and push configurations.
    - **SEG/PowerShell**: Customers will utilize **SEG/PowerShell** to secure mobile access to its mail application running on endpoint. This system utilizes mail-compliance rules to provide administrators with visibility to mobile email access and to enable a cohesive device security posture.
    - **App Config**: **VMware AirWatch** integrates with the **App Config** standard, which allows application-specific configurations for certain use cases.
    - **AirWatch Tunnel**: The VMware **AirWatch Tunnel** secures access to enterprise systems (such as internal websites).
- **VMware AirWatch Content Locker**: This secures access to backend content sources. This server component confirms that only enrolled, secure devices have access to sensitive corporate data.
- **Mobile Devices**: The following device platforms have been selected by customers:
    - Apple iOS
    - Android
    - Windows 10

- **Network**: Existing physical networks are used for this system. Detailed network connections are outlined in VMware Workspace ONE Design and deploy service-engineering specifications.
- **Virtual Machines**: An existing virtual machine infrastructure is used for this system.

Top ten use cases of Workspace ONE Intelligence

Workspace ONE takes the guesswork out of access to cloud, mobile, and Windows applications. IT can rest easy knowing both **bring your own device** (**BYOD**) and corporate-owned devices are secure, and can keep the network safe with simple-to-use conditional access settings. Managers don't have to worry about employee productivity with secure applications, including mail, calendar, documents, and social media. And employees never miss a beat with real-time app delivery and automation.

Identifying and mitigating mobile OS vulnerabilities

Customer challenge: Known vulnerabilities are discovered, such as Spectre or Meltdown. Each manufacturer quickly release OS updates but manufacturers vary in how they implement fixes. Each OS has its own update schedule and update version; iOS uses OS version, while Android uses security patches. IT admins are not able to determine impacted mobile devices and deploy fixes across their entire environment.

Workspace ONE Intelligence can help to quickly assess and report on the impact of a threat or vulnerability, and share these reports with management and IT teams across the organization. It easily identifies assets with known vulnerabilities by creating a visualization of all devices with an out-of-date OS version (iOS) or old security patch date (Google). It segments the data by organization group, device type, or model to see which devices are the most out of date and most vulnerable. It leverages automation to target vulnerable devices and add actions to force OS update (iOS-supervised devices only), notify the end user via email or Slack, notify the InfoSec team of the most vulnerable devices, move devices to an org group with stricter access requirements, and monitor how many devices have been patched or upgraded across Android and iOS.

Key benefits: This increases security hygiene across the organization, increases compliance, and increases collaboration between the IT ops and InfoSec teams.

Insights into Windows 10 OS updates and patches

Customer challenge: A customer is requesting a list of devices without specific KBs installed, that are the most at risk (severe security or critical Windows updates).

Workspace ONE Intelligence can help customers to create a real-time dashboard for all current devices that do not have critical KB installed and can segregate the data by model or OS version to identify OS versions with risk. Automation will help to notify users for all updates of their devices and will monitor whether devices have been patched or upgraded across all Windows 10 devices.

Key benefits: Customers can save time, improve user experience, and better protect their endpoints.

Predicting Windows 10 Dell battery failures and automating replacement

Customer challenge: Users are using Windows endpoints that require charging during a full day of work, and it sometimes affects end users' productivity by limiting their mobility.

Workspace ONE Intelligence can help these users by limiting their mobility. Customers need a solution that can monitor Windows 10 Dell devices with poor battery health as well as the overall life of the battery reports or dashboards. It should provide visibility to end users about battery life. It is known that the maximum charge capacity is reduced as the battery life decreases. It can create a workflow to tag devices with poor battery life in Workspace ONE UEM . It will also help in reporting and in creating ServiceNow ticket with device information to order new battery. Then, it will notify employees via Slack or email for a battery replacement by automating all manual tasks.

Key benefits: Automation will reduce costs linked to user-generated support tickets or calls, and increase employee experience and productivity by enhancing the lifespan of devices.

Identifying unsupported OS versions and platforms

Customer challenge: A big challenge for IT is to understand how many users have devices that are no longer supported by the organization and can be security risks. Another challenge for IT, especially for organizations that are building their own applications, is the lack of visibility into device and OS distribution across the organization.

Workspace ONE Intelligence can help to identify devices that are too old to upgrade to the latest OS and are exposed to the latest security threats and create a report or a widget on a dashboard that identifies devices that are potential end-of-life candidates. It gives visibility into most popular device types among users, recommends new hardware to employees, and easily communicates device and OS version adoption to app developers to ensure they are building for the most popular device/OS combinations and maximize adoption of their in-house applications. It quickly determines which device and OS versions to stop supporting based on usage.

Key benefits: This can optimize development efforts, understand user needs per geography, save time, and increase productivity.

Tracking OS upgrade progress

Customer challenge: Every year, Apple and Google release new major OS updates that include new UEM features for better management, and new usability features that administrators want their end users to take control of to improve productivity. When a major OS releases, administrators need near-real-time visibility into how an OS version is adopted so they can forecast how long they have to pilot new features and to determine when is a good time to deploy the new UEM feature (for example, security policy) to all of their devices.

Workspace ONE Intelligence can help to create a dashboard to monitor the adoption of old and new OSes and monitor the increase of devices reporting the latest version of an OS while seeing the decrease of devices reporting the previous version. It also compares OS adoption between different vendors year after year, and forecasts when a major OS release will reach the majority of their devices.

Key benefits: This can help to make informed decisions about the entire environment, give quantitative insights to app developers, and prioritize feature development based on OS distribution.

Monitoring device utilization or usage

Customer challenge: In business use cases, devices have a single or multi-purpose use, where they are either shared by a group of users, as in retail stores, or dedicated to one user, such as an electronic flight bag for an airline pilot. In either case, IT needs visibility to ensure that all of these assets are online and active. In retail, stores with devices that are inactive are most likely stolen. Airline pilots can't fly without their devices, so there should be almost zero inactive devices.

Workspace ONE Intelligence can help IT teams get visibility into understanding where and what stores have the most inactive devices and use automation to notify store managers of potentially stolen devices. It also helps to create tickets (ServiceNow) and deploy devices in need to the right location, and use dashboards to monitor the types of devices most used across the organization or per location. It also uses intelligence to make data-informed decisions when the time comes to purchase new devices.

Key benefits: This can help to improve store performance, increase efficiencies within an organization, and optimize resources.

Increasing compliance across Windows 10 devices

Customer challenge: IT teams have to work together to quickly identify what their device posture is at any moment on Windows 10 PCs. They have to install multiple agents to pull basic OS and model information or report on more granular device states, such as BIOS version and Secure Boot status.

Workspace ONE Intelligence can help only one agent needed to gather and report on all of the numerous device states that IT team cares about and understand devices at high risk. Query entire environment to identify most at risk devices such as out-of-date BIOS version, Secure-Boot-disabled, TPM-Chip-disabled, Firewall-disabled, AV-disabled, and BitLocker-note-encrypted. It can sort and segment these devices by OS version, region, and model and create rules that automatically quarantine high-risk devices and remove access to sensitive data sources. It use automation to enforce compliance by pushing down security policies: removing access to VPN/Wi-Fi, re-enabling BIOS settings, and moving the device to an org group with less entitlements and app access.

Key benefits: This can save time, as there's no need to aggregate multiple reports from different sources; increase compliance across the environment; and increase IT Ops efficiencies.

Comprehensive mobile app deployment visibility

Customer challenge: As an IT administrator, deploying an app update is critical to meet business and security needs. Sometimes, there is only a small window of opportunity to deploy applications. In retail, it can only be in the middle of the night; for security, it's as soon as possible; and for 24-hour healthcare workers, there may not be a good time to push an update.

Workspace ONE Intelligence can help to get visibility on the best time to deploy an app based on usage patterns and accurately report on how a deployment is going. It also gives information about app adoption, app engagement in real time to app development teams, management and the helpdesk by providing full 360 degree view of any application. It gets insights into app performance per device manufacturer, model, or OS version by quickly detecting the root cause of deployment issues or poor app adoption. Devices on older app versions can be notified to update to the latest version and app developers can stop maintaining older versions when the user base is low. It leverages automation actions to remediate issues, such as notifying store managers of an issue to redeploy a previous release of the app if the new version is not stable.

Key benefits: This can reduce costs linked to user-generated support tickets or calls and increase employee experience and productivity. Help developers prioritize features and get insights into older app versions that can be retired.

Tracking migration and adoption of productivity applications

Customer challenge: IT regularly evaluates productivity applications based on user feedback and license costs, and often migrates end users from one productivity app to another. IT's challenge is understanding how the migration is going and whether users are adopting the new productivity app with the objective to EOL the older solution., for example, moving from WebEx to Skype to Zoom.

Workspace ONE Intelligence can help to quickly determine which devices have which productivity app installed and monitor the popularity of each app per location or group. It determines whether a location or group has completed the migration to the new app and uses automation to notify users that they need to migrate to the new app, based on usage and adoption. It makes data-based decisions on which applications to buy or renew during the next refresh cycle.

Key benefits: This can optimize resources, reduce risk, increase compliance, increase employee experience, and increase IT Ops efficiencies.

Adopting internal mobile applications

Customer Challenge: Organizations are investing a lot of money into building and maintaining internal applications, and they don't have visibility on how many are used and how they're used.

Workspace ONE Intelligence can help **line of business** (**LOB**) owners can easily monitor usage and engagement of the applications they are responsible for, and can prioritize feature development using real-time and historical data available in the app's detail dashboard. It easily determines why applications are not used and rules out any performance or compatibility issue. Least-used applications that are mandatory can have adoption-remediation action plans; those that are not critical can be EOL-ed and resources can be redirected to more important projects.

Key benefits: This will optimize resources, improve user experience, increase productivity, and maximize developer efforts.

Workspace ONE Trust Network

Workspace ONE Trust Network provides customers with an extensive and new security approach to secure their emerging digital workspace. Customers can create fully-compliant security process across organizations from employees, applications, endpoints, and networks, with new features to defend, identify, and recover cybersecurity risks based on a framework of trust and validation.

Workspace ONE Trust Network has built-in security functionalities developed on the Workspace ONE platform, which integrates them with third-party security partner services to provide security across their digital workspace.

Workspace ONE Trust Network offers the following:

- Customers can configure rules for data encryption and application blacklisting. It can monitor for threats, such as malware and malicious applications, and helps in remediating with its feature-like access-control.
- End users can utilize a self-service app catalog and single-sign-on into applications for efficiency and multi-factor authentication across all applications, which will help in application protection.
- It helps with end-to-end monitoring for security threats such as OS vulnerabilities, authentication issues, and application-based attacks. It can automate actions against risks by wiping, isolating, and patching in a short amount of time.
- It can identify suspected applications or files and attacks by isolating and remediating the root cause.
- It has a data-loss-prevention component with end-to-end visibility and prevents unauthorized data transfer by using its data analytics engine.

We will get valuable data through data analytics and avoid too much data to verify and check by automating data filtering.

The digital workspace is an innovative domain and, by integrating third-party security tools with Workspace ONE, improves end user experiences.

Workspace ONE AirLift

Workspace ONE can provide end-user-device life cycle management tasks using cloud-based services with intelligent data analysis and automation. The VMware digital workspace is the only unified endpoint-management solution that is suitable for all use cases and different phases of the endpoint devices.

Workspace ONE can assist customers by transforming Windows 10 management with the following features:

- Customers can deliver day-one productivity for new employees with Zero-Touch Onboarding and improve productivity.
- Customers can do real-time configuration on the fly through cloud-powered policies from firmware to the OS/applications layer. Workspace ONE can integrate with Dell Client Command Suite for over-the-air BIOS configuration.
- Workspace ONE Intelligence can patch in real-time on or off the customer network so they are always up to date and protected from high-severity exploits.
- It is a completely web-based solution with peer to peer Win32 app distribution, which needs zero server footprint.
- It has AirLift co-management and co-existence with Microsoft **System Center Configuration Manager** (**SCCM**), by assisting any **PC lifecycle management** (**PCLM**) task and also support current SCCM deployment with Windows 10 versions.

Workspace ONE platform updates

Customers are using multiple platforms, such as Windows 10 and macOS, so they require regular and secure application delivery across all platforms. Workspace ONE has security, life cycle management, and compelling features for all applications, irrespective of OS platforms across mobile and desktop. These features help IT team to provide better security with maximum usability.

Expanded Win32 app delivery

Windows applications are an important part of any digital workspace even most of the organizations are adopting OS-neutral applications . Workspace ONE combined both applications and desktop provisioning from a single console hosted in either on-premises private cloud or from cloud service providers (public cloud). VMware Horizon Cloud on Microsoft Azure VDI is an extension of the VMware support for published applications on Microsoft Azure.

Customers can manage on-premises desktops and applications to the cloud using the VMware software-defined data center tools, such as NSX, **virtual storage area network** (**vSAN**) and vSphere, across Amazon's data center networks beyond regional boundaries. They can utilize Horizon 7 **Cloud Pod Architecture** (**CPA**) across AWS pods to support federated users source across on-premise and cloud-based infrastructure with the single Horizon 7 management console for their daily operations.

Simplified macOS adoption

Workspace ONE client for macOS provides a uniform platform even users will move to different OS platforms. Users can consume all applications, including virtual Windows applications, from their macOS.

Extended security for Microsoft Office 365 (O365) applications

Workspace ONE extends Intune app protection rules in Microsoft Graph to provide IT O365-specific security capabilities, such as data-loss prevention controls and continuous device risk-monitoring, which disconnects O365 on the fly if a threat is detected. Customers will secure critical business data as their end users are using Office 365 for their daily utilization which can be easily integrated with other critical applications.

VMware Boxer with Intelligent Workflows

Customers can assist their end user's contents on their mobile devices with mobile flows powered by context-based moves and accurate understanding in VMware Boxer secure email. Users can do their work across multiple backend business processes, such as Salesforce, Concur, and Jira, within the Boxer app with automated workflows. They have Boxer tool with automated workflows features to design predefined connectors with third-party services to assist their users to be productive within Boxer.

Extended management for rugged devices

Rugged devices need remote management and intelligent remediation in the field, and both are important to have maximum availability. Workspace ONE assists customers to get maximum up-time by supporting battery management for Android devices. Customers can fix a defined clause, such as battery or memory level, network connectivity, or the time to trigger a particular action, such as force-quitting mission-critical applications or backing up files.

Customers can retrieve battery health, cycle count, and identification from the rugged device to recognize bad batteries and change them before it is not performing as it should.

Workspace ONE has developed an extensive API framework that integrates with existing enterprise systems and services, as well as third-party applications. The Workspace ONE API framework allows external programs to invoke core Workspace ONE product functionality, extending security measures and strengthening the overall enterprise infrastructure. The Workspace ONE architecture incorporates RESTful and **Windows Communication Foundation** (**WCF**) **Simple Object Access Protocol** (**SOAP**) enterprise APIs to enable automated, real-time event notifications to integrated solutions.

Summary

Workspace ONE Intelligence has features that give us a deep understanding of the digital workspace with intelligent unified endpoint management for automated delivery. Customers can enhance their security, compliance, and end users' productivity with these features. Workspace ONE Intelligence assists in data-based decisions, which provide all critical data information across the digital workspace system through digital workspace analytics.

It is impossible to manage mobile work environments with massive data aggregation without any tool. It is a herculean task to make data-driven decisions in the digital workspace without a single visible console across all devices, applications, and end users. Manual tasks are reactive to user demands and external actions rather than being proactive.

In the next chapter, you will learn about how VMware helps customers to automate data centers and the public cloud running on vSphere by injecting advanced analytics into its VMware vRealize Suite components to manage IT operations based on intent.

4
Proactive Operations with VMware vRealize Suite

In this chapter, we will focus on how VMware helps customers to automate data centers and the public cloud running on vSphere by injecting advanced analytics into the solution to manage IT operations based on intent. The capacity analytics engine with vRealize Operations leverages ML techniques to proactively alert you about future events based on past trend analysis.

We will learn about different analytics engines in vRealize Suite and how vRealize tools work across different clouds. Also, we will learn about the automation of containers on vSphere by reducing the **total cost of ownership** (**TCO**) and improve ROI with better optimizations.

We will cover the following topics in this chapter:

- Unified end-to-end monitoring
- Intelligent operational analytics with the **Software-Defined Data Center** (**SDDC**) journey
- The vRealize operations architecture and capacity planning
- VMware container management services
- VMware Cloud on the AWS implementation plan

Technical requirements

Refer to this link for VMware Cloud on AWS `https://cloud.vmware.com/vmc-aws.`

Unified end-to-end monitoring

Monitoring solutions should collect and monitor end-to-end service-level and infrastructure-level KPIs, such as response times by transaction and service availability, and alert on deviations. It can understand and map all of the components of the end-to-end service, such as applications and application components, and monitor the performance and availability of all of the application platform components, such as the web server, application server, message bus, and database. We should understand and map all of the virtual and physical infrastructure components, including VMs, server, storage, and network, by monitoring the performance and availability of all of the virtual and physical infrastructure components. We can combine and correlate all these parameters to generate alerts by identifying the root cause of alerts. IT Operation team can get all of the information on a customizable dashboard as per their roles with all reporting capabilities. It should add a predictive element to the analysis capability in order to prevent business outages.

Intelligent operational analytics

The highly dynamic and complex nature of virtual environments requires a holistic perspective and making essential correlations with the applications and other parts of the infrastructure. It requires a new class of data management and analysis technique(tools designed for physical infrastructure do not work well with the dynamic and decentralized nature of virtual environments).

Operational analytics consists of two key areas:

- Performance analytics help customers to adopt a proactive approach in IT operations for faster issue-detection and resolution by enabling the following:
  - Proactive control of service performance and availability based on automatic learning, near-real-time adjustment of baselines, statistical and trending algorithms
  - Service impact analysis and prioritization
  - Problem isolation and root-cause analysis

- Capacity analytics enable a predictive approach through current and historical data analysis, simulation, and what-if scenario-enabling:
  - Capacity planning and forecasting for medium to long-term provisioning
  - Predictive alerts
  - Near-real-time capacity optimization through automated provisioning and scaling

The vRealize Operations Manager architecture

vRealize Operations Manager collects and analyzes information from multiple data sources within the enterprise. vRealize Operations Manager uses advanced analytics algorithms to learn and recognize the normal behavior of every object it monitors. This information is presented to users through views, reports, and dashboards.

The user interface allows users to access the results of the analytics in the form of badges, alerts, charts, and reports.

vRealize Operations Manager can be download as a **virtual appliance** (**vApp**) and run as a VM. It will be configured to perform one of the following roles within the complete vRealize Operations Manager cluster design:

- **Master node**: The critical first node in the cluster or it will be a single standalone node in a small deployment architecture
- **Master replica node**: An optional instance for high availability
- **Data node**: Used for scalability purposes
- **Remote collector node**: Helps to overcome data-collection issues, such as poor network performance across the network

vRealize Operations Manager is available in two different deployment models:

- A pre-configured vApp
- As a Windows or Linux installable package

The customer can choose the vApp model for ease of deployment.

Application architecture overview

We will learn about the vRealize Operations Manager's logical node architecture with all functional capabilities :

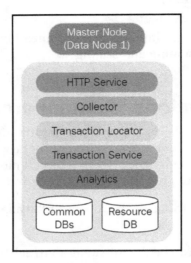

HTTP Service is the main product UI. It supports the main product UI, administrator UI, and suite API. This explains how vRealize Operations Manager calculates stress, and then how stress is used for capacity-planning calculations of recommended size, capacity remaining, and time remaining. This provides enough detail that people can understand how vROps calculates these values, can defend when they are reasonable, can recognize when a fluke in data is causing recommendations that should be overruled and explains the concepts behind parameters that can be tuned in vROps.

Capacity planning

Stress is a measure of the severity of performance problems because of being undersized in the worst hour of the past month. It is an intelligent way of dealing with peaks and fluctuations in demand, which considers both how hot the resource ran and for how long in a continuous period.

Total capacity versus usable capacity: Total capacity is the raw capacity. Usable is the capacity we pretend we have for planning purposes, allowing for host failures and subtracting some headroom to be safe.

Total capacity – Buffers (HA and general) = Usable Capacity. You can see this in **Analysis |
Capacity Remaining** in the vROps UI.

The capacity defines the stress zone. For stress calculations, do we use total or usable as the
capacity? It depends on whether we want to know what actually happened (total), or
whether we're planning for the future and want to be more cautious (usable).

For actual stress calculations, we use total capacity as the capacity. When planning and
finding suggested right-sizes, we want to be cautious, so we do stress calculations where
the capacity is the usable capacity and given the measured demand, at what capacity would
we barely have avoided performance problems, without wasting resources, after allowing
for possible host failure and some headroom to be safe.

Critical success factors

The following are the critical success factors:

- Improve **mean time to repair** (**MTTR**) and operational efficiency to prevent
  severe service impact
- Implement unified end-to-end monitoring
- Combine ongoing capacity and performance management with policy-based
  automated remediation to dynamically optimize performance and capacity usage
  and promptly remediate performance issues
- Introduce operational analytics to augment real-time visibility and provide
  actionable intelligence for problem isolation and troubleshooting with
  foundational policy-based automated remediation capabilities
- Introduce proactive issue-detection by alerting and improving **mean time
  between failures** (**MTBF**) with advanced proactive and automation capabilities
- Gain full proactive control of capacity, performance, and availability
- Adopt predictive analytics capabilities to enable proactive issue identification
  and resolution
- Day-to-day performance, capacity, and availability issues are largely managed by
  adaptive-process automation

Kubernetes solution from VMware

Kubernetes is the accepted container orchestrator being adopted by enterprises, but operationalizing Kubernetes in production is not an easy task. Enterprises need a comprehensive solution that supports multi-cloud environments with networking services, security, policies, persistence, monitoring, and analytics. As more containers are being used, customers need orchestration tools to manage operations, such as scaling up and down, scheduling containers, and handling failure, in order to run and manage these containers. Container-orchestration tools, such as Docker Swarm and Mesosphere, are available but the most accepted is an open source system called Kubernetes. Kubernetes has a perfect solution for running containerized apps but operating Kubernetes in a production environment is still a complex task. Production capabilities (such as storage, networking, security, multi-tenancy, and persistence) need more enhancement and complementary tools to reliably deploy, maintain, scale, monitor, and self-heal the underlying infrastructure.

Pivotal Container Service and VMware Kubernetes Engine

VMware has **Pivotal Container Service (PKS)**, a joint product developed by VMware, Pivotal, and Google that deploys and manages enterprise-grade Kubernetes on top of the VMware SDDC stack as well as on public cloud providers such as **Google Cloud Platform (GCP)**. VMware PKS helps enterprises to run Kubernetes in production on vSphere and in the public cloud. It radically simplifies the deployment and operation of Kubernetes so you can run containers easily at scale. We can help customers with PKS so they can quickly set up and manage a Kubernetes service within their existing vSphere environment. Customers are looking for a Kubernetes solution that is simple to deploy and operate by helping them to take care of all of the day-one and day-two needs and eliminate the lengthy steps of setting up and maintaining the platforms. They are also demanding that the solution offer hardened production capabilities in the areas of networking, storage, security, and multi-tenancy.

VMware Kubernetes Engine (VKE) is an enterprise-grade **Kubernetes as a Service (KaaS)** offering that provides easy-to-use, secure-by-default, and cost-effective Kubernetes. VKE will launch first on AWS.

Forrester had a 31-criteria evaluation of hybrid cloud-monitoring and -management providers; here are some of them:

- Must have core capabilities in multi-cloud management across workloads
- Must support at least the AWS, Azure, and vSphere-based clouds
- Must be sold as a standalone tool

Containers are productive as a container offers developers a simple, lightweight, and portable way to package and deploy applications across various hosts or cloud environments. The use of containers is expected to grow exponentially in the coming years because of these benefits. Containers are not a new technology, but a company called Docker successfully popularized this technology and Docker is the most-known container format today.

SDDC journey stages

VMware defines the following journey stages toward SDDC:

- **Cost center**: IT operates as a cost center. The focus is on reducing costs through CapEx and OpEx savings by improving IT efficiency with uniform anarchitecture and by virtualizing the infrastructure.
- **Service provider**: IT becomes a service provider by delivering secure, highly-available, and resilient IT services that meet business demands and service-level requirements.
- **Business partner**: IT transforms to become a business partner by automating the delivery of infrastructure and application, resulting in faster delivery times and more responsive IT, enabling a quicker time to market.

There are three stages of capability maturity for this data center virtualization and standardization:

- Compute virtualization, virtualization for business critical apps, big-data application support
- Software-defined storage, network virtualization, extension to hybrid cloud, data center migration
- Management across hybrid, heterogeneous data centers

The following capabilities are crucial:

- **Financial model and measurement**: Awareness and understanding of the costs of assets and underlying infrastructure capacity
- **Process and control**: IT processes are adapted for virtualization but are largely manual, with ad hoc inter-process integration
- Establishment of standard operating procedures for consistency in operations
- Focus on limited, continuous improvement

VMware container-based services

This requires the following VMware SaaS and third-party products:

- Deploy a network virtualization foundation (NSX-T)
- Deploy and run containerized workloads (VMware Pivotal Container Service)

The following prerequisites are required to deliver this service:

- **Deploying NSX-T (virtual appliance) foundation**:
    - The minimum requirement for virtual appliance virtualized CPU capacity (GHz) is that enough CPU capacity must be available to deploy NSX Manager and NSX Controllers
    - The minimum requirement for virtual appliance virtualized RAM capacity (GB) is that enough memory capacity must be available to deploy NSX Manager and NSX Controllers
    - **Network time protocol** (**NTP**) must be set up and time-verified to be correct.
    - DNS must be configured and tested for forward, reverse, short, and long name resolution.
    - Shared storage must be provisioned. Enough storage capacity must be available to deploy NSX Manager and NSX Controllers.
    - **Maximum transmission unit** (**MTU**) size : 1700 (minimum)

Deploying NSX-T for network virtualization on ESXi and deploying PKS for use in a private cloud

Deployment of a network virtualization solution based on NSX-T according to a VMware standard architecture is implemented and verified in the customer environment. The service includes technical verification of platform prerequisites, the deployment of network virtualization using NSX-T, and functional testing for the customer.

The following table shows the installation and configuration of all components associated with NSX-T:

Specification	Description
NSX Edge VMs deployed and configured	NSX Edge VMs deployed and configured as a transport node
NSX logical switches	Logical switches configured
NSX-T tier-0 logical router instance(s)	NSX tier-0 logical routers to provide an on and off gateway service between the logical and physical network using static or dynamic routing **border gateway protocol** (**BGP**) peering
VMware ESXi™ hosts configured as transport nodes	ESXi hosts prepared, registered to the NSX-T management plane, and configured as transport nodes

Deploying the NSX-T foundation

Foundational VMware NSX-T deployment: This includes the preparation work, deployment, and verification of NSX Manager and NSX Controllers:

Specification	Description
Data center location(s)	This means the data center deployment of NSX-T components.
NSX Manager instances	NSX-T Manager appliances are installed and configured.
NSX Controllers	NSX-T Controllers are installed and associated to an NSX Manager. For every NSX Manager instance, a control cluster of three NSX controllers will be formed.

Deploying and running containerized workloads

Deploying PKS for use in a private cloud: Deploy the PKS platform to help customers create a private cloud environment for provisioning Kubernetes workloads.

The following table shows installation and configuration of all components associated with PKS:

Specification	Description
Deploy pivotal operations manager into vSphere	This means the deployment of pivotal operations manager within a single data center.
Configure pivotal operations manager	This is the configuration of the pivotal operations manager instance.

Install PKS	This refers to the deployment of the PKS tile within a single pivotal operations manager.
Configure PKS	This is the configuration of PKS within vSphere, connections to pre-existing NSX-T objects, Kubernetes cluster plan sizing, **User Account and Authentication** (**UAA**), errands, syslog, resource configuration, and stemcells.
Create Kubernetes clusters using PKS	This is the installation and use of the PKS command-line interface to create Kubernetes clusters according to defined cluster sizing plans.
Install and configure Harbor container registry into vSphere	This means the installation of Harbor Container Registry instance, without replication, using the **open virtualization application** (**OVA**) so that the single instance can serve many clusters. VMware will assist in certificates between Harbor, and Kubernetes cluster nodes, and other environments are configured to enable pushing and pulling of container images to Harbor.
NSX-T preparation for PKS integration	This means the creation of NSX-T objects needed for PKS integration.
Logical switches	Logical switches are created for the PKS management network and service network.
IP pool for external access	An IP pool is configured to provide load-balancing address space for each Kubernetes cluster created by PKS. The network will also provide IP addresses for Kubernetes API access and Kubernetes exposed services.
IP block	An IP block is configured to assign address space to Kubernetes pods through the **Container Networking Interface** (**CNI**).
NSX-T tier-1 logical router instances	These are Tier-1 logical routers, one dedicated to PKS management components and one dedicated to Kubernetes cluster nodes.
PKS and NSX-T integration	This means the configuration of PKS on vSphere to integrate with NSX-T.

VMware Cloud on AWS

VMware Cloud on AWS is a vSphere-based cloud service. The service brings VMware enterprise class SDDC software to the AWS cloud. It is delivered, sold, and supported by VMware as an on-demand, elastically-scalable service that leverages the global footprint and breadth of services from AWS.

Along with VMware vCenter Server® management and optimizations, it presents a full cloud solution that runs on next-generation, elastic, bare-metal, AWS infrastructure.

This will help in the quick deployment of secure, enterprise-grade AWS cloud-based resources that are operationally consistent with vSphere-based clouds. This will result in a complete turnkey service that operates seamlessly with both on-premises private clouds and advanced AWS services.

In addition, new features enable new functionality that revolutionizes business functions:

- **VMware Cloud on AWS disaster recovery**: This is an add-on on-demand service that will help to reduce cost, simplify disaster recovery strategy, and accelerate time to production for an environment.
- **VMware Hybrid Cloud Extension (HCX)**: This helps to accelerate cloud adoption by making bulk migrations available for zero downtime live migrations that can be scheduled. This solution is multisite-aware, WAN-optimized, and secure to allow for migrations to occur as quickly as possible to VMware Cloud on AWS.

VMware Cloud on AWS differs from on-premises vSphere

VMware Cloud on AWS has vSphere running on Amazon's bare-metal hardware with its cloud-automation engine. VMware administrators have access to all of the required interfaces, including VMware vSphere Web Client, both HTML5 and Flash-based, with all of the needed API integrations. This is a VMware-managed service and **role-based access control (RBAC)** will be properly working.

Following is the configuration with specific users profile:

- VMware manages the VMware Cloud on AWS environments and as such, rights are assigned to `cloudadmin@vsphere.local` for user access. This might cause incompatibilities with products that require `administrator@vsphere.local` access to an environment.
- Users are expected to place workloads in the `Workloads` folder because permissions are denied on the other folders.
- Networking is configured through the VMware Cloud on the AWS user interface as the NSX user interface is not available.
- VMware Cloud on AWS is a managed environment, so all upgrades and maintenance procedures are performed by VMware.

VMware Cloud on the AWS implementation plan

VMware Cloud on AWS has the benefit of being an architected solution that can be deployed on-demand. It is quite difficult to make sure that requirements are met successfully to connect a pre-existing on-premises environment to the VMware Cloud on AWS.

The current on-premises installation, software revisions, and configuration determine the steps required to successfully connect a VMware Cloud on the AWS instance. This section discusses the implementation path that VMware recommends.

The following diagram shows the steps required when assessing an environment for compatibility to connect to a VMware Cloud on AWS environment. The following is a flow chart based on a standard process starting with authentication:

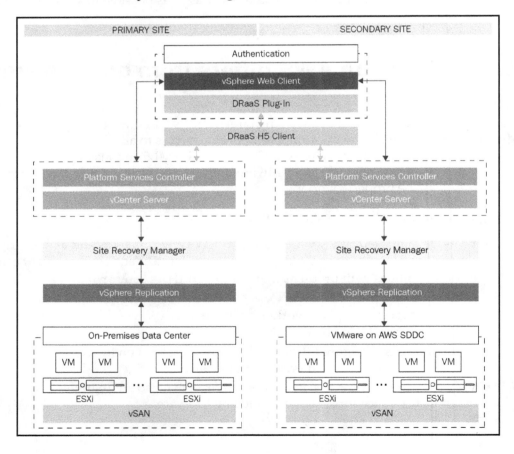

Implementation plan for VMware Cloud on AWS

Use the following implementation plan to configure the on-premises environment to support VMware Cloud on AWS connectivity. After completion, the environment is a fully-configured hybrid cloud that can be used for the defined use cases.

Here's a summary of the steps:

	Action	Impact	Required	VM downtime
1	Creation of VMware Cloud on AWS account and having it linked to the customer Amazon account details	None; timelines are dependent on having the accounts created	Yes	No
2	Create the SDDC data center in VMware Cloud on AWS	None	Yes	No
3	On-premises vSphere upgrade performed (if required)	vSphere is upgraded, so VMs might require downtime, for assistance with upgrades, contact your VMware sales representative for information about the VMware vSphere upgrade service	Yes (if version is earlier than 6.0U3)	Yes (if upgrade required)
4	VPN connectivity between the on-premises and AWS	Network changes required to create the VPN tunnel	Yes	No
5	Test hybrid linked mode in the environment	None	Recommended (if hybrid linked mode is supported)	No
6	Use case configuration	Dependent on the use cases being designed	No	Depends on use case being designed

	Action	Impact	Required	VM downtime
7	Create or migrate workloads	VM downtime for cold migrations	No	Depends whether cold migration is required

Detailed initial steps to configure VMC on AWS

The detailed initial steps to configure VMC on AWS are as follows:

1. Log in to VMware Cloud on AWS
2. Invite users to join the cloud instance
3. Link credentials to an Amazon account
4. Create the VMware Cloud on the AWS SDDC data center
   This step includes the creation of the data center in the VMware Cloud on the AWS instance. During this process, customer will be asked to provide the details for the configuration, including a name, sizing, data center location, and most importantly, the IP address subnet information. The IP address details cannot be changed without deploying the SDDC again, so be sure to specify the correct address.

5. On-premises vSphere environmental upgrade:
   The environmental upgrade of vSphere must occur at this point so that there is feature compatibility with the VMware Cloud on the AWS instance. This process can be time-consuming, but verify that all features are compatible. The environment must be at the vSphere 6.0 update 3 or later to be supported, but preferably at vSphere 6.5 to utilize the hybrid linked mode and other functionality.

Installation, configuration, and operating procedures

The following section describes several basic procedures for the installation, configuration, and operation of a VMware Cloud on the AWS environment.

The following are basic tests for testing a new VMware Cloud on the AWS environment:

1. Log in to the test console:
   1. Open a web browser
   2. Navigate to `https://vmc.vmware.com/`
   3. Log in with your VMware Cloud on AWS credentials

2. Create an SDDC:
    1. Click **Create SDDC:**

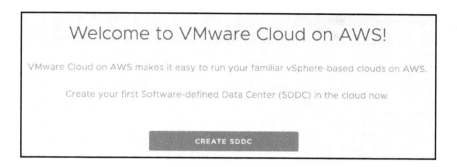

2. Fill out the details as prompted to provision your data center:

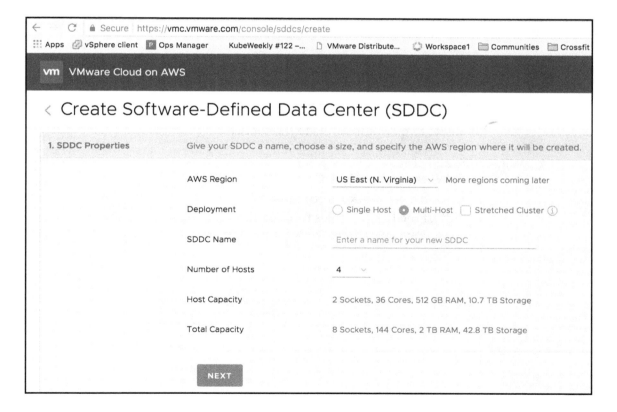

3. Invite users:
   1. Click **INVITE USERS:**

   2. Invite two or more users to the service

4. Adjust firewall rules:
   1. Select the created SDDC
   2. Click the **Network Information** tab
   3. Adjust the firewall rules through the VMC console to allow access from your internal network (or the appropriate security policy for your company):

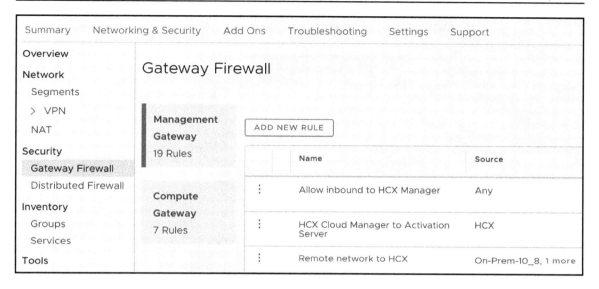

5. Log in to the vCenter Server instance:
    1. Select the created SDDC
    2. Click the **Connection Information** tab
    3. Log into the VMware vSphere Web Client™ (HTML5) using the specified credentials

The following represents basic workflows to test VMware Cloud on AWS:

1. Create a VM using the OVF deploy feature using the vSphere Web Client (HTML5):
    1. Go to the workload resource pool

2. Deploy an OVF to create a VM:

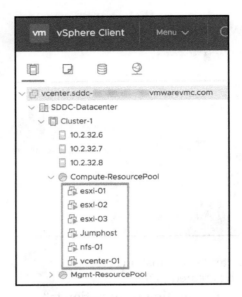

2. Create a local content library:
    1. If you do not already have one, create a content library in your on-premises data center.
    2. Add your templates, ISO images, and scripts to the content library. All .vmtx templates are converted in to OVF templates.
    3. Publish your content library.
    4. In your VMware Cloud on AWS SDDC, create a content library that is subscribed to the content library you published from your on-premises data center. The content is synchronized from your on-premises data center to your SDDC in VMware Cloud on AWS.

3. Create a VM and boot an OS using an ISO:
    1. Upload an ISO to the content library
    2. Create a VM and mount ISO from the content library
    3. Then start the VM

4. Perform basic VM operations on a VM:
    1. Migrate a VM
    2. Clone a VM
    3. Migrate a VM using VMware vSphere vMotion®

4. Snapshot a VM
5. Connect to your VM using the vSphere Web Client (not the remote console)
6. Create a logical network using the vSphere Web Client (HTML5):
    1. Go to **Global Inventory Lists**
    2. Go to **Logical Networks**
7. Assign the previously-created VM to this logical network and power on the VM and then Edit the settings of the VM
8. Create a rule that allows VMs on `sddc-cgw-network-1` to reach the internet:
    1. Create a new firewall rule on the compute gateway
    2. Ping from your VM to a known IP address on the internet

Hybrid-linked-mode testing functionality

This section describes the hybrid-linked-mode testing functionality. To test the hybrid linked mode, perform the following steps:

1. Log in to the cloud vCenter Server instance using the credentials specified in the **Connection Information** tab.
2. Navigate to the hybrid linked mode configuration by clicking **Menu | Administrator**.
3. Under **Hybrid Cloud**, click **Linked Domains:**

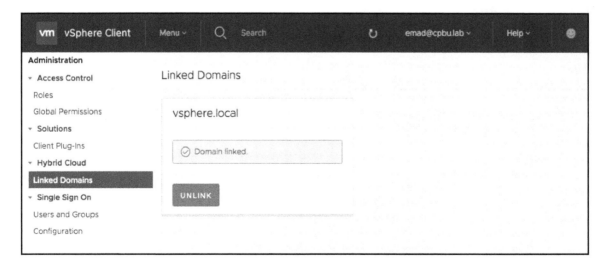

4. Follow the steps on the screen to configure **Hybrid Linked Mode**:

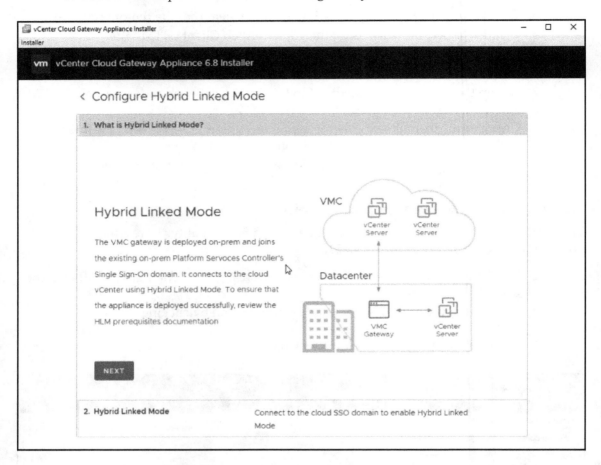

5. Add an on-premises identity source (Active Directory or Open LDAP) to cloud vCenter Server instance.

6. Grant the cloud vCenter Server access to the on-premises Active Directory group (the one identified in the prerequisites):

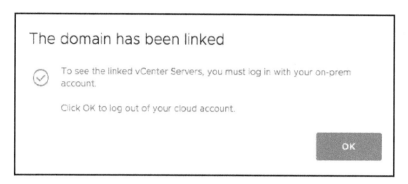

The domain has been linked

To see the linked vCenter Servers, you must log in with your on-prem account.

Click OK to log out of your cloud account.

OK

7. Link to the on-premises **Single Sign-On** domain (you are prompted to log out).

8. Log back into the cloud vCenter Server instance using an Active Directory user from the on-premises Active Directory group. Both on-premises and VMC vCenter Server inventories should be available.

9. Perform VM operations in both on-premises and cloud vCenter Server instances:
    1. Create and delete a VM
    2. Power a VM on and off
    3. Snapshot a VM
    4. Clone a VM
    5. Migrate a VM

vSphere vMotion is not supported between on-premises and cloud vCenter Server instances at this time.

Support and troubleshooting

There are several options for getting help and support for your VMware Cloud on the AWS environment. This section will brief you about some known issues and workarounds that can help you resolve problems.

There are several options for getting help and support for your VMware Cloud on the AWS environment.

1. Before you contact VMware for support, have the support information for your SDDC ready:
    1. Log in to the VMC Console at `https://vmc.vmware.com`
    2. Click **View Details** on the SDDC card
    3. Click **Support** to view the support information
2. Select a method for getting help or support:
    - **Chat**: Click the Chat icon and click **New Conversation**. Type your message in the chat window. You can include images by dragging them into the chat window. Currently, chat is monitored Monday through Friday, from 6 A.M. to 6 P.M. PST.
    - **File a support request on My VMware**: Click the Help icon and click **My VMware**. You are taken directly to a form for submitting a support request.
        - **View contextual help**: Click the Help icon. Browse the topics under the **Help Topics** heading or type a question or keywords in the **Type your question here** field to search the available topics.
    - **Ask a question in the forums**: Click the Help icon and click on **Community Forums**. You can post questions and discuss the product with other users in these forums.

Summary

vRealize tools can automatically correlate all IT data and events into a unified view with a complete picture of the IT environment, and use predictive analytics to help customers to improve performance and avoid disruption by enabling them to proactively identify and remediate issues before they affect the business. Customers can monitor performance, optimize their infrastructure capacity, and perform log analytics while getting comprehensive visibility into their applications and infrastructure in a single solution.

vRealize Operations Insight provides an on-ramp to the SDDC by helping customers to prepare for storage and network virtualization with management tools that are designed with the SDDC in mind. With vRealize Suite, virtualization customers have one solution to do it all, including vSphere, container management and compliance, log analytics, storage and network visibility, application dependency mapping, and OS monitoring.

In the next chapter, `Chapter 5`, *Intent-Based Manifest with AppDefense*, we will explore VMware AppDefense, which enables organizations to tackle the challenges associated with keeping data safe across on-premises to the public cloud. It is a data center endpoint security solution that embeds threat-detection with responses directly into the kernel of the virtualization layer on which applications and data reside.

Further reading

- For details on the account creation, linking, and inviting process, see the *VMware Cloud on AWS documentation* at `https://docs.vmware.com/en/VMware-Cloud-on-AWS/services/com.vmware.vmc-aws.getting-started/GUID-9CAB2B3E-42D5-44A1-9428-E8FFD22BDD01.html`

- For testing, the following prerequisites listed in `https://docs.vmware.com/en/VMware-Cloud-on-AWS/services/com.vmware.vmc-aws.getting-started/GUID-BE75F0F1-2864-4926-97FE-37E635471C43.html` must be met

- Hybrid-linked mode is only supported if the prerequisites are met; see the guide for details at `https://docs.vmware.com/en/VMware-Cloud-on-AWS/services/com.vmware.vmc-aws.getting-started/GUID-BE75F0F1-2864-4926-97FE-37E635471C43.html`

- For details on network configuration, see configuring management gateway networking at `https://docs.vmware.com/en/VMware-Cloud-on-AWS/services/com.vmware.vmc-aws.getting-started/GUID-3A7090C5-836C-4DBA-9E69-A4A1D9B6F139.html`

- See the *Deploying a Software Defined Data Center* section of the *VMware Cloud on AWS Getting Started* guide at `https://docs.vmware.com/en/VMware-Cloud-on-AWS/services/com.vmware.vmc-aws.getting-started/GUID-BC0EC6C5-9283-4679-91F8-87AADFB9E116.html`

- For details on upgrading the vSphere environment, see the *VMware vSphere Upgrade Guide* in the vSphere documentation center at `https://docs.vmware.com/en/VMware-vSphere/index.html`

5
Intent-Based Manifest with AppDefense

This chapter will cover the strategies you can use to host applications, so that you can provide freedom to end users and full control to administrators. You will learn about business values by using AppDefense, which uses machine learning to create an intent-based manifest for an app running in a VM. It can properly secure the app against malicious behavior with an algorithm that measures the running state against the intended state.

After going through this chapter, you will have learned how to get relevant alerts in a security operations center by defining an application-centric policy to detect, protect, and enforce the desired state of an application. This will also help you to design a **security operations center** (**SOC**) based on a precise decision engine, rather than having to perform guesswork.

In this chapter, we will cover the following topics:

- VMware innovation for application security
- Application-centric alerting for the SOC
- AppDefense and NSX

Technical requirements

You can download VMware AppDefense plugin 2.1.1 for the Platinum Edition from `https://my.vmware.com/web/vmware/details?downloadGroup=APPDEFENSE-211 amp;productId=742amp;rPId=31142`.

VMware innovation for application security

The problem lies in the existing security strategies that customers are employing to protect data center endpoints. We are specifically referring to the endpoints within the data center where applications are hosted, not end user endpoints, like laptops or phones.

The legacy approach to protecting applications is to monitor endpoints for known threat signatures. Think of antivirus software. AV software has a massive database of known malware signatures, which it uses to identify threats on an endpoint.

The problem with this approach is that if the security solution hasn't seen the threat before, there is no signature to match, and therefore, the threat will be missed. This means that any brand new (or zero-day) threats will go undetected.

ML approaches to endpoint threat detection have become more prominent in recent years, in order to address this problem of identifying unknown threats. The idea is that by aggregating data from as many parts of the environment as possible, machine learning and AI algorithms can be used to sort out and distinguish normal behaviors from threats. The problem with this approach is noise. These solutions take in so much data, from so many different corners of the environment, that it is incredibly difficult for them to accurately detect threats. As a result, they tend to produce a high number of false positives:

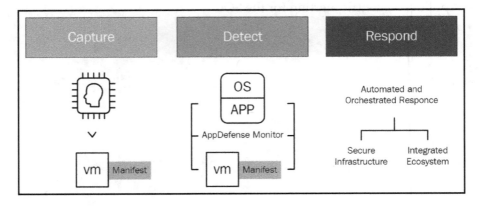

Application security must evolve to keep up with the speed of modern development practices, and VMware has developed a unique approach to solving this problem. In contrast to traditional security solutions, which focus on chasing threats, VMware AppDefense leverages its position in the hypervisor to learn the intended state of an application and immediately respond to deviations from that state. This level of application visibility results in more accurate security policies and faster remediation, simplifying the prevention of malicious behavior. This result is a common source of truth for IT and security teams, making it easy for them to collaborate on compliance, security incident investigation, and incident response.

AppDefense builds context by gathering the inventory of virtual machines and the application details from automation and provisioning tools, such as vCenter, Puppet, and Ansible, in order to understand the intent of a particular machine and application. It then monitors the behavior of the VM, operating system, processes, and application, and correlates this information with the intent that's defined during provisioning. AppDefense creates a blueprint based on known good behavior for how the machine and application should be functioning and communicating, by using machine learning.

Once the blueprint has been established, it is stored in a secure partition of the hypervisor. AppDefense monitors for any changes, detecting and preventing any deviations from the intended, established state, ensuring the integrity of applications, infrastructures, and the operating system. When a threat is detected, it can natively respond through a variety of capabilities and through NSX Data Center for enforcement and containment.

Digital governance and compliance

VMware government solutions enable customers to securely modernize government IT, strengthen cybersecurity, and streamline operations across infrastructures, clouds, apps, and endpoints, with their data center transformation approach. Government customers can innovate IT for greater impact and deploy a digital-first vision to achieve mission objectives with VMware solutions.

New Technology is always the key enabler for customers to deliver same services in better way. IT modernization is now an integral component of the cybersecurity solution. IT is working harder than ever to meet increasing demands on infrastructure to develop costly, ineffective systems for modern, cloud-capable platforms that are able to support both legacy investments and next-generation applications.

VMware provides a secure, practical, and accurate approach to modernizing the foundation of IT operations in the data center, by extending investments in compute virtualization to storage, networking, and management. The modern government data center is software-defined, virtualized, and centralized, providing customers with the availability, scalability, and operational efficiency that are needed to run today's dynamic services on demand. VMware's SDDC architecture leverages a globally consistent infrastructure to enable seamless application and workload portability across on-premises, private, and public clouds, enabling customers to operate a truly hybrid cloud environment with flexibility. This will ultimately span on-premises and public clouds across common infrastructure and management environments.

Intelligent government workflows with automation

IT is innovating the way it delivers and supports applications, to keep up with mobile innovation and to better respond to internal requests for flexible access to government resources and services. Pivoting from a locked-down, hardened approach to mobility, customers are leveraging virtualization and the cloud to put the right apps and productivity solutions into the hands of the right users, at the right times. VMware digital workspace solutions empower government workforces to more effectively and efficiently serve citizens through secure, remote access to resources and data, across devices, locations, and applications. It transforms applications and IT service delivery for greater productivity and impact on mission programs.

As the foundation of a mobile workforce, the VMware digital workspace represents a fundamental shift in the way that applications and IT services are delivered and consumed. Based on a software-defined architecture, the digital workspace isolates applications from the operating system, enabling agile, over-the-air delivery and management of Windows, cloud-native, web, and mobile applications. Complimenting Microsoft's approach to managing Windows 10, VMware digital workspace solutions abstract device and application life cycle management to support Windows 10 PCs and applications over-the-air. An enterprise-secure application catalog, backed by identity-based access and unified endpoint management, provides users with a consumer-like work experience without compromising data security or compliance. It provides additional security features, including the full visibility and management of all endpoints, such as macOS and Windows desktop and laptop devices, device and data-level encryption, granular **data loss prevention** (**DLP**) policies, and automated compliance monitoring, to further protect data and prevent data loss.

Transforming networking and security

Customers have to strengthen cybersecurity by reducing the total threat attack surface. They do this by transforming IT infrastructure and governance. Applications and data are living in increasingly stretched out and distributed IT environments; end users are no longer neatly contained behind perimeter firewalls, and attackers are smarter than ever, so cybersecurity efforts must bind more than just the core infrastructure by extending to the cloud, the user's identity, and their device. VMware helps customers to stay on top of changing security needs with a multilayered, software-defined approach to cybersecurity, which enhances the visibility and control of interactions between users, applications, and data.

Network virtualization reduces the risk and inefficiency that's inherent in a physical networking environment by embedding networking in the hypervisor and enabling micro-segmentation, which reduces the infrastructure's attack surface by ensuring that network, security, and automation policies follow the individual workload or application. This abstraction layer also provides a platform for IT to insert additional third-party services for more advanced security protection, and provides an ideal point to encrypt data at rest at the workload level.

With highly distributed computing environments, greater cross-organization and defense collaboration, and stricter privacy regulations, such as the **General Data Protection Regulation** (**GDPR**), organizations must accommodate perimeterless computing. VMware helps IT to transform security by building on a virtualized foundation and moving to a security architecture that's layered, segmented, and policy-driven. VMware solutions work in tandem with traditional security measures to reduce the attack surface and prevent the lateral movement of threats.

Business outcomes of the VMware approach

VMware helps customers to transform government data centers, in order to increase efficiency, expand into the cloud, and support shared services. The VMware approach is to leverage virtualization and a **hyperconverged infrastructure** (**HCI**) to build an agile, service-oriented data center that is standardized, centralized, and hybrid cloud-ready through the following methods:

- Reducing the data center footprint, hardware, and operating costs to optimize the data center
- Building a best-in-class private cloud that bi-directionally extends to the public cloud with only required resources

- Consolidating IT systems, functions, and services across multiple organizations to support shared service models
- Supporting cloud-native application development and platforms, in addition to legacy applications
- Increasing efficiency and agility, and improving IT service levels with a faster, on-demand delivery of IT resources
- Reinvesting savings into app development and agility

The following are the VMware solution approaches for different use cases:

- Reduces the total threat attack surface with a comprehensive and modern security platform:
    - **VMware approach**: Enable a software-defined security and governance framework by applying a ubiquitous software layer across application infrastructure and endpoints that are independent of the underlying physical infrastructure:
        - Decouple security functions from the underlying physical infrastructure and place protections closer to data/workloads across the entire IT environment
        - Embed intrinsic security across the data center and cloud infrastructure
        - Mitigate risk and improve security posture
        - Reduce operational complexity

- Serves and protects with IoT:
    - **VMware approach**: VMware offers an enterprise-grade, IoT device management and monitoring solution that addresses the challenges agencies face to onboard, manage, monitor, and secure their IoT use cases, from the edge to the cloud. There's just one console to configure, secure, manage, and monitor IoT infrastructure. The benefits of the VMware approach are as follows:
        - Reduces complexity
        - Improves reliability
        - Transforms security
        - Innovates faster and accelerates ROI

- Builds new capabilities, operating models, and services, including the following:
    - Smart buildings
    - **National defense**: Improving asset tracking and supply chain management; network-centric warfare, which provides shared awareness of the battlefield via cameras, infrared sensors, detectors, drones, and satellites
    - **Fleet telematics**: The use of sensors to remotely monitor the location, performance, and behavior of vehicles within a fleet
    - Monitoring weather and atmospheric conditions
    - Enhancing safety and public health
    - Smart cities
- Developing e-government and security frameworks to achieve digital citizenship:
    - **VMware approach**: VMware helps governments to modernize IT with digitization from data centers to end user devices by automating every layer of IT infrastructure. This abstraction enables the full visibility and control of system components programmatically across the life cycle, strengthening security, increasing efficiency, and supporting modern frameworks, now and in the future:
        - Improves the cost and quality of public service delivery
        - Delivers new capabilities
        - Speeds up innovation
        - Maintains citizen trust, data security, and privacy
- Adopts a zero-trust security model:
    - **VMware approach**: Enables software-defined networking to segment and isolate networks and control lateral movements inside the data center. It embeds networks in the hypervisor layer, to attach network, automation, and security services to policy-driven workflows that move with the workload or application, enabling a layered, defense-in-depth approach to security:
        - Expands network protection to applications and data
        - Ensures that security policies move with the application
        - Systematically enforces policies through automation and orchestration across individual workloads

- Exercises the capabilities of least-privilege and unit-level trust across the network
- Contains a lateral spread of attacks
- Reduces errors and inefficiencies

Expanding globally with AppDefense

AppDefense is based on the ML technique for threat detection and response solution. Customers trust digital information, but any data breach will impact their consumer confidence, as well as their reputation. Data is very critical for organizations to be competent in today's market, so data security cannot be compromised.

AppDefense helps organizations to solve a few challenges in relation to keeping their data safe. It is a data center endpoint security solution that has built-in threat detection and response solutions embedded into the vSphere kernel, with host applications and associated data. It consolidates intuitive information about the correct state with all required services on each end point. It can also detect unauthorized changes as it happens.

The following is a screenshot of an AppDefense dashboard with three uncleared alarms:

VMware AppDefense focuses on validating the *known correct* parameters of an endpoint by removing the need to drill the whole environment, chasing *known* or *unknown incorrect* behaviors that might be a threat. Security teams can detect anomalies as true threats with full confidence by minimizing the occurrence of false positives. AppDefense resides in isolation from the attack surface, so that it can't be compromised itself.

Application-centric alerting for the SOC

AppDefense raises a smart alarm, which is significant for the environment. Only trusted alerts with an automated response allow the security team to concentrate on finding and destroying threats from their environment as compared to searching for threats from incorrect data. SOC can use this tool to detect with trust and to automate responses to threats. The **Chief Information Security Officer** (**CISO**) organization is split into security architects and security operations. Security architects are responsible for devising the policies that are used to secure a given application, and security operations are responsible for actually monitoring and identifying threats in the environment.

Security architects review new applications and determine how they should be secured. Today, they have very little insight into how apps are composed, which processes should (or should not) be running, and how they should be communicating (and with whom), and they often don't even know who to go to for answers to their questions. The review process can take months, and often, the policies that they use are generic and focus on ensuring that the app is patched and that the logs are monitored.

With AppDefense, architects get a trusted manifest of the application's intended state and behavior from the outset, which allows them to define specific, app-centric policies that will remove the guesswork for the SOC when the app is ultimately deployed. This makes the review process more effective, less manual, and far quicker, which is particularly important as organizations move to more agile application development methods.

Once the app is deployed, it comes down to the SOC to detect when an app is compromised. Today, they are bombarded with false positives and a ton of noise that they need to make sense of. If they do find an issue, remediation is manual and labor-intensive. With AppDefense, when an alert comes in that something is wrong, the SOC can have faith that the alert is legitimate. Furthermore, they can automate the remediation actions so that the threat is neutralized quickly and efficiently, minimizing the damage that's done to the environment.

Transforming application security readiness

Apps are developed, changed, and destroyed rapidly within the DevOps environment. Application codes coming with enhanced features change frequently, and it's tough for security teams to have regular updates/knowledge about new amendments in applications. Customers can't take risks with their businesses by having critical data compromised, which may also damage their precious reputations. Customers have to ensure that the security services across all platforms tightly secure their network, applications, and data center endpoint positions.

It is possible for virtually anyone with a computer to initiate an attack against a specific organization, and new kinds of threats are being developed every day. We can't focus on following threats continuously to disrupt all of the challenges related to IT security.

CISOs are responsible for securing the applications and data that are residing in dynamic and distributed IT environments. Customers have to opt for new cloud-native application development processes, and must also implement security that strengthens their business objectives.

AppDefense protects applications with a specific approach, by *ensuring good* rather than *chasing bad*. AppDefense understands application behavior with its objective and keeps a check against application desired state. AppDefense automates responses when applications are manipulated. This is a simple and powerful tool that shrinks the attack surface by providing more context and controls.

AppDefense can also work in container environments and assist customers in securing their applications on any platforms, across regional boundaries. AppDefense provides a base layer to secure data center applications. AppDefense is the only solution that can span across all platforms with a consistent approach to discovering context, defining rules with alerts, and remediation. Customers can initiate least-privilege enforcement across all of their applications by integrating container support.

Innovating IT security with developers, security, and the Ops team

The security team can use AppDefense to establish the security review process for customers with frequent application development and deployment processes.

Applications and infrastructures expand more rapidly today, due to ever-changing end user demands. This will challenge security teams to leave their traditional, manual ways of investigating and managing amendments when applications are regularly being revamped and redeployed. The security team should understand what the application intends to do and define a security policy for its desired state.

We use AppDefense by integrating it into the CI/CD pipeline with provisioning tools and automation frameworks. We can define the desired state with real-time monitoring by maintaining a trusted map of an intended state that keeps in sync with on-demand application teams, in order to support the DevSecOps approach.

Least-privilege security for containerized applications

AppDefense exposes an API that enables container security partners to integrate into the platform. AppDefense can get a workload context from container orchestration systems, and can also configure policies that are enforced by container security vendors.

Aqua Security is one of the third-party tools that can integrate with the AppDefense container ecosystem; it enables runtime assurance for containers when the containers execute by investigating and enforcing behaviors. AppDefense along with Aqua Security will help container runtime profiles so that VMware can manage/maintain security scopes across the data center, and Aqua will also transfer compelling alerts to the AppDefense, console for management and resolution. Containers come with an automation engine and defined techniques for the desired state by integrating into container security solutions that can extend into a mixed cloud model.

AppDefense supports the VMware vCenter inventory for container workloads that are running across all platforms, like virtual servers, bare metal servers, and any cloud environments. AppDefense is available to customers in Europe via support from European-based data centers that support the data localization policy.

The **General Data Protection Regulation (GDPR)** (Regulation [EU] 2016/679) is a regulation that builds up and merges data privacy rights for people within the European Union. GDPR also focuses on the export of personal data outside of EU regional boundaries. The GDPR's first objective to have control over personal data, such as the name, address, and national identity numbers of the individual, which is a basic right, and also makes it simple to understand the regulatory environment for global business by coordinating data protection prescriptions within all EU countries.

The GDPR extends the scope of current EU data protection laws to non-EU organizations that are processing personal EU data. The coordination of data protection ratification should make it simpler for non-EU organizations to comply with a tight data protection compliance authority, with maximum punishment for non-compliance. VMware will be aligned with the European Union's GDPR.

VMware can tackle the export of personal data from the EU by constructing its compliance framework within the standard contractual clauses. We can guarantee a high level of protection for a customers' personal data, as needed, under current EU laws. VMware's standard contractual has clauses like internal consensus for the global movement of personal data between VMware and its subsidiaries across the globe. VMware's customers depend on VMware's certification underneath the Safe Harbor plan, with reference to VMware's processing of customer personal data. VMware's internal standard contractual clauses can be utilized by any of VMware's customers.

VMware helps customers to align with the GDPR regarding data security, so that customers can exchange ideas with privacy experts and enforce business processes by supporting the intended law.

AppDefense is a cloud-based security tool with many advantages, but it's important to have local data centers for performance and data localization. European customers have to obey regulatory compliance regarding data localization. AppDefense services will only be delivered to customers in Europe from European-based local data centers. AppDefense has launched a critical cloud security service to maximize customers across the globe with regional data centers.

The Indian government also has this policy that they can only take services from cloud service providers that have datacenters in India.

AppDefense collects and leverages end user and business data, from a compliance perspective. It is also used with different global data laws/regulations. AppDefense collects the customer email addresses for authentication, which are then placed into the service and examined for personally identifiable information. AppDefense also fetches hostnames, IP addresses, and process information from customer protected applications. All these critical data are important from compliance perspective. AppDefense supports applications that are hosted in the different kinds of clouds.

Enhanced security with AppDefense

Customers are updating their data center's infrastructures, and are also working on all severe security breaches without spending any extra money. AppDefense, along with VMware NSX, will enhance network security with micro-segmentation and will safeguard servers from unknown threats.

Most of the security breaches cannot be tackled with a point product (can only handle single problem and not have complete solution) or tool, as these are more basic and architectural in character. AppDefense makes security an inherent part of the network and application fabric where in businesses are running. Security is a native part of data center endpoints, which consist of applications, by implanting AppDefense within vSphere kernel. AppDefense helps its customers tackle the growing frequency and costs of security incident points in security models, which mostly focus on unidentified threats. AppDefense conveys a purpose-based security model that determines what the applications are supposed to do—the known correct. Compare this to what the hackers will do—the known incorrect.

AppDefense and NSX

AppDefense shield applications run in vSphere environments and various cloud environments. NSX and AppDefense complement each other, but NSX is not mandatory for AppDefense services. If AppDefense is integrated with NSX, automated response techniques like automatically quarantine a compromised data center endpoint can be leveraged. AppDefense is outstanding in a new security model which has a native, purpose-based, and application-centric approach. AppDefense will do the same job for compute that NSX does for the network, by creating least-privilege environments for business applications. We can monitor running applications against their desired states and can investigate them with an automated response to attacks that try to exploit applications.

AppDefense is distinctive, as it is located in the hypervisor kernel to better interpret the desired state and conduct of a data center endpoint. It monitors endpoints in real time for unapproved changes from the *known correct* state. AppDefense uses vSphere with NSX for automated responses when a threat is detected for applications.

AppDefense complements a number of security solutions, but it competes with two main endpoint security solutions, as follows:

- Legacy signature-based products (antivirus, anti-malware, IPS, and so on)
- Next-generation endpoint security (**Endpoint Detection and Response** (EDR), machine learning, behavioral analytics, and so on)

AppDefense is evolving from the preceding solutions by recognizing deviations from the application's desired state, as compared to following possible warnings. AppDefense also has automated response capabilities, which can be integrated with other security tools in various aspects.

VMware assists its customers with security and data protection features, from the data center to the end user. It secures a customers' environments end to end, by identifying potential data protection gaps:

- **Data access and data transfer (using VMware NSX)**: Creating security policies to prevent data movement across unapproved networks
- **Data access (using Horizon and Workspace ONE)**: Creating a policy engine to impose role-based access to data with identity checks and validation
- **Data storage (using VMware vSphere and vSAN)**: Enabling data encryption
- **Data deletion (using VMware vSphere and AirWatch)**: Wipe out data, including individual data

AppDefense differs from Microsoft's **virtualization-based security (VBS)** tools, like Device Guard, Credential Guard, and AppLocker, since these are built for Windows only, and will not support Linux workloads. Additionally, none of these solutions are designed to detect and respond to threats on data center endpoints. VBS uses the hypervisor to help protect the kernel and other parts of the operating system. AppDefense is focused on the application. Protecting the application means protecting the integrity and behavior of the application components, not just the OS. AppDefense provides OS protection, even if VBS is not present or enabled. AppDefense also provides the SOC with the ability to detect and respond to any compromises. Device Guard is focused on whitelisting which executables are allowed to run on a machine. It does not perform behavior whitelisting. It doesn't take an application-centric view of creating, updating, and monitoring these policies. It doesn't support automated response integration. All of these are essential parts of delivering a solution that can be used efficiently by SOCs. AppLocker is the older application whitelisting solution that's focused on end user endpoints, and it suffers from all of the problems that is had with traditional whitelisting. There is significant confusion about when to use AppLocker, as opposed to Device Guard.

AppDefense does whitelisting and behavioral analysis for an application. Traditional whitelisting is based on monitoring and validating what is allowed to be installed on a machine. However, this approach misses the behavioral component. What is the machine allowed to do? AppDefense incorporates both of these components into its approach to determine the application's intended state. AppDefense also takes a holistic view of application behavior, rather than focusing solely on individual data center endpoints. AppDefense stores VM inventory, machine names, expected process behaviors, expected network flows, and security alarms in the cloud. AppDefense holds metadata about the customer's data center environment and security status. AppDefense won't store any application data in the cloud, and does not handle any actual application data from customers. The only data that's stored is what is required to maintain the security posture of the infrastructure.

We secure the information that's stored in the cloud because we take the security of the AppDefense service very seriously. The service is managed and protected by the VMware SOC, which is the same team that manages the security of all of VMware's Cloud Services, as well as VMware's on-premises data centers. Any configuration changes or behaviors within AWS are closely monitored by the SOC and require an authorized change control process. All data is sent to and from the AppDefense service via encrypted tunnels, and all of the data that's stored is encrypted at rest.

AppDefense uses third-party service providers and makes use of a select few third-party SaaS services. All third-party vendors are vetted by internal security and legal teams and have a data privacy agreement in place with VMware.

AppDefense is managed from the cloud, and customers get a number of benefits by consuming AppDefense as an SaaS service:

- Security teams are not required to deploy, manage, and maintain software, which is not typically their core competency.
- Customers get the benefit of the collective knowledge of the vSphere installed base. This means that we can baseline behaviors running across a large number of machines from different tenants, in order to recognize anomalies and security threats more quickly.
- A cloud delivery model allows us to update and change some of the anomaly detection logic on a regular basis, without requiring customers to install and manage software updates.
- Delivering as a cloud service allows customers to manage the security postures of their environments from a single location.

AppDefense understands the application's intended state, and the application's intended state includes application composition information like the VMs, services, and binaries that make up the application, in addition to other software that co-resides with in the core application, like security and management software. It also includes behavioral information, like the network interactions between the various processes. AppDefense also ties into provisioning systems like vRealize Automation, Puppet, and others, to get composition information about the intended state. It then augments that with the runtime discovery of behavior to create a comprehensive and verified intended state. If a VM moves between hosts or clusters using vMotion, the AppDefense policy moves with it, similar to NSX. The administrative domain boundary for AppDefense is vCenter, so moving VMs across vCenters is not currently supported.

Intended application changes that may create false alerts come in two forms: updates to software and behavior that was not exhibited during the learning period. To limit false alarms, do the following:

- We recommend an extended and variable learning period for applications
- We support wildcards and do smart and auto-wild carding

AppDefense won't consume a lot of system resources on the endpoint or the host, as it is surprisingly lightweight and consumes minimal resources on the host. AppDefense uses the simple method of understanding the intended state of an application and monitoring for changes, rather than relying on complex algorithms and computation, which is how other next-generation endpoint security solutions typically work. AppDefense integrates with **security information and event management** (**SIEM**) and other next-generation security solutions, as it is an open platform that allows SIEMs and other security systems to consume its alarms and application context information, as well as leverage its automated response capabilities.

AppDefense integrates with configuration management tools, orchestration engines, and cloud management portals by integrating with DevOps automation tools to get trusted intended state data. You can also integrate with vRealize Automation and add support for tools like Puppet for automated provisioning and orchestration.

Detailed implementation and configuration plan

The following section covers the required components and steps for the successful deployment of AppDefense. A target application environment that will be protected by AppDefense needs to have the following:

- A minimum of two ESXi hosts, running ESXi 6.5a or above
- vCenter 6.5+ managing ESXi hosts
- VM hardware version 13
- IP address for AppDefense appliance OVA and HTTPS connectivity to the internet
- At least one production-like application that runs on Windows Server 2012 or 2016 64-bit
- Preferably, the selected applications should be distributed (for example, Web-App-DB)
- NSXv 6.3 or above
- vRA 7.2 or above

Environment preparation for AppDefense deployment

The environment preparation for AppDefense deployment is as follows:

- **Phase 1**:
  - Install vCenter
  - Install ESXi Hosts
  - Install NSX Manager
  - Install vRealize Automation

Install and deploy AppDefense components: The application and infrastructure team is responsible for the installation and support of the AppDefense platform components and for selecting the target application. Provisioning the target applications to be tested against and simulating standard changes to provisioned applications are also performed by the application team.

- **Phase 2**:
  - Provision AppDefense login
  - Download AppDefense appliance
  - Deploy AppDefense appliance OVA

AppDefense deployment will be successful if the following conditions are met:

- AppDefense is successfully deployed (all components) in the environment
- AppDefense is successfully connected to all external components (vCenter, NSX, and vRA)
- VM inventory from vCenter is visible from the AppDefense management console
- The key workflows that are described should be completed successfully

It starts with capturing the intended purpose, state, and behavior of your virtual machines. Here, we are leveraging a unique property of vSphere, which is application visibility. The hypervisor allows you to see both the runtime state (what's running in the VM) and the provisioned state (what was provisioned there in the first place).

- **Phase 3**:
    - Provision an AppDefense Manager instance
    - Copy UUID and API-KEY
    - Modify the `application.properties` file
    - Verify AppDefense Appliance connectivity
    - Verify NSX Manager connectivity
    - Verify vRealize Orchestrator connectivity

Complete the AppDefense deployment by configuring AppDefense components: All of the technical requirements for these solutions (IP addresses, DNS, VMs, NTP, and so on) need to be fulfilled. The customer has to help the implementation team by reviewing the permitted behavior practices in their environment, configuring protection policies, monitoring the protected application, and testing detection capabilities, using VMware provided tools, internal tools, or manually triggering violations. Running and protecting the test applications with AppDefense installed will be evaluated from time to time, depending on the current and upcoming security threats.

- **Phase 4**:
    - Install the host module on the ESXi hosts
    - Deploy a guest module to application servers
    - Enable guest integrity
    - Verify that the application servers show a ready status

Create an application scope with foundational detection and response capabilities: At the core of AppDefense is the definition of the application's intended state. The intended state includes the application's composition, process-level, inbound and outbound connection behavior, and their relationship in the context of a broader application, as these apps are used to connect or integrate as per customer demand. One or more of these methods will be used to create the intended state during deployment.

- **Phase 5**:
    - Create a scope in AppDefense for application
    - Create services in AppDefense for application
    - Verify that the capture process has been running for a few weeks

Create an application scope: You can utilize infrastructure blueprints from vRealize Automation to create services and application scopes/composition in AppDefense, and you can also manually define the application composition in AppDefense.

- **Phase 6**:
    - Create a multi-machine blueprint
    - Tag VMs in the blueprint with scope and service
    - Verify the scope creation in AppDefense

Verify and protect mode: We can get Application behavior by running AppDefense discovery mode on the application for a few weeks for automatically learning the application behavior. You can also modify and verify the application's intended state (allowed behavior).

- **Phase 7**:
    - Verify behaviors
    - Add/modify/remove behaviors, as necessary
    - Change action to verify and protect
    - Observe default rule violations in alert logs

Remediation testing: Test automatic and manual workflows to perform the following remediation actions:

- Suspend
- Power off
- Snapshot
- Block and alert
- Detection testing and incident investigation
- Intended state deviation testing by triggering unauthorized behavior
- Incident investigation
- Alarm with detail notifications
- Provisioning events

- **Phase 8:**
  - Modify rules for power off
  - Trigger unauthorized behaviors
  - Verify power off and associated alarm in the log
  - Modify rules for suspension
  - Trigger unauthorized behaviors
  - Verify suspend and associated alarm in the log
  - Modify rule for block and alert
  - Trigger unauthorized behavior
  - Verify block and alert and the associated alarm in the log
  - Modify rule for snapshot
  - Trigger unauthorized behavior
  - Verify snapshot and associated alarm in the log

Remediation testing with NSX Manager:

  - Ease of creating and updating the intended state
  - Ease of incident response automation
  - Low noise-to-signal ratio when using deviation from the intended state as a signal for a security or compliance events
  - Quarantine
  - Configuration of protection policies

- **Phase 9:**
  - Modify the rules for quarantine
  - Trigger unauthorized behaviors
  - Verify NSX AppDefense Security tag applied
  - Verify NSX AppDefense Security group inclusion
  - Verify NSX AppDefense Security policy applied
  - Verify that the VM can no longer communicate

Summary

Digital transformation has the potential to revolutionize the way that governments connect with citizens/constituents, protect sensitive information, and achieve the organization's mission. Yet revolutionizing the business of the government is a complex task. Primary obstacles include siloed legacy systems, applications, and processes; funding and talent shortages; complex procurement processes; and cultural dissonance. Despite these universal challenges, government leaders recognize that digital transformation is necessary to serve the public in the digital age. VMware AppDefense helps to strengthen data security across infrastructure and endpoints, protecting sensitive citizen data and privacy by reducing cybersecurity risks.

In the next chapter, `Chapter 6`, *ML-Based Intelligent Log Management*, you will learn about how vRealize tools can automatically correlate all IT data and events into a unified view with a complete picture of the IT environment, and you will use analytics to predict and provide support to customers. We will also improve performance and avoid disruption by enabling them to proactively identify and remedy issues before they affect the business.

Section 2: ML Use Cases with VMware Solutions

VMware has to deal with things in a fully automated fashion and requires machines that can make decisions. They are currently trying to figure out at least automatic initiation of the first remedial actions, and only if the machine doesn't respond or behave in an expected way is it then calling out for help. This is where the trend is heading today, as people innovate with machine learning techniques. VMware is gearing up for machine learning-based responses to the infrastructure and applications to be able to take action in relation to them and should not depend on any subsystem by precisely mentioning the impact on the system in real-time scenarios. We will learn about management toolsets, with a focus on machine learning techniques, in the next few chapters.

This section contains the following chapters:

- Chapter 6, *ML-Based Intelligent Log Management*
- Chapter 7, *ML as a Service in the Cloud*
- Chapter 8, *ML-Based Rule Engine with Skyline*
- Chapter 9, *DevOps with vRealize Code Stream*
- Chapter 10, *Transforming VMware IT Operations Using ML*

6
ML-Based Intelligent Log Management

In this chapter, we will explore the architecture of vRealize Log Insight and how it works. We'll also discuss how intelligent data summarization happens and its ability to cluster similar messages together. vRealize Log Insight also has automatic schema extraction. It has the capability to perform rapid troubleshooting across physical, virtual, and cloud environments by indexing and intelligent grouping, which assists in searching for quick resolutions with exact root cause analysis.

We will learn to leverage vRealize Log Insight for automated remediation, and the logic behind indexing and message grouping, by integrating vRealize Log Insight with third-party tools.

We will cover the following topics in this chapter:

- Intelligent log management with vRealize Log Insight
- Cloud operations stages
- **VMware vRealize Network Insight (vRNI)**

Technical requirements

You can download the following:

- VMware vRealize Log Insight 4.6.2 from `https://my.vmware.com/web/vmware/details?downloadGroup=VRLI-462productId=676rPId=28154`
- VMware vRealize Operations Manager 6.7.0 from `https://my.vmware.com/web/vmware/details?downloadGroup=VROPS-670productId=676rPId=28154`
- VMware vRealize Network Insight 4.0.0 from `https://my.vmware.com/web/vmware/details?downloadGroup=VRNI-400productId=832rPId=29784`
- Log Intelligence from `https://cloud.vmware.com/log-intelligence`

Intelligent log management with vRealize Log Insight

It's important that VMware customers understand comprehensive cloud-management platform offerings, and that this is a small part of automating and streamlining their data center operations efforts.

We can plan a log-management solution with vRealize Log Insight as a single point solution. We should understand the larger and more strategic SDDC management story. Log management is a point solution and it fits into the bigger picture and elevate the discussion. Log Insight is extensible with the vast array of content packs available. Unlike other solutions, it will not charge more as the data volume grows.

Log Intelligence value propositions

VMware vRealize Operations and vRealize Log Insight assist cloud service providers to provide services across physical, virtual, and cloud infrastructures. Both can together correlate structured and unstructured data from applications to storage in a simple, easy-to-use, unified console. This is achieved by providing control over performance, capacity, and configuration for accurate future-planning, which helps in taking proactive action with policy-based configuration. vRealize Log Insight adds value to vRealize Operations by providing real-time log management based on intelligent grouping with innovative search capabilities for a quick resolution and enhanced operational analytics.

The following table shows **Log Intelligence** (**LInt**) core to VMware Cloud on AWS features:

VMC on AWS + LInt features	LInt core to VMC	LInt 30 day free trial	LInt paid (price per GB/month)
Audit log collection	Unlimited	Unlimited	Unlimited
Non-audit log collection	1 GB/Day	Unlimited	On-Demand/Customer Chosen Level
Log retention	7 Days	30 Days	30 Days
Audit log content	Available	Available	Available
Visualization (dashboard)	Available	Available	Available
Search and save query	Available	Available	Available
Long term archiving		Available	Available
Alerts		Available	Available

Notifications		Available	Available
Event forwarding		Available	Available
Non-audit log content		Available	Available
External web hooks		Available	Available

DevOps end-to-end troubleshooting with **Wavefront** and **Log Intelligence** has the ability to cross-launch based on context (time, source, and custom tags) and to extract metrics from logs.

The following diagram shows the data movement flow across Wavefront and Log Intelligence:

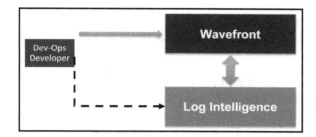

Developer teams get precise data from the Log Analytics tool after going through extensive filtering and they push this data to the **Wavefront** dashboard to get the desired output, which will help them to enhance application capabilities. This is a continuous cycle and all three tightly integrate with each other to achieve the final common objective.

Log Intelligence metrics have the following features:

- Ability to provide Number of critical errors and the along with number of warnings
- Uses Wavefront as the centralized alerting dashboard
- Forwards alerts raised from logs to Wavefront
- Cross-launch of Alerts related to logs correlation
- Application-aware correlation and cross-launches
- Content across both metrics and log

Wavefront is a cloud-native metrics-monitoring and analytics platform that is specifically designed to handle the high scale of modern cloud applications' velocity and dynamism. DevOps and developer teams who run true cloud-native apps (such as Box, and so on) use Wavefront to monitor their cloud services. Wavefront has capability to reach an **unprecedented scale**. The Wavefront platform collects metrics from distributed applications, containers, microservices, hybrid public cloud infrastructure, and even business data. Once metric data is in the Wavefront time-series database, we can apply powerful and flexible analytics in the form of the Wavefront Query Language.

Engineers use Wavefront to understand the performance of their cloud services and distributed applications at an unprecedented scale. We get instant visibility across all of our cloud services. We can troubleshoot faster and proactively alert and detect the leading indicators of anomalies with Wavefront. We have instant access and unified visibility drives agility in code release, enabling the same visibility across everything. Once Wavefront enters an organization, its adoption spreads across hundreds of engineers, enabling a self-service approach.

Wavefront is easy to implement and easy to scale with its analytics engine, the Wavefront Query Language, which has over 100 analytics functions within the Wavefront Query Language. It's easy to customize dashboards with analytics-driven visibility across cloud applications and infrastructures. Wavefront pricing is defined as per rate of ingestion and per host with vRealize Operations Manager. Customers can see metric rate consumption clearly, tweak it as needed, and use it for budgeting without any hidden costs. Wavefront data sources are native metrics ingestion by integrating open source agents, API, code libraries and events, metrics from logs, and other tools (DevOps and so on) . It can easily scale up to 4,000,000 **packets per second** (**pps**) . It has enterprise adoption across thousands of engineers within developer/DevOps teams. Wavefront has already proven SaaS offerings and successfully integrated with popular SaaS apps such as Box, Lyft, Intuit, Workday, and so on across thousands of developers.

Wavefront supports container technology, such as Docker, **Pivotal Container Service** (**PKS**), Kubernetes, and **Elastic Container Service** (**ECS**), out of the box. Container metrics are added and scaled without any issues or performance degradation. It is built from the ground up to scale. Greenfield customers can also leverage LInt/Insight with Wavefront while non-greenfield customers can opt for conversion of logs to metrics for other logging tools.

Wavefront is not an **Access Policy Manager** (APM) tool, but ingests APM metrics as any other APM tool. It also supports correlation with any other long term trending data source. It also supports code instrumentation with open source libraries, delivers applications visibility (StatsD, Micrometer, and DropWizard), and is ideal for microservices and dynamic custom applications at a high scale. Wavefront can complement existing APM tools. It supports predictive forecasting with Holt-Winters and **Autoregressive Integrated Moving Average** (ARIMA) forecasting algorithms. It can also integrate with more than 125 applications, and supports Azure, GCP, and AWS.

Log Intelligence key benefits for service providers

LInt's key benefits for service providers are as follows:

- Proactive identification and remediation of emerging performance, capacity, and configuration issues achieve the highest levels of availability.
- Continuous monitoring and automatic capacity management optimize scarce infrastructure resources.
- There's comprehensive visibility across multiple tenants, applications, compute, storage and networking in a single console.
- It has automated enforcement of IT policies, configuration standards, and regulatory requirements.
- There's workload balancing for optimal placement of workloads based on the operational characteristics of the environment.
- **Custom data centers** (CDCs) allow service providers to combine hosts, clusters, and data centers from one or more vCenter environments and map those CDCs to individual tenants to create logical groupings of objectives, delivering full capacity management, planning, and support for all analysis badges.
- It provides reduced OpEx and increased operational efficiency from accelerated troubleshooting times and improved **mean time to resolution** (MTTR) and reduced manual effort.

Log Intelligence for VMware Cloud on AWS provides unified visibility into infrastructure and application logs across VMware Cloud on AWS, AWS, and on-premises SDDC. VMware Cloud on AWS support its native audit logs through Log Intelligence for faster monitoring results and troubleshooting as a core service for real-time alerts on anomalies based on custom triggers/dashboards to visualize trends and effective notifications on custom alerts. It will provide a high-performance search function within logs for faster root-cause analysis with support for a broad range of applications from a single-pane-of-glass console.

Audit log examples

VMC customers can use the explore logs Log Intelligence capability to view the audit log examples within the **Log Intelligence** tab. Samples of **VMware Cloud** and **Log Intelligence** tabs with sample view of VMC audit log information are as follows:

- Virtual machine created; virtual machine deleted; virtual machine modified; firewall rule created
- Firewall rule deleted; firewall rule modified; NAT rule created; NAT rule deleted
- IPSec VPN created; IPSec VPN deleted; IPSec VPN modified; Number of failed logins
- Virtual machine power on failures; logical networks created; logical networks deleted

The following screenshot shows the **Log Intelligence** dashboard:

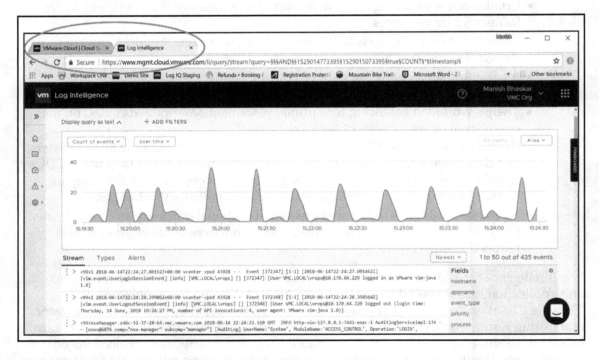

vRealize Operations and vRealize Log Insight can be used to manage workloads on service providers, private or public clouds, including vCloud Air. **VMware VRealize Business (vRB)** Operations and vRealize Log Insight are shipped as vApps and will run on any vSphere installed/certified hardware infrastructure.

VMware Integrated OpenStack (**VIO**) is a version of OpenStack that includes adapters to VMware compute, network, and storage virtualization solutions. There are several use cases for VIO, which include more than just basic developer access to infrastructure resources. vRealize Operations and vRealize Log Insight can be used with OpenStack to use OpenStack in deploying the open API set. VIO is used for web-scale applications that rely on the open API, a management solution is needed to ensure SLAs and ongoing infrastructure management. We will go through cloud operations stages in the next section, which will explain how we can streamline the cloud operations process to save more OpEx with optimal service.

Cloud operations stages

VMware provides a set of best practices for organizing, operating, and measuring success as customers move to the cloud. The goal is to give customers access to best practices so that they can get the most out of this transition.

Financial transparency, process maturity, organizational setup, and technology implementation are critical factors for success at every stage of the journey.

VMware defines the following stages for the journey into VMware Cloud computing:

- Standardize
- Service Broker
- Strategic partner

The stages are described in the following sections.

Standardize

We can include this stage with server consolidation and emphasize a cloud solution with a service catalog that end users can access on-demand from anywhere, anytime, and on any device. This will help in rapid deployment of services for all kind of users and applications, irrespective of their domain. Service catalog assists business users in a cloud environment by helping to do their daily tasks more efficiently and with more productivity.

We need the following capabilities in this stage:

- **TCO/ROI**: Clear visibility of operating costs and assets value with their capability
- **Business and IT users**: Specialized skill sets on cloud computing

- IT processes should be automated with all regulatory compliance
- Continuous innovation with continuous improvement
- Self-service on-demand provisioning portal for application provisioning
- Seamless adaption of SaaS-based applications
- Intelligent operations based on predictive analysis

Service Broker

We have to first design a common platform for service-driven cloud deployments. IT will act as a Service Broker to deliver business services in a cloud environment. IT can host cloud environments internally and externally by adding external capacity for current infrastructure or to give access to vendor-based SaaS applications to their business users. This way, IT can minimize development and provisioning times and better assist business objectives with enhanced quality of service and agility.

We need the following capabilities in this stage:

- Define application life cycle and design application with continuous development processes
- Delivering services in a pay-as-you-go model
- Automating most of the operation tasks by integrating all tools with a single interface
- IT infrastructure/applications usage metering through showback/chargeback tool
- Bifurcating CapEx and operating expenses
- Transforming a project-based approach to demand-based for Cost optimization
- Integrating all IT operational processes to get a single, unified console
- Design on-demand service and development processes
- SLA should be tightly aligned with the business objective
- Services are defined and offered through the customized service catalog
- Design cloud-level disaster recovery beyond regional boundaries

Strategic partner

Customers want efficient, scalable clouds, with a hybrid capability for their cloud environment in the final stage. IT can be consumed as a service with automation, policy-driven governance, and control across the cloud environment.

This will also help with zero-touch operations supported by predictive and self-healing operational tool capabilities. Application mobility and device-independent access are perfect use cases of cloud computing.

IT is now acting as a strategic partner for any organization to achieve its business objective by improving the following:

- On-demand help in meeting the market requirement
- Better utilization by reducing **Total Cost of Ownership** (**TCO**)
- Improving **quality of service** (**QoS**) will increase stability
- Budgeting and services should align with each other
- Resource optimization will improve business agility and efficiency
- Continuous innovation based on predictive analysis and proactive actions
- Applications adaptability in a hybrid cloud environment
- Single-pane-of-glass management across the private and public clouds
- Service-level disaster-recovery across different geographies
- Intelligent remediation and self-healing process

The Log Insight user interface

Log Insight has two interfaces for log monitoring and analysis:

- **Dashboards**: Dashboards are GUI of the log data absorbed by Log Insight and included with content packs for better customization having one or more widgets per dashboard. Widgets are customized per pre-built or user-created queries and come with charts to represent the log data.
- **Interactive Analytics**: This will help administrators to check log messages, locate problem areas, and work on root-cause analysis. The vSphere content pack has customized dashboards that contains details on log data related to specific events. These dashboards will provide high-level overview information through particular events, such as **Distributed Resource Scheduler** (**DRS**)/HA, vMotion, security, and different performance parameters. Content packs cumulate and show correlated log data across the vSphere environment by allowing a quick view of trouble areas in the environment to find possible connecting reasons, find the root cause, and resolve the problem.

Content packs are read-only plugins to vRealize Log Insight that give predefined data information about particular event types, such as log messages, to provide data in a specific format that is easily understood by the operations team.

A content pack should answer questions such as "Is the product/application healthy?" In addition, a content pack should create a greater understanding of how a product/application works.

A content pack comprises information that can be saved from either the **Dashboards** or **Interactive Analytics** pages in VRealize Log Insight. This includes the following:

- **Queries**
- **Fields**
- **Aggregations**
- **Alerts**
- **Dashboards**
- **Agent Groups**
- **Setup Instructions**

Log Insight is capable of performing real-time log management to gain insights across physical, virtual, and cloud environments. Featuring tight integration with vRealize Operations Manager, Log Insight delivers the operational intelligence and enterprise-wide visibility needed to proactively enable service levels and operational efficiency in dynamic hybrid cloud environments.

Splunk Enterprise is a competitive solution to Log Insight, with similar log management and operational intelligence. Splunk Enterprise is a general-purpose log-management solution that looks closely into machine data to provide insights (which Splunk calls *operational intelligence*). When compared with vRealize Log Insight, the performance of Splunk suffers and falls far behind Log Insight in terms of time needed to perform search queries and time needed to show search results.

Indexing performance, storage, and report export

Splunk Enterprise provides a distributed management console that lets administrators view information about the overall Splunk infrastructure. It can collect data from virtually any source and provides multiple options to input data from the web, **command-line interface** (**CLI**), and apps. Administrators can also configure advanced archival and data-retirement policies.

However, Splunk becomes remotely inaccessible when network-intensive operations are performed and has multiple issues with viewing reports and dashboards on the console.

vRealize Log Insight tightly integrates with vRealize Operations Manager to provide deep insights into the VMware virtual infrastructure. An integrated network load balancer enhances the availability of clusters, helping to build robust solutions. Historical log data can be archived to NFS servers, but with limited capabilities.

The user experience

Splunk Enterprise provides a unified user console for log management. Splunk Enterprise can be accessed through one of two authentication methods: using **Lightweight Directory Access Protocol (LDAP)** authentication or via proprietary Splunk authentication. Splunk offers numerous options for visualizing results including reports, charts, and gauges, but legend values are not shown for pie charts from the dashboard. XML dashboards can be converted into HTML dashboards, but once dashboards have been created, administrators cannot modify the date and time of the result to be displayed. In addition, while configuring the **simple mail transfer protocol (SMTP)** server for alerts, Splunk does not verify SMTP server details; it requires a test connection with Splunk Server each time a PDF report is scheduled.

VMware vRealize Log Insight is a truly streamlined log-management tool. Log Insight simplifies result visualization, new field extraction, and changing date/time criteria from the search page itself. Unlike Splunk Enterprise, Log Insight also allows date and time values to be modified for preconfigured dashboards. However, when the field definition for any saved query or chart is changed, it stops updating the respective results. Log Insight seamlessly integrates with vRealize Operations Manager but alerts sent to Operations Manager do not show the severity level. All alerts shown in the Operations Manager are the same as ordinary information alerts. This can create a problem for administrators trying to identify critical or important issues.

The following screenshot displays the dashboards with all of the warnings:

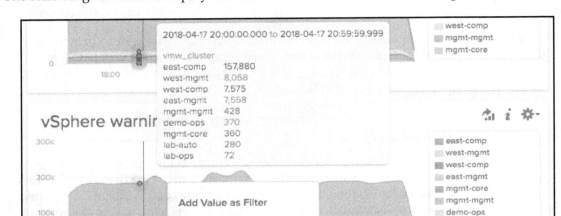

We open the **Interactive Analytics** interface with query and filter out information related to specific customer by linking widgets with other widgets. We can also link multiple dashboards by clicking their dashboard, which brings up a list of dashboards to further refine how a set of logs can be viewed as we get dashboards of all vSphere events by hostname widget in the vSphere content pack general **Overview** dashboard by dashboard linking. We can also select another dashboard on a specific widget that will bring up a list of dashboards that contain specific info or problem areas in the content pack for a selected host.

We adapt **Interactive Analytics** with the query filter information and time range configured. We will reset the overview chart and query to default by clicking **Interactive Analytics**. We will first see the overview chart on the top of the **Interactive Analytics** page, which is a graphical interface of log data. This is based on the chart type, query, and chosen accumulative functions. The search box and query builder assist users to filter and locate relevant log information. Query criteria is automatically entered if a user transformed from a widget in the **Dashboard** view and the bottom view shows individual log events.

It shows fields related to log messages that sustain for the specified time range. Log Insight takes out a subset of the log data to use as a column in a database. This helps unstructured log data to be queried. We can view fields related to specific events in the fields pane. Fields that are included in the index or extracted manually are static. These fields data can be taken out or included through agent parsers, content pack fields, syslog fields, or manually extracted fields. A mini-chart is shown in the field pane by clicking a field.

Events

Absorbed log events can be shown within **Interactive Analytics**. All log events are presented by default even when no filters are added and provide event-based information as per the following conditions:

- As soon as a log message reaches the Log Insight server, it is timestamped.
- Log messages have relevant fields to create rapid and efficient queries, for example, hostname and appname are in syslog RFC-compliant fields.
- Fields can be also included by content packs and third-party tool integrations, such as the `vmw_datacenter`, `vmw_object_id`, and `vmw_vcenter` fields added by VMware integrations. We can make queries related to these fields to get specific log messages.

Query created by Log in to Log Insight Interactive Analysis:

- **Create a query**: Log Insight assists to use plain English words while searching for log messages. We can also create queries by leveraging regular expressions:

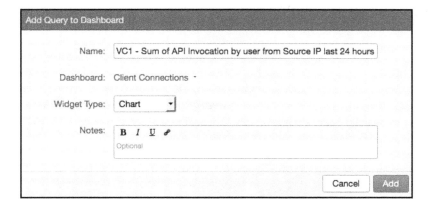

- Select the time range:
    - Explore the time range drop-down menu by listing all options
    - Check the **Latest 24 hours of data**:

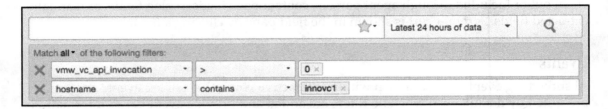

We can get a display of only those log events with timestamps that are within the selected time range. The time zone set in the client web browser discovers the visible log messages. The event list will get amended with the last 24 hours of log messages.

Log message output is related to matched values and operators in the filter.

The following are a few of the filter options to get the desired output:

- Operators manage filtering functions as we used to do with dashboards. Fields that have numeric values, such as latency numbers, have additional operators, such as <, >, or =.
- We have the option to match all or match any values in the filters while two or more filters are created.
- We can select a new field by clicking the down arrow and scrolling to the required field. We can also type the filter into the search box and Log Insight will match results as per the typed word. By default, new filters have a text field.

Log Insight leverages using globs in queries. * helps to match various characters. ? only supports one character while using `fail*` could give back (failed, failure, or failing) as outputs but `erro?` will mostly come back with the word error as output. Log Insight will verify a match corresponding to what we typed while inputting a value. The OR constraint can be used for multiple values for a single filter line, such as text containing `esx-03a OR esx-01a`.

Cumulative functions: We can also manage the data that operates the **Overview** chart in Log Insight with cumulative functions. The default cumulative function count of events over time is presented above the search box, and clicking the drop-down menu will give us additional functions. Multiple functions can be included in a chart. This assists in displaying a single event in two different ways. The overview chart will amend and add the unique count of hostnames in the console as a line. Each column and line will present information. The column will display the count of events for a specific time frame. The line can give a view of the number of hostnames which have matching error logs during the mentioned time frame. We will group the results/events by hostname and information will come by that displays the time range and count events for a specific hostname. Different charts are also accessible and Log Insight will by default automatically choose the best chart for the dataset. We can manually select charts to display the data in various ways.

Now, we will explore the vRealize Network Insight tool, which provides end-to-end visibility about all network packets and how they are travelling from one object to another, along with predictive analysis for better planning and design.

VMware vRealize Network Insight

VMware vRealize Network Insight provides customers intelligent operations for software-defined networking and security. It helps customers to build an efficient, always-on, and secure network infrastructure across different cloud infrastructures. We can plan, design, and deploy micro-segmentation to have visibility across virtual and physical networks. It is very useful in managing VMware NSX deployments and is available as a service offering as VMware Network Insight. vRNI polls third-party devices periodically (between 5 and 10 minutes on average) on a read-only basis. The protocols used include **Secure Shell (SSH)**, **Simple Network Management Protocol (SNMP)**, and **Representational State Transfer (REST)**.

vRNI administrators must configure the vRNI data source interfaces with the read-only credentials that have been predefined on these devices. Additionally, vRNI must be able to access these devices where there are no firewalls and other types of security restrictions (specific to these protocols). In particular, SNMP is typically configured as highly restrictive. In most cases, the vRNI proxy node, in which the SNMP read-only requests are made, is commonly located locally, within the same layer-2 management network, as the third-party devices it needs to poll.

vRNI is not polling these devices in real-time, nor is vRNI listening to or collecting SNMP traps or log data. vRNI is a time-based analytics product and is again polling data every 5-10 minutes (depending on the device and use cases) in support of the use cases offered in this product. The following shows various ways of collecting data for the vRNI dashboard:

- **SSH**: vRNI uses SSH version 2.0 to access the third-party data source(s). Third-party devices are polled every 10 minutes by default (except for Brocade VDX, which is polled every 15 minutes). No persistent session is maintained.
- **REST**: vRNI also uses the REST APIs provided by the data source(s). Third-party devices are polled every 10 minutes by default. No persistent session is maintained.
- **REST/SSH user credentials and privileges**: vRNI requires read-only third-party device credentials (passwords) to access the REST and SSH data. These passwords are added when configuring the third-party data provider within the vRNI user interface.
- **SNMP**: vRNI uses SNMP to collect metrics information from third-party devices (switches, routers, firewalls, and so on). The third-party devices much have SNMP enabled and be accessible from vRNI. vRNI queries the device(s) every five minutes to collect the metric information.

Depending on the exact SNMP version used, different parameters are needed:

- **SNMP version 2C**: Needs the SNMP community string configured on the switch
- **SNMP version 3**: Needs all of the credentials of the user authorized to poll the SNMP service on the switch

Supported data sources

The following table summarizes the data sources currently supported by vRNI:

Datasource	Version/model	Description
AWS (Enterprise license only)	Not applicable	It connects to AWS over HTTPS.
Arista switches	7050TX, 7250QX, 7050QX-32S, 7280SE-72	It connects to Arista switches over SSH v2 and SNMP.
Brocade switches	VDX 6740, VDX 6940, MLX, MLXe	It connects to Brocade switches over SSH v2 and SNMP.
Check Point Firewall	R80	It connects to Check Point Firewall over HTTPS/REST.

Cisco **Adaptive Security Appliance** (**ASA**)	5x series (without FirePower) ASA OS Version 9.4	It connects to ASA device over SSH v2 and SNMP.
Cisco Catalyst	3000, 3750, 4500, 6000, 6500	It connects to Cisco Catalyst switches over SSH and SNMP.
Cisco Nexus	5000, 6000, 7000, 9000, VSM N1000	It connects Cisco Nexus switches over SSH v2 and SNMP.
Cisco **Unified Computing System** (**UCS**)	Series B Blade servers, Series C Rack servers, Chassis, Fabric interconnect	It connects UCS Manager over HTTPS and UCS Fabric Interconnect over SSH to fetch information. It also connects to the SNMP service on UCS.
Dell switches	PowerConnect 8024, FORCE10 MXL 10, FORCE10 S6000, S4048, Z9100	It connects to Dell switches over SSH v2 and SNMP.
HP	HP OneView 3.0	It connects to HP OneView Manager over HTTPS/REST.
HP	HP Virtual Connect Manager 4.41	It connects to HP Virtual Connect Manager over SSH v2.
Infoblox	Infoblox	It connects to Infoblox over REST.
Juniper switches	EX3300, QFX 51xx Series (JunOS v12 & v15, without QFabric)	It connects to Juniper switches over Netconf or SSH v2 and SNMP.
Palo Alto Panorama	7.0.x, 7.1.x, 8.0	It connects to Panorama over HTTPS/REST.
VMware NSX	6.4, 6.3 (upto 6.3.5), 6.2 (upto 6.2.9), 6.1(upto 6.1.7), 6.0	It connects to VMware NSX over SSH v2 and HTTPS.
VMware NSX T	2.0	It connects to VMware NSX T over HTTPS.

All REST APIs vRNI use the following:

API	Description
`/api/v1/sessions`	It creates a session with the API. This is the equivalent of login. This operation exchanges user credentials supplied in the security context for a session identifier that is to be used for authenticating subsequent calls. To authenticate subsequent calls, clients are expected to include the session key.
`/api/v1/version`	It gets the version of Log Insight installation.
`/api/v1/content/contentpack/${id}`	It fetches the details of a vRNI content pack identified with given ID.
`/api/v1/alerts`	It fetches list of alerts that correspond to this user.
`/api/v1/events`	It fetches a list of events that match content pack alerts that occurred in the queries timeframe.

Summary

In this chapter, we learned how LInt can access VMware Cloud on AWS audit logs for faster monitoring and troubleshooting as a core service with real-time alerts on anomalies based on custom triggers. It will also provide you with custom dashboards to visualize trends for effective notifications on custom alerts and high-performance searches within logs for faster root-cause analysis. We went through how it provides a single console across a broad range of applications such as VMware Cloud on AWS, cloud-based applications, and Native AWS EC2-based applications along with Wavefront integration for faster troubleshooting with logs and metrics. We saw how to determine the health of an on-premises SDDC environment quickly by identifying anomalies across infrastructure and applications and accelerating troubleshooting with out-of-the-box dashboards for VMware SDDC solutions, such as vCenter and NSX.

In the next chapter, we will explore **machine learning as a service (MLaaS)** by using vRealize Automation. The ML workflow includes data-cleaning, model-selection, feature-engineering, model-training, and inference. Production ML environments are always complex to build and maintain as each ML process may require customization of the hardware and software. We can eliminate this complexity by automating the deployment of hardware resources (such as **Load Balancer as a service (LBaaS)** and **network as a service (NaaS)**) by configuring them with the required operating system and application stack and providing them to different tenants.

ML as a Service in the Cloud

7

This chapter will help you to learn about **machine learning as a service** (**MLaaS**) by using vRealize Automation. The ML workflow has data cleaning, model selection, feature engineering, model training, and inference. The production of the ML infrastructure is complicated to develop and manage because all ML processes will need to have their hardware and software modified.

We can minimize this complication by automating the provisioning of hardware resources, configuring them along with the operating system and application package, and giving access them to the related IT team. This process customization can be introduced as MLaaS. We will learn how vRealize Automation provides MLaaS with use cases of MLaaS. It will also help in the design and configuration of the blueprint to define the process with workflows in vRealize Automation. We'll also look at **load balancer as a service** (**LBaaS**) and how **network as a service** (**NaaS**) can remove bottlenecks in hardware-based network architectures.

We will cover the following topics in this chapter:

- VMware approaches for MLaaS and its architecture
- LBaaS with use cases
- Transforming network and security services

Technical requirements

You can download VMware vRealize Orchestrator Appliance 7.5.0 from `https://my.vmware.com/web/vmware/details?downloadGroup=VROVA_750productId=742`.

MLaaS in a private cloud

ML helps computers to acquire a knowledge without extensive programming and its performance enhances in compute and data by improving its development.

High-performance computing and big-data applications leverage virtualization as it helps in concurrent support for different software infrastructures, creating resource pools, consistent research surroundings, multi-domain data security, problem diagnosis and elasticity, effective load balancing, and QoS. **High-Performance Computing** (**HPC**) and big data merged together so ML can be consumed as services from different cloud environments. These applications have huge data volumes with data-compliance and security policies to follow. Customers like to opt private cloud for hosting these ML applications with huge data which required more compute resources.

We can configure MLaaS in a private cloud using vRealize Automation to provide GPU-powered ML services for design/power users. The workflow can help to build an ML-based blueprint that can fulfill the particular requirements of design users.

VMware approach for MLaaS

We have two private-cloud options for building **Infrastructure as a Service** (**IaaS**) with VMware:

- vRealize Automation
- Integrated OpenStack

vRealize Automation helps to achieve IT automation by creating a tailor-made infrastructure, workloads, and applications hosted across hybrid cloud. VMware Integrated OpenStack is an OpenStack distribution with direct support from VMware, which helps customers to build an enterprise-class OpenStack cloud on the ever-reliable vSphere engine. It enhances performance with easy-to-use and vendor-independent OpenStack API access to the VMware environment. This chapter will brief you on creating MLaaS using VMware vRealize Automation.

MLaaS using vRealize Automation and vGPU

We can configure a TensorFlow service that end users can consume through a self-service provisioning portal built with vRealize Automation. We have the NVIDIA card installed with vSphere, vRealize Automation, NVIDIA GRID drivers to support NVIDIA vGPU and a recommended guest OS on certified servers.

NVIDIA GRID vGPU Manager for ESXi driver should be configured on ESXi to provision vGPUs. The physical GPU should be shown in ESXi as a vGPU device rather then default vSGA device.

NVIDIA vGPU configuration on vSphere ESXi

We can build a vRealize Automation template for end users to leverage a TensorFlow service. The workflow for creating and provisioning a TensorFlow service is mentioned in the next diagram. There will be five steps to build and provision a TensorFlow service for end users with a CentOS VM:

1. Add an NVIDIA GRID vGPU to the VM
2. Customize the guest OS environment
3. Convert the VM into a template and create a customization specification
4. Design the blueprint
5. Publish the blueprint

In `Chapter 1`, *Machine Learning Capabilities with vSphere 6.7,* we learned that the first three steps are configured in vCenter Console and the last two steps can be configured with vRealize Automation. The last two steps are mentioned in the following diagram:

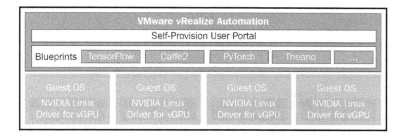

Customizing the vRealize Automation blueprint

First, we have to power off the VM installed with the driver/all tools and vGPU configured. We have to convert it into a template, which we can use as a blueprint with vRealize Automation. Once the template is created, we can then build a uniform tailor-made blueprint with defined parameters once the required template is created. Cloud Admin can use this to create clone blueprints for TensorFlow VMs:

1. Log into the vSphere web client as administrator.
2. Right-click on the VM object and select **Template** | **Convert to Template**.

3. Click on **Customization Specification Manager** and create a new specification based on the template on the home page.

4. Create a software stack that defines the software life cycle for all software to be installed and configured within a blueprint while creating the VM.

5. The blueprints have to be designed to leverage the custom functions of vRealize Automation:

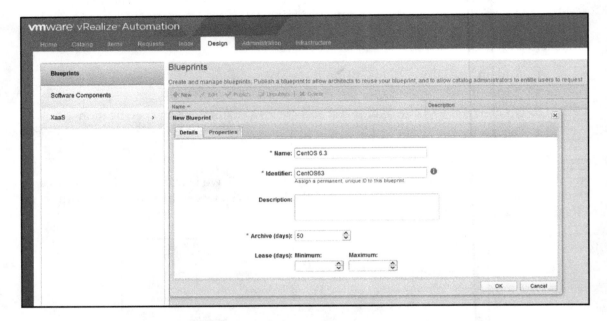

6. Bundle the software stack to design how the software will be installed, configured, started, upgraded, and uninstalled within a blueprint's VM in vRealize Automation. We can drag and drop this software stack onto a specific container variation on the design console.

7. Install TensorFlow by creating a software component. Explore the **Design** tab, then select **Software Components**, and choose **New.**

8. Define a name and details for the software stack. We have to mention the container specification as the machine in the general section and then click on **Next** to continue.

9. Create a command script that will fetch a TensorFlow GPU container image and customize the /etc/motd file to show instructions to the end user when they log in to the TensorFlow VM. vRealize Automation will install the container image and the example bash script type can be changed as per required configuration and installation steps.

10. Design the blueprint. Blueprints define the process for services to be implemented using vRealize Automation. We can opt for a basic blueprint that can deploy only a single VM, and a multi-VM blueprint that has software stacks, networks, security, and storage policies:

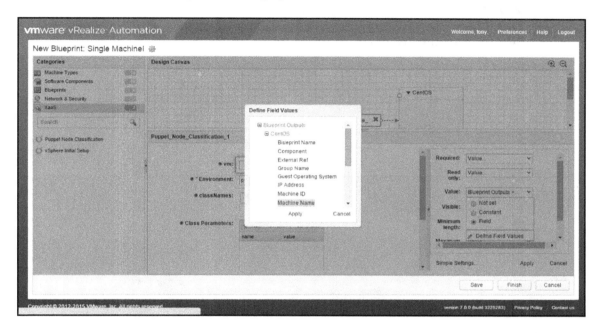

11. Create a blueprint than has only a CentOS VM, TensorFlow application, and associated virtual network: explore the **Design** tab, choose **Blueprints**, and select **New**.

12. Mention the name and details in the new blueprint section so a unique ID will be generated.

13. Add an ESXi host to the TensorFlow blueprint by choosing **Machine Types** from the **Categories** section and dragging the ESXi host to the design console. We have to define other parameters and mention the prefix in the **General** tab to be used with all VM names built by the blueprint and gave access to users for self provisioning of up to four TensorFlow VMs.

14. Access the **Machine Resources** tab to get information about the virtual CPU, memory, and storage to be configured for the VMs created by this blueprint.

15. Specify the virtual network under the **Network** tab when the VM gets created.

16. Choose the required network from the drop-down menu and select **DHCP** or **Static**. If we include a passthrough PCI device to a VM, we have to allocate full memory reservation for this configuration. The template called VM memory reservation will be not able to keep this configuration during the cloning process. To manage this, we have to add the specific **VMware.Memory.Reservation** parameter with a defined memory size by exploring the **Properties** tab.

We can provision this blueprint as service through the vRealize Automation service catalog from the **Machine learning** category and nominate users to use it. Edit the **Custom Properties** tab and follow the below steps:

1. Choose **TensorFlow-GPU** in **Blueprints**
2. Click on **Publish**:

We can see various ML/DL services with and without GPUs from a self-service provisioning portal in the preceding screenshot, which design users can use defined resources.

LBaaS overview

Customers can use LBaaS by integrating it with NSX and the vRealize automation engine, which create a workflow to include applications requirements. They can also integrate with third-party tools with this service for automated deployment and monitoring of services. We have many options to design a load balancer as a service by using the VMware software-defined approach.

The load balancer must offload SSL to enhance performance and its output. A global load balancer has to fail over to application services between multiple data centers. It has to use the most productive load-balancing algorithm to increase the productivity of the application services. It can monitor the application services and generate alerts as soon as it finds any threats.

VMware **vRealize Orchestrator (vRO)** assists us in building LBaaS by automating F5 virtual server deployments as per predefined workflows that contain parameters such as number of steps, virtual server addition associated with IP address, protocol, port, profile, and a monitoring report of a specific virtual server. LBaaS has to provide HTTPS as a service and offload SSL. vRO can execute scripts on a PowerShell server to generate Microsoft CA signed certificates and transfer it to the F5 server. It ensures SSL is attached to the F5 profile.

LBaaS design use cases

LBaaS use cases are as follows:

- Deploying a single-site load balancer
- Deploying a multi-site load balancer
- Customizing a load balancer
- Removing a VM

Let us see the use cases in detail:

- **Deploying a single-site load balancer**: Create the VMs and then define the load balancer with specific VMs. Users can log in through the **Self-Service Portal** (**SSP**) and request a virtual server. As per design, the load balancer is configured at one site. Users can choose data with list boxes and combo boxes along with pre-populated data to provide data entry process. vRealize has the capability to invoke vRO, which in turn will execute predefined workflow steps to provision a F5 virtual server for the group of virtual servers selected by the user.
  Once vRealize Automation receives the application-specific data, it can create an F5 **Local Traffic Manager** (**LTM**) virtual server with a **VMware Infrastructure Planner** (**VIP**) and DNS name as per workflow:

Step	Actor	Actions
1	User	• Logs in to vRealize SSP • Requests LBaaS provisioning using a XaaS Blueprint • Provides necessary data to the request form
2	vRealize Automation	• Receives and validates the data entered by users • Invokes vRO workflows to provision the F5 virtual server
3	vRO	• Provisions the F5 virtual server • Attaches the F5 virtual server with the virtual machines selected by the user

- **Deploying a multi-site load balancer**: A multi-site load balancer configuration is different from a single-site load balancer as two F5 LTMs associated with a Big-IP DNS are configured in two data centers. Big-IP DNS is not mandatory and required only as global load balancers. Its workflow helps users with various alternatives for traffic flow methods (that is, 50/50, 80/20, 60/40, 40/60, and 20/80) across two sites.
  Users will enter the data into the vRealize Automation request form. vRealize Automation will invoke vRO workflows to process the data, create two F5 virtual servers (one on each site), and a F5 Big-IP DNS system:

Step	Actor	Actions
1	User	• Logs in to vRealize SSP • Requests LBaaS provisioning using a XaaS Blueprint • Chooses the **Global Traffic Manager** (**GTM**) checkbox to create a multi-site load balancer • Inputs LTM and GTM information to the request form
2	vRealize Automation	• Receives and validates the data entered by users • Invokes vRO workflows to provision three F5 virtual servers—one per site on LTM and one for Big-IP DNS
3	vRO	• Provisions the F5 virtual servers • Attaches the F5 virtual server with the VMs selected by the user

- **Modifying a load balancer**: The load balancer can be customized on F5 with a new VM and then we can execute a XaaS blueprint to a new VM configured with the load balancer. If the user selects the incorrect load balancer algorithm during the load balancer deployment, they can amend it through a XaaS blueprint. The following table describes the actions for this use case:

Step	Actor	Actions
1	User	• Logs in to vRealize SS • Requests LBaaS modification using a XaaS Blueprint • Provides the necessary data to modify an existing load balancer
2	vRealize Automation	• Receives and validates the data entered by users • Invokes the vRO workflows to modify the F5 virtual server
3	vRO	• Modifies the F5 virtual server

- **De-provisioning a VM**: We can de-provision any member VM of the F5 virtual server member pool with a vRealize Automation workflow, otherwise F5 will release alerts with the message that **The virtual machine is unavailable**. Users can also remove the VM from a F5 virtual server pool with a modified XaaS workflow. The F5 virtual server member pool will be automatically finished as the last VM is deleted:

Step	Actor	Actions
1	User	• Logs in to vRealize SSP • Requests VM de-provisioning using an existing blueprint
2	vRealize Automation	• Calls the LBaaS XaaS workflow as part of the VM de-provisioning blueprint
3	LBaaS XaaS Workflow	• Receives all necessary data from the VM de-provisioning request • Calls the vRO workflow
4	vRO	• Creates the XaaS workflow to add/remove VMs from the F5 virtual server member pool

- **LBaaS workflow**: To provision a multi-site load balancer, two identical load balancers are deployed at each site in a multi-site design. A Big-IP DNS wide-IP is also created and the user is asked to enter other input along with the primary site and traffic flow ratio:

Lane	Action	Notes
vRO	Advanced F5 GTM Workflow using REST API	• Click the GTM checkbox and enter the Big-IP DNS parameters to run a workflow to build a BIG-IP DNS global load balancer

The following diagram shows the workflow:

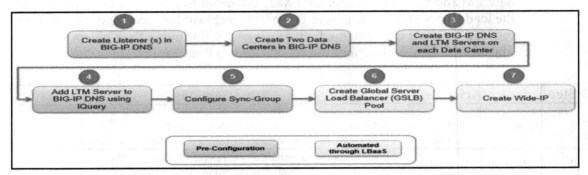

Let's go through all of the functions mentioned in the preceding diagram. As we know, the first five steps were already discussed in the LBaaS workflow and are needed to execute the LBaaS workflow. All functions are given from a reference point of view:

1. Create a listener. From the Big-IP DNS UI, select **DNS | Delivery** to provide the values to the listener parameters. A listener needs to be created on each site. This is a prerequisite for the LBaaS workflow.

2. Create the data centers. From the Big-IP DNS UI, select **DNS | GSLB | Data Centers | Data Center List | New Data Center** to provide the data center name and other parameters. You will need to repeat this step for both data centers. This is a prerequisite for the LBaaS workflow.

3. Create the Big-IP DNS and LTM servers. From the Big-IP DNS UI, select **DNS | GSLB | Servers | Server List | New Server** to add LTM servers to Big-IP DNS. You will need to repeat this step for both data centers: the Primary and Secondary sites. This is a prerequisite for the LBaaS workflow.

4. Configure the (bigip_add utility) iQuery:
   1. Log in to the BIG-IP DNS at Rancho Cordova.
   2. Run the # `bigip_add <rc-ltm-ip>` command to add Rancho Cordova LTM to the GTM.
   3. Upon successful communication between BIG-IP DNS and LTMs, the status in the BIG-IP DNS UI will turn green. This is a pre-requisite for the LBaaS workflow.

5. Configure sync-group:
    1. Add both DNS servers (RC_DNS and FX_DNS) to the BIG-IP DNS system.
    2. Create a sync-group.
    3. Use the #gtm _add <fx-gtm-ip> command to add the Fairfield Annex BIG-IP GTM appliance.
    4. Use the #bigip_add <fx-ltm-ip> command to add the Fairfield Annex BIG-IP LTM appliance. This is a pre-requisite for the LBaaS workflow

6. Create the **Global Server Load Balancer (GSLB)** pool:
    1. The GSLB pool will be created as part of the LBaaS workflow. The pool name will be provided by the user as part of the XaaS UI.
    2. If created manually, select **GSLB | Pools**. Click on **Create** to create a global pool.

7. Create wide-IP:
    1. Wide-IP will be created as part of the LBaaS workflow.
    2. If created manually, select **GSLB | Wide IPs**. Click **Create** to create a wide-IP. The wide-IP name will be provided by the user as part of the XaaS UI.
    3. An IP address will be assigned to wide-IP through the vRO IP reserve workflow from Infoblox.

Challenges with network and security services

Network and security were always the bottleneck of the infrastructure.

Below are the major pain points with rigid hardware defined infrastructure :

- Placement and mobility were limited by the physical port
- Provisioning was slow due to lack of advanced automation capabilities, as it is not designed for automation
- It was operationally intensive and hardware-dependent

The following can be done to achieve IT as a service model:

- Cloud networking architectural and operational model support the evolution of **IT as a service** (**ITaaS**) model
- End-to-end visibility with real time monitoring and troubleshooting (across virtual and physical networks) for integrated network availability and performance management
- On-demand automated network provisioning and configuration to support rapid application deployment
- New organizational model to facilitate collaboration between new cloud/SDDC team and existing functional teams (application, server, network and storage)
- Skills to support the new operational model and service-oriented approach

To gain an understanding of the concepts of a new IT operating model and why network and security should be part of it.

Different phases of NaaS Model

- Review the ITaaS and NaaS operating models
- Identify the capabilities required to deliver and operate NaaS
- Understand the journey to the NaaS operating model from both an operational and organizational standpoint

The NaaS operating model

NaaS is one of the important part of the ITaaS operating model which help customers to achieve specific IT (network,security, and so on) outcomes. We have to review current network and security operating model across people, processes and technology and how to offer NaaS using the VMware Operations Transformation model and framework.

We should first discover the operational capabilities required to manage and operate NaaS based services with a structured approach.

It focuses on three main areas:

- Proactive operations management
- Network and security service provisioning
- Security operations

The key operational capabilities are identified, as well as how to transform from the current operational capabilities to operating a network virtualization environment that enables the NaaS vision for each of the following areas:

- Defining the vision and strategy
- Defining key operational capabilities
- Assessing operational readiness
- Building an operations transformation roadmap and plan
- Developing and implementing the target operating model with the NaaS vision

The VMware NaaS transformation workshop service provides customers with an operational and organizational view on how to leverage the network virtualization architecture to move toward a NaaS operating model and ultimately toward the ITaaS operating model.

VMware defines ITaaS as a new delivery and operating model that leverages cloud technologies to enable business agility and value-based choice through readily-consumable IT services that have transparent prices and established service levels. The network plays a key role in enabling the ITaaS vision. Until now seen as a barrier to agility and speed, the new and emerging network architecture, based on network virtualization and SDDC/cloud, makes a new way to deploy, manage, and operate network and security possible.

The new operating model implies a paradigm shift from a device-centric operating model to a service-oriented operating model called NaaS. Though network virtualization is the technology enabler, the technology alone is not enough to achieve the full benefits of software-defined networking (and SDDC in general) but it has to be complemented by streamlined, integrated, and automated processes and a cross-functional organization that breaks silos with new skills.

This paradigm shift is actually an operations transformation that goes beyond the technology aspects that impact operational and organizational aspects. The operational and organizational aspects shouldn't be considered as an afterthought—they should be planned and designed in parallel to the technology plan and design.

The NaaS transformation workshops are directed to support the customer in the vision and strategy-definition phase, as well as in the planning of the operational and organizational capabilities required to deploy, manage, and operate the network virtualization solution that the customer is going to implement.

The goal of the workshops is to facilitate the customer to understand the NaaS operating model and identify the operational and organizational impact and challenges of network virtualization adoption as well as the capabilities required to fully leverage the benefits of the emerging network architecture.

The workshop service also provides an introduction to the VMware Operations Transformation model and framework and how it applies to driving the operational and organizational maturity growth toward the NaaS operating model.

The NaaS service can be divided into two parts:

- **NaaS transformation envisioning**: We have to assist customers with a clear understanding of the VMware NaaS operating model, its role as part of the ITaaS operating model, and the benefits of adopting this model in terms of IT outcomes. We will also discuss the customer's operational strategy, goals and objectives, the current network and security operating model across people, processes and technology and how it can be transformed to NaaS using the VMware Operations Transformation model and framework. This is oriented to network and IT infrastructure and operations teams that are willing to explore how network virtualization can drive the adoption of a new network and security operating model to make IT more agile, flexible, efficient, and business-aligned.
- **NaaS transformation discovery**: Discover the operational capabilities required to manage and operate NaaS starting from a process perspective. The end-to-end operational processes are decomposed in common process elements and the operational capabilities required to optimally execute the process elements are identified. The discovery activity focuses on three main areas: proactive operations management, network and security services automated provisioning, and life cycle management and security operations. For each area, the key operational capabilities are identified and high-level observations on how to evolve and transform from the current operational capabilities to operating a network virtualization environment that enables the NaaS vision.

Transforming traditional network by consuming NaaS:

- **Traditional networking challenges**: Networking is all about ports and its capabilities related to performance, configuration, and the power dissipation of custom **application-specific integrated circuits (ASICs)**. It's also connected with related skillsets and OpEx cost-related with network operations. Network services will not be agile if it sticks with particular physical device with manual deployment, which raises the risk of configuration changes and human errors. It is not justified to write a script for each device interfaces to orchestrate automation as it creates hindrance to utilize the full capabilities of virtualization and cloud model.
- **Networking is a service**: It always has been, and will continue to be, a service by abstracting, creating resource pools, and automating the network. Networking services are instantly provisioned from a capacity pool, decoupled from specific hardware, made equally mobile, deployed using templates, and controlled and managed through policies. The NaaS operating model enables us to deliver the agile data center of the future, the service velocity and agility that modern applications need, and the OpEx and CapEx efficiencies and cost savings we desire.

LBaaS network design using NSX

VMware NSX can assist us in building **Virtual Extensible LAN (VXLAN)** based virtual networks automated deployment to produce micro segmentation across different web, app, and DB servers. A **Distributed Logical Router (DLR)** will be provisioned to enable routing between networks produced by leveraging NSX logical switches. Since a DLR supports up to 1,000 logical interfaces, logical switches for several applications can be connected to DLR to leverage its routing capabilities.

Application-level segmentation can then be provided using NSX Service Composer features, such as security groups and security policies. BIG-IP DNS helps to maintain applications redundancy with native intelligence. Two BIG-IP DNS systems deployed at two sites will work as a single unit but accountable for primary and secondary authoritative name service.

The users get the most favorable IP address (which is the LTM VIP) from site A (primary) or site B (secondary) based on defined rules, such as resource redundancy, SLA, load, geographical location, or QoS.

BIG-IP DNS assists with various kinds of queries when the *A* type query is used extensively. A BIG-IP DNS gets a query by matching the domain name and type with a wide-IP, then it chooses a pool (GSLB pool) to justify the response. Then it gets a virtual server from the pool by reacting with an IP address. GSLB pool will help in choosing a virtual server across both sites based on the load-balancing policy on each site and resources availability at runtime.

BIG-IP DNS high-level design

Wide-IP is a **Fully-Qualified Domain Name** (**FQDN**) to get the application URL, which is a web application hosted on a group of web servers, such as Apache or IIS. BIG-IP DNS resolves queries to define wide-IP FQDN association with a virtual server (VIP) from a GSLB pool that has two virtual servers at each site.

The load-balancer pool algorithms for the LTM virtual server and BIG-IP DNS virtual server are not the same, and the LTM virtual server load-balancer algorithm is chosen by the user from a drop-down field. The BIG-IP DNS GSLB pool algorithm is defined on user input. There are three kinds of GSLB pool algorithms that were chosen for the LBaaS design: global delivery, ratio, and round robin.

Customizing the BIG-IP DNS component

The BIG-IP DNS configuration has the following components:

- **Listener**: This is the BIG-IP DNS object that operates and answers to DNS queries. The listener configuration on BIG-IP DNS should be defined before executing the LBaaS workflow.
- **Data center**: This is a container object which host the place for application delivery components and has two LTM virtual servers from each site. The data center configuration on BIG-IP DNS should be defined before executing the LBaaS workflow.
- **Server**: This is a container object which host application components reside and can be a BIG-IP DNS, LTM server, or physical server instance. The server configuration on BIG-IP DNS should be defined before executing the LBaaS workflow.
- **Virtual server**: The virtual server has the IP address and service port configured on a physical server. BIG-IP DNS use these IP addresses and service ports to resolve queries and choose suitable virtual server.

- **Pool**: This is a logical object configured on the BIG-IP DNS system. Virtual servers can be set with different pools to resolve queries in a smart way. GSLB pool can be created by grouping all concerned virtual servers. Pool configuration for LBaaS will be customized on-demand using LBaaS workflow.
- **Wide-IP**: This is a logical container that is known as FQDN by grouping GSLB pools and have a batch of all concerned virtual servers. This object is developed and customized in the LBaaS workflow. The IP address for the FQDN will be restrained on Infoblox by leveraging a vRO workflow.
- **DIG**: The DNS resolution utility is a tool to experiment with wide-IP configuration and can be downloaded to a system. Users like to download the utility to the PowerShell desktop to check the acceptance of wide-IP configuration with the LBaaS workflow. The `#dig @listener-ip wide-ip-name` command will post a DNS query to the listener and show the response from BIG-IP DNS.

The BIG-IP DNS load-balancing algorithm

We have three kinds of load-balancer algorithms based on the LBaaS design, which we'll explore here; they should be registered effectively to the BIG-IP DNS GSLB Pool.

Global availability

This load-balancing algorithm will be suitable for the active/standby scenario and BIG-IP DNS disperse DNS name resolution requests to the first accessible virtual server from the configured list in a pool and, if the virtual server is not accessible, then BIG-IP DNS post requests to the next virtual server in the configured list.

The vRO workflow should define the GSLB pool load-balancing algorithm as globally available when a user chooses Active/standby in the XaaS form. It also makes sure that the first reachable virtual server will be from active site.

Ratio

The LBaaS workflow has to manage traffic flow across two sites. The BIG-IP DNS Ratio load-balancing algorithm can assist you in fulfilling this use case. The ratio load-balancing method disperses DNS name resolution requests between the virtual servers in a pool by leveraging a weighed round robin. Weights for both virtual servers should be measured in the vRO workflow and registered by using the REST APIs. We can choose the ratio as a user from a drop-down list in XaaS form.

Round robin

The LBaaS workflow can distribute inbound requests by keeping an active state at both sites. The BIG-IP DNS round robin algorithm can be configured for the GSLB pool. BIG-IP DNS name-resolution requests can be distributed between the virtual servers of a GSLB pool in sequence so each virtual server will get a similar number of requests.

The LBaaS LTM design

LBaaS design used to suppose that BIG-IP virtual editions are installed on both sites. It also suppose that **Device Service Clustering (DSC)** can be used for every pair of BIG-IP appliances with the active/active scenario. The LBaaS design also understands that a sync failover device configuration survives on the virtual editions pair to sync the device configuration among the members pair so the devices can failover vice versa.

Configuring BIG-IP LTM objects

The following objects are configured automatically by using the LBaaS workflow in the F5 LTM:

- **Node**: It represents the IP address of a physical or virtual instance in a network, such as a web server or an application server. A single node can have many application services running different or same kind of services associated with a pool member.
- **Pool Member**: It is union of an IP address and a port number that defines an application service that resides on a node. A pool member is obtained by a BIG-IP system.
- **Pool**: Load balancing can be accomplished by grouping one or more pool members and choosing suitable pool members. Load balancing policy should be configured on a pool with the specific pool members.
- **Virtual server**: It is a kind of listener which permits matching traffic types consisting of virtual server IP and port and forward them to pool members as per load balancing policy. All traffic gets blocked as the F5 LTM is a default-deny system. Virtual servers are ideal units that connect the clients.

Designing the LTM load-balancing method

We can configure many load-balancing techniques with the LTM virtual server traffic operations. Users get a drop-down box to choose one of the following load-balancing techniques:

- **Round Robin** (Default)
- **Least Connections**
- **Weighted Least Connections**
- **Ratio**
- **Observed**
- **Dynamic Ratio**
- **Least Sessions**
- **Fastest**
- **Predictive**

The **LTM** tab is shown in the following screenshot:

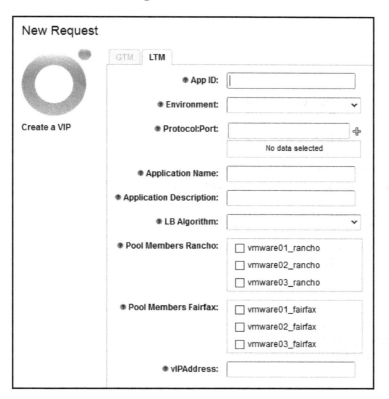

Designing the LTM virtual server

VMware Cloud on the AWS L2 network extension service provides customers with the capability to extend the on-premises networks to VMware Cloud on AWS over any IP network using an SSL VPN tunnel (L2VPN) by creating subnets with a single broadcast domain. This enables customers to move workloads between an on-premises network and VMware Cloud on AWS without changing the IP address.

This service starts by introducing it's offering and collecting details to perform a technical gap analysis and recommendation, which helps the customer to prepare the environment for L2 network extension. VMware Cloud on the AWS environment is configured, and extended network functional testing is performed.

Objectives with this service initiative to perform below two activities:

- Establishing an SSL tunnel (L2VPN) between on-premises and VMware Cloud on the AWS network
- Extending the L2 subnets across on-premises and VMware Cloud on AWS networks using the SSL tunnel

Summary

We can choose from various kinds of cloud-based offerings, including SaaS and IaaS. **Machine Learning as a Service** (**MLaaS**) is one of the latest innovations in the IT industry. ML deployment basically needs huge amounts of data and advanced users who can investigate patterns from the data volumes. The ML algorithm is always a hit-and-miss scenario. MLaaS will play a crucial role in AI adoption as it'll help developers and businesses reap the benefits of ML features. It will assist in embedding AI in business apps and enable organizations to use data in better ways to achieve their business objectives.

VMware SDDC products and approaches can be utilized to automate various services, and not just for the VMware-offered products but even for third-party tools. The entire process of provisioning and de-provisioning services using vRealize products can be automated along with vRealize Orchestrator, vRealize Log Insight, and NSX on top of vSphere hypervisor.

The next chapter, Chapter 8, *Machine Learning-Based Rule Engine with Skyline*, will give you a detailed overview of VMware Skyline. We will collect information from a customer and use ML as an intelligent rule engine to monitor and provide proactive support for a faster resolution by preventing upcoming threats.

8
ML-Based Rule Engine with Skyline

This chapter will show you how VMware Skyline collects information from a customer and uses machine learning techniques to create an intelligent rule engine. This is used to monitor abnormal behavior and then raise a red flag to enable proactive support.

You will learn how to create policies and rules to avoid future incidents and minimize downtime, and you will also learn about the features and configuration of the Skyline tool. This tool is able to automate monitoring and management to prevent attacks from unknown threats.

In this chapter, we will cover the following topics:

- Proactive support technology
- Overview of Skyline Collector
- Customer experience improvement program

Technical requirements

You can download VMware Skyline Collector 2.0.0.2 from `https://my.vmware.com/web/vmware/details?downloadGroup=SKYLINE10productId=790rPId=26633`.

Proactive support technology – VMware Skyline

VMware Global Services have built an intelligent support engine called Skyline, which collects customer-specific VMware products related data without any manual effort or compromise of security policies. It aggregates and analyzes this data to help the support team attain a quick time-to-resolution and take action to prevent upcoming issues.

We can get a full 360-degree view of VMware products in the customer's environment, from a deployment and usage perspective. We can help customers by providing them with more information and allowing them to interact with all customer endpoints for an overview of known and unknown issues. Skyline is necessary for mission-critical applications running on a VMware infrastructure, which is available 24/7, 365 days a year, and is highly optimized to achieve maximum performance from its resources. Customers want quick resolutions and suggestions, with all the supporting data analytics to recognize problems before they create issues in the customer environment. Skyline can take care of all of these requirements with its smart support system, which helps support engineers learn information and data about the specific customer's deployment of VMware products.

If we knew our customer's environment just like they did, then we would be able to suggest proactive, prescriptive, and predictive recommendations about a problem that might occur in the future, in advance. It would also help support teams with their reactive support cases, since these could be resolved more quickly to help customers get back to their businesses faster. VMware Skyline consists of three technology (Collector, rule engine and Advisor) components. Global Services has innovative new support capabilities.

Proactive support with VMware Skyline offers many benefits, including the following:

- A customized support experience will deepen the relationship with the customer
- Knowledge of customer usage will enable adoption of applications and value realization through customer success initiatives
- Faster, higher quality support resolution
- Optimum design, configuration, and software versions for customer-specific implementations
- Improved reliability, with advanced warning systems
- **Support request** (**SR**) deflection to fix identified errors before they occur
- Shorter time to resolution; that is, data is collected proactively and solutions are provided to allow for a faster diagnosis and resolution

- Protection of a huge amount of money in **Support and Subscription Services (SnS)** bookings by delivering continuous incremental value
- Increases the total deal size and compensation, and upsell customers from production support to premier services
- Improved tools and technology
- Visibility into customers' environments

Collector, viewer, and advisor

Skyline Collector helps gather details about changes and occurrences in near real time and is isolated from the customer environment, as no customer-specific data is saved in the collector. VMware Skyline data is accessed on an as-needed basis by VMware support teams.

VMware Skyline Advisor will be a customer-facing, self-service dashboard that will be delivered as an SaaS application for customers. This will provide detailed analysis about the outcomes of identified alerts and suggested operations, so that customers can configure smart remediation. An advisor can be utilized and connected with a viewer to fully utilize this policy-based analysis engine, which is comprised of support intelligence libraries, product information, and logic to analyze the internal customer-specific product deployment data. This is used to get suggestions and detailed reports that can be shared with customers. It is well integrated with VMware validated design, best practices, and **Knowledge Base (KB)** articles, to send alerts, identify faults and issues, and any deviations from recommended design. It then initiates a remediation process with support assistance by support engineers, or faults and issues can be solved through self-service steps. Skyline has a single collector instance to collect and transfer VMware product-related information back to the **VMware Analytics Cloud (VAC)** infrastructure. Customers who have active product support can use Skyline Collector. It can analyze changes, activities, and patterns related to specific information such as faults by using a machine learning engine. The Skyline policy engine supports intelligence libraries, and product information and the relevant logic is saved to analyze the customer's internal flow of data that's relevant to VMware products. It send notices if the customer is not following VMware validated design practices to make configurations or patch management for VMware products. All of the problems that are identified are fed into the analytics engine, which has hundreds of detection policies to help us rectify the same kinds of problems for multiple customers.

VMware Skyline collects information about vSphere and NSX in a customer's environment. It can analyze telemetry information from vSphere and NSX. We plan to rapidly add support for more VMware technologies in the future with vSAN, which is next on our roadmap. Eventually, the full stack of products will be available on VMware Skyline. Our insights will get better with time, adding more predictive recommendations to reduce downtime and performance issues. VMware Skyline matures as the rules engine evolves in scope and complexity, so the value to customers will continue to grow. Customers will also be able to add and remove individual product deployments from collection. Skyline is available through the VMware managed access program at no cost for premier support customers (Mission Critical, Healthcare Critical, and Business Critical) with vSphere and NSX on-premises environments.

Release strategy

VMware's plan is to deliver incremental benefits and expand the scope of product and solution awareness to drive toward introducing customer self-service opportunities within the development and release a roadmap.

This will help us add value quickly as we introduce the VMware Skyline Viewer for support engineers, which is to be utilized in both proactive and reactive support engagements with customers. We plan to make the VMware Skyline Advisor workbench available to various support teams, along with product engineering teams, so that they can actively participate in the creation of new rules and analysis as we expand our ability to automatically detect known issues or recommendations. VMware Skyline will also provide added support service capabilities to customers in future who have production support and Premier Support Services in the form of self-service solutions.

VMware Skyline fits into Global Services' overall vision, as VMware strives to provide best in class support to our customers, as represented by our high customer satisfaction and **net promoter score** (**NPS**). As the competition attempts to close that gap, we innovate. VMware Skyline is one of those innovations that puts us ahead of the competition in both reactive and proactive support. No other full stack software company provides this level of capability. VMware Skyline focuses on transforming the customer experience, and the key way that we do this is by building customer intimacy. If we know and understand what our customers are doing, we can more readily engage with them proactively, in order to provide assistance and guidance.

VMware Skyline can be rolled out in a very large customer environment, phase-wise and during the initial rollout. It is best to collect from a single vCenter, have the customer give us feedback on the value that we're providing, and then keep adding incrementally. There will be some scale scenarios that we will hit in the real world that we will never encounter in testing, and we can identify those through a measured adoption plan. We don't recommend any aggressive approaches to an initial enterprise software drop. The collector attaches itself to a vCenter. It can connect to multiple vCenters, as well, but it can always be split on a per-vCenter basis. Very large, multi-vCenter environments will also require multi-collector setups. The collector appliance should also be as near to the vCenter as possible, in terms of network traffic, so as to not stress sending data over the WAN. Multiple physical data centers will also lean toward multi-collector setups for each location. Data is tied together on the backend, so we know that it all came from the same customer.

At any point in time, customers can opt out of the **Customer Experience Improvement Program** (**CEIP**). Customers can unregister Skyline Collector from operations and disable all Skyline functionality from their environment. Data that's been collected will be retained for a 13-month period for customer-identifiable information, and for up to four years for other collected data. Product-related data is saved and used for different processes, along with the end-to-end security for this data. We can manage data and de-identify as required. We can encrypt data in storage and in motion, as well as all kinds of all kinds of physical security such as firewall, HIPS, IDS, and so on. We can also design data backups, disaster recovery, and other security processes for this data with proper auditing. VMware is responsible for managing this collected data to provide better technical support, along with product enhancement.

We must meet the criteria to gain access to VMware Skyline product usage data. This includes completing training for the product usage data policy, acknowledging your responsibility for how this data is used, and submitting a formal request that identifies other details about our intended use. The process continues with our manager's review, and, in exceptional cases, with the data trustee's review. If your request is approved, then your access can be provisioned at the approved system(s). We are planning to expand the requesting process to an enterprise identity access management system. This will be part of an external facing website that we can share with customers.

Customers can download Skyline Collector via the following simple steps:

1. Click on the `https://my.vmware.com/web/vmware/details?downloadGroup=SKYLINE10productId=790rPId=26633` link to go to the VMware Skyline download site:
2. Log in to Skyline Collector using your credentials:
3. Once you have accepted Skyline's privacy policy, you can start to install the Collector appliance.

4. Fill out a few simple configuration web pages with My VMware credentials and entitlement account information to register the collector to learn the basic setup.

Overview of Skyline Collector

Skyline Collector is available in the form of a virtual appliance and can collect critical information about vSphere and NSX from the customer's environment so that the support team can deliver better support.

After registration, customers will have the following benefits:

- Better support with CEIP
- The customer's data will be secure and safe with this clear approach
- VMware's My VMware customer portal will authenticate the validity of the customer
- The My VMware customer account will be integrated with the Skyline Collector appliance
- The customer will be entitled to Skyline services after the account is authenticated
- The customer support experience is improved by the customer's direct connection to VMware's technical support services

The requirements for Skyline Collector

There are a few system prerequisites to install Skyline Collector, with hardware and software configurations.

The software requirements are as follows:

- vCenter Server, 6.0 or later
- ESXi, v6.0 or later
- NSX for vSphere, 6.1 or later

We can deploy Skyline Collector on any system that has the required minimum system prerequisites. The following are the prerequisites for the Skyline Collector virtual appliance:

Number of vCPUs	Memory	Disk Space
2	8 GB	87 GB (1.1 GB initially, if thin provisioned)

Networking requirements

The external network connectivity requirements are as follows:

Machine	Connection to	Connection type	Protocol	Port
VMware Skyline Collector	`vcsa.vmware.com`	HTTPS	TCP/IP	443
VMware Skyline Collector	`vapp-updates.vmware.com`	HTTPS	TCP/IP	443

Most customers want data to be scrubbed, and VMware provides an in-house log scrubber script to customers. It removes IP addresses, hostnames, and so on from customer logs. Instead, a placeholder is added and a key is provided to the customer to associate the IP addresses and hostnames to the names that are inserted in the logs. This capability needs to be included in the Skyline appliance locally, so that the customer host and IP data are not transmitted. The customer may want some control (radio buttons or check boxes, for example) for different data if not all of their data needs have been scrubbed. The following table summarizes all of the required ports and protocols for Skyline's operation:

Machine	Connection to	Connection type	Protocol	Port
VMware Skyline Collector	vCenter Server	HTTPS	TCP/IP	443
VMware Skyline Collector	**Platform Services Controller (PSC)/Single Sign-On (SSO)** service provider 5.5	HTTPS	TCP/IP	7444
VMware Skyline Collector	PSC/SSO service provider 6.0 / 6.5	HTTPS	TCP/IP	443
VMware Skyline Collector	NSX Manager	HTTPS	TCP/IP	443
Web browser	Skyline Collector admin interface	HTTPS	TCP/IP	443
Web browser	Skyline Collector **vCenter Server Appliance Management Interface (VAMI)**	HTTPS	TCP/IP	5480

Skyline Collector can use different network connections to fetch and transmit relevant data. The following diagram illustrates how the ports work:

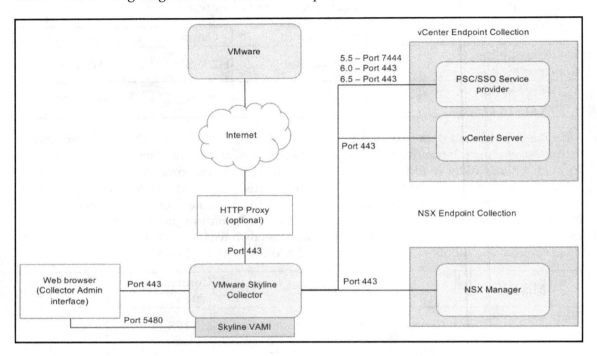

Skyline Collector user permissions

Skyline Collector's admin account authenticates and logs in to the Skyline Collector admin interface, and then it registers the application to manage collection endpoints. The admin account's password will be defined as the deployment starts and the collector is registered. Skyline Collector's root user will be used for updates with VAMI interface access at `https://<Skyline_Collector_Appliance_IP_Address>:5480`, when that user is notified of a pending update.

Skyline Collector needs read-only user access to connect to the VMware product (with license information) that's been installed on the customer premises, so that it can gather data and tie it to its respective deployment.

It needs a user account in all concerned vCenter Server instances with the following privileges:

- The collector can integrate with the default vCenter Server, with built-in, read-only access
- **Global | License** permissions are required

Skyline Collector needs read-only access with an auditor (or the same kind of access with APIs) to send queries for NSX Manager. The following diagram shows how the authentication process works:

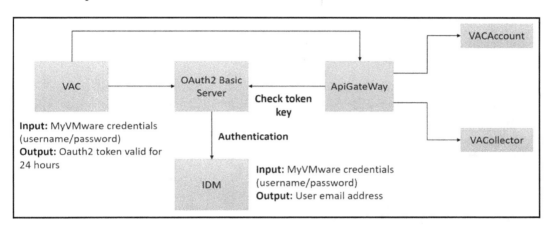

Skyline Collector is available in an **open virtualization appliance** (**OVF**) format, and it can be installed via the OVF deployment wizard from the vCenter Console. A virtual appliance consists of a preconfigured VM with a pre-installed guest OS, application, and other related software. We can access the collector admin interface through a web browser by including the IP address or hostname associated with the appliance after installing it.

Integrating the client plugin: The client plugin provides access to the collector console and other vSphere capabilities through the vSphere Web Client. This plugin also helps to install other virtual appliances by using Windows session authentication through the vSphere Web Client.

Skyline Collector appliance: We can power on a collector appliance and then access the admin interface and obtain the IP address for the collector appliance, in order to explore the collector console:

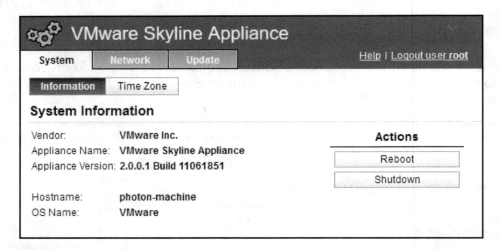

Skyline Collector should be registered before it is configured for a specific customer environment.

VMware Skyline Collector admin interface

After powering on the Skyline Collector appliance, we can obtain the IP address for that appliance. This can be done as follows:

1. As an administrator, log in to the vSphere Web Client
2. Right-click on **Collector virtual appliance** and choose **Power**. Then, click **Power On**
3. We can view the IP address of the collector appliance in the **Summary** tab by refreshing the vSphere Web Client after powering on the virtual appliance
4. Browse to `https://<Collector_Appliance_IP_Address>` through the web browser

Skyline Collector admin interface: Because the collector certificate doesn't match the hostname/IP address for the environment, a browser security warning will appear the first time we connect. First, we must log in with our default username and password:

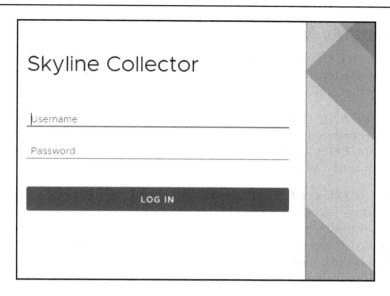

Our default username is `admin`, and the password is also `default`. A password should have a minimum of eight characters, with one uppercase letter, one special character, one digit, and one lowercase letter.

Click on **Change** after entering a new password for the admin account. We must log in to the Skyline Collector admin interface again after changing the password; we will get a **Your password was changed successfully!** screen.

The connectivity is always one-way, from the Skyline Collector going outward to VAC or the Photon OS update library services. We have two methods of returning data to the Skyline Collector appliance. This can be done through the Photon OS VAMI interface for product updates/patches, and so on, and through manifest updates, where we can post an updated manifest that describes what data has been collected, at what interval, and so on. The appliance checks for manifest updates periodically, and when an update is available, it pulls the new manifest down to utilize its current configurations. The collector must upload encrypted data to VMware via the internet. If the collector requires an HTTP proxy to reach the internet, toggle the switch to **Yes** and configure the settings that are required by the proxy administrator. Click on **TEST CONNECTIVITY** to validate the network's connectivity, and then click on **Continue.**

The collector will not be registered upon the first login. Registration of the collector is required to configure data collection. The registration wizard will automatically appear upon the first login.

Linking with My VMware account

We can participate in CEIP while registering Skyline Collector and initializing its process. Skyline Collector data is vastly utilized for both support and product improvement purposes with the the CEIP:

Then, select **AGREE AND CONTINUE**. Collector registration requires an active My VMware account connected to an active VMware production support or premier services support entitlement. Enter your My VMware account email, password, and Entitlement Account ID. When ready, select **Link Account:**

Once the collector has successfully validated your credentials, click on **Continue**. If customers have issues with their My VMware account login, please go to `https://my.vmware.com` to reset the account credentials. You can get the health report of the Skyline Collector and all associated data endpoints from the system status page, in the **Overview** section. We can manage collector services through restart, stop, or de-register through the collector section. It will also show the Skyline Collector ID and the My VMware user that was used for the registration process. The Skyline Collector ID is a particular identifier for every Skyline Collector instance and is used to recognize the data transfer back to VMware:

We can also customize the Skyline Collector name so that we can recognize the entitlement number and support type (production/premier services) associated with a Skyline Collector instance; that way, we can connect to a VMware Global Support Services team. This entitlement account connects Skyline Collector data to its respective support requests. These entitlement accounts can be accessed and driven through `https://my.vmware.com`, and Skyline Collector log activities can be shown through the admin interface in real time.

Managing endpoints

Skyline Collector is integrated with vCenter Server, and three endpoints will be configured with every vCenter instance. These are shown in the system **STATUS** tab, along with all of the endpoints' health statuses:

The following data is collected from vCenter endpoints:

- The **VC_CHANGES** endpoint fetches the vCenter topology and configuration data
- The **VC_EVENTS** endpoint fetches vCenter event-related data
- The **VC_HOSTS** endpoint fetches ESXi event data from vCenter Server

Skyline Collector is integrated with NSX Manager, and every NSX Manager is configured with three endpoints:

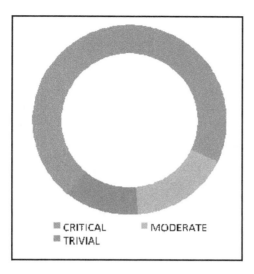

The following is the description of each endpoint:

- The **NSX** endpoint fetches NSX product and configuration related data
- The **NSX_TELEMETRY** endpoint fetches NSX operational parameters, like CPU, memory, and disk
- The **NSX_EVENTS** endpoint fetches NSX event-related data

All of the endpoints will show the related VMware product instance integrated with the Skyline Collector and the associated account reading all the recent and past data that was retrieved by particular collection endpoints. All active collection endpoints will be displayed in green, while passive endpoints with faults will be displayed in red.

Configuring VMware Skyline Collector admin interface

All administrative actions can be performed by clicking on **Configuration** at the top of the VMware Skyline Collector admin interface.

We can add/delete a vCenter Server for/from data collection and also add/delete an NSX Manager for/from data collection. We can configure an auto-upgrade and set the collector's name from the same console. This console also helps to configure Active Directory authentication, and NSX for vSphere has to set up an account with these privileges.

Auto-upgrade

VMware Skyline Collector has the ability to auto-upgrade the virtual appliance. Auto-upgrade will check for and install updates as per a schedule. We can get email notifications, as we mentioned during the registration phase of the VMware Skyline Collector. Select **Set Upgrade** after each auto-upgrade.

You can go to **Configuration** to enable and save the **Auto-Upgrade** settings that we have configured:

You will have to either enable the **Enable Collector Auto-Upgrade** option or follow these steps to update the Skyline Collector appliance to the latest version, using the VAMI:

1. Open a web browser and browse to
   `https://Skyline_Collector_IP_address:5480`:

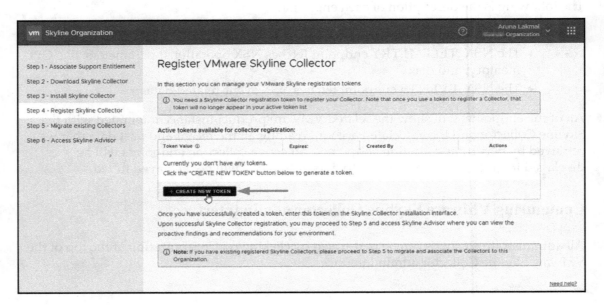

2. Log in with the root username and password:

3. Select **Update**
4. Select **Check Updates**
5. If a new update is available, select **Install Updates**

CEIP

Participation in the VMware CEIP is necessary and is a part of VMware Skyline. As a part of the initial Skyline Collector registration process, it is necessary to join this program. Skyline Collector sends data back to VMware for related product endpoints that are connected with specific product instances for quick support through the CEIP, which is included during the initial configuration or in the configuration page after installation. Customers can opt out of this program by following the de-registration process.

Types of information that are collected

VMware product/service technical data consists of the following:

- **Configuration data**: Every customer infrastructure is unique from a design and configuration point of view, even with the same VMware products and services. They have their own use cases, as per their business objectives, and data contains information such as the product's version/edition, deployment related information, settings, and the data logs of all of the devices that are connected to these products and services.

- **Feature-related data**: Customers deploy products with their functions in various ways, so that customers can achieve specific business case, for their respective customer's domain.
- **Performance data**: This includes information about products and services, along with all of the relevant supporting reports, such as performance and scale parameters, the user interface's response time, and API call related information.
- **Product log data**: They have related product logs that are produced by products from the installation stage to the production stage. These logs have details about the system's activity. This will also help with the actual status in real-time production data, excluding end customer application data.

Product usage data utilization

Product-related data is securely managed and used in certain internal scenarios with proper customer intimation. It is also agreed upon and accepted by the Information Governance Executive Council. Product-related data can be utilized for different purposes, including the following:

- **Product deployment reports**: We can correlate a customer's actual product adoption to purchased product licenses. Account managers can only assess this report so that they can have a fruitful discussion with the customer and use the purchased products in an optimal way by enhancing their design and settings.
- **SDDC analysis**: This is used to analyze the deployment of SDDC products across the customer base. This can be used to identify customers that meet certain SDDC deployment criteria, which can be provided to VMware executive management.
- **Customer advocacy surveys for new SDDC product releases**: This is used to identify customers who have deployed new SDDC product releases. These customers can be contacted by executive management to request their responses to specific customer surveys.
- **Customer support**: Technical support engineers may use a VMware license key and derived customer ID values to contact the customer in order to help resolve a specific support request or to proactively give advice on a support issue the customer may encounter, based on the analysis of the product usage data.
- **Customer profiles and advanced analytics**: This is used to analyze customer interactions with VMware, in order to create customer profiles and advanced analytics models. These must only be made available to VMware management and need to be approved by the product usage data trustee.

We can find details on the VMware Skyline deployment architecture, especially in a customer environment containing internal firewalls that segment different portions of the customer's network, each of which includes VMware products, in the product documentation. This covers the directional connectivity and networking port requirements for communications within customer networks and out to the internet/VAC destinations. We don't document on the northbound and southbound APIs of the collector, which are used to communicate with both the products that they are collecting and to the VMware Cloud. The APIs that we utilize for transmission of data back to the VAC can be found on the VAC confluence pages.

VMware Skyline is designed for the one-way communication of data back to VMware, and it ensures that the architecture has been developed to allow for closed-loop feedback to the collector and back to the products. The connectivity is always one-way from the Skyline Collector outward to VAC or the Photon OS update library services. We have two methods of providing return data to the Skyline Collector appliance:

- Through the Photon OS VAMI interface, for product updates/patches, and so on
- Via manifest updates, where we can post an updated manifest that describes, for example, what data is collected, at what interval, and so on

The appliance checks for manifest updates periodically, and when an update is available, it pulls the new manifest down to utilize its current configurations. The system will look to identify whether the **distributed firewall** (**DFW**) rules are active at the host or the VM level, in order to better troubleshoot connectivity issues as they arise. Skyline collector uses secure protocols to transmit the collected product usage data over HTTPS or SSH, back to VMware. The encryption algorithm is used to transfer the Skyline Collector data back to VMware.

Skyline pulls telemetry information from the product APIs and customer's inventory automatically over time, so that we can identify changes, patterns, and trends. This will help us to lower the time to solve an issue and identify problems before they turn into service availability, performance, or patch/security issues. Data that's collected by Skyline is stored in US-based VACs that are only operated by VMware. Snapshots of the protocols and encryptions are used with Skyline. Upstream encryption is done via TLS 1.2, using the cipher suite `TLS_RSA_WITH_AES_128_CBC_SHA256`. The data that's collected is retained in the system in VAC and **Operational Summary Reports** (**OSRs**) for a period of 13 months, as per policy guidelines.

Summary

VMware Skyline's breakthrough of being able to dramatically transform our visibility of the customer's environment has many benefits. If we know and understand what our customers are doing, we can more readily engage with them proactively, in order to provide assistance and guidance. We can start to focus on the core problems when supporting them, so that we do not only rely on the symptoms that our customers describe. This drives confidence as we build and strengthen those relationships. At the core of VMware Skyline is a focus on transforming the customer experience, and the key way that we can do so is by building customer intimacy. We can start to focus on the core issues of customers with these reliable data rather then relying only on the symptoms or, customer's inputs.

The next chapter, Chapter 9, *DevOps with vRealize Code Stream*, will provide you with a detailed architectural design that enables the application and platform to be deployed on the VMware vRealize Automation private cloud platform, using **continuous integration (CI)** and **continuous delivery (CD)** processes, alongside **VMware vRealize Code Stream (vRCS)** and other industry standard products. The architectural design recommendations will be based on a VMware vRA/vRO/vRCS product reference architecture and industry best practices, along with customer-specific requirements and business goals.

DevOps with vRealize Code Stream

9

The DevOps operating model and its supporting CI/CD toolsets implementation approach to managing IT is changing the roles and responsibilities of IT resources, as well as the traditional design, delivery, and operation processes. This chapter will enable you to make the process changes that are required for the adoption of DevOps. We will look into the highest priority processes to transform and apply techniques to compare and contrast the key differences between legacy operating models, processes, and team structures with the strategic operating model that's required for DevOps. We will also go through **VMware vRealize Code Stream (vRCS)** and its orchestration for DevOps release processes and continuous application delivery.

You will learn about the DevOps Cloud operational model for the private cloud. which enables developers to seamlessly deploy, configure, and manage production-ready applications by leveraging VMware Cloud Automation services, along with configuration management tools such as Puppet to accelerate DevOps operations. You will also learn about CI/CD with **VMware Kubernetes Engine (VKE)**.

In this chapter, we will cover the following topics:

- Application development life cycles
- Automation with vRealize
- vRCS

Technical requirements

You can download VMware vRealize Code Stream from `https://my.vmware.com/web/vmware/info/slug/infrastructure_operations_management/vmware_vrealize_code_stream/2_x` and VMware Wavefront from `https://www.vmware.com/download/eula/wavefront-terms-of-service.html`.

Application development life cycles

It is important to understand the change that has taken place in terms of application development life cycles in order to understand application transformation. When the pace of change was slow, application development always had a pre-determined plan with a finite end goal. The design of the application was thought through and agreed up-front, including capturing all of the user's requirements. Then, a series of steps followed that involved developing the plan, testing the functionality of the application, testing whether the application would run efficiently and to the right scale (non-functional testing), user acceptance testing to agree that the application had been built the way it was supposed to be, before finally going live in its final format.

The pace of change in some modern applications, coupled with the fact that they can be very experimental in nature, means that the waterfall approach (where the final application design is fully understood upfront) just doesn't work. Instead, application development, application design, user, and even customer testing occurs in rapid iterations, meaning that the application develops with a continuous feedback loop. Development teams are also typically assigned to individual components, so there is no concept of a controlled state that everyone has to comply with. Development occurs in simultaneous streams with frequent code check-ins to confirm overall functionality.

We can apply these results in terms such as CD, DevOps, and Agile. While these principles can be applied to traditional application architectures, they tend to be best suited to cloud-based application tools, platforms, and architectures. It should be noted that this area has several models and is still maturing, despite being widely practiced.

One very important thing to realize is that Agile and DevOps is not a replacement for waterfall. Customers will use both disciplines, which are dependent on the application development requirements. Applying Agile principles of development to a mission-critical traditional application could have terrible consequences, and conversely you could use as many cloud technologies as you want, but using a waterfall approach for application development that is exploratory in nature would fundamentally cripple the ability to deliver effectively.

CD pipeline

DevOps helps with the CD pipeline process by going through the following procedure:

- **Plan**: We have to first plan and define software release cycles; user-defined use cases; Agile planned actions; and a proper plan for backlogs and problems with a follow-up plan.
- **Code**: This is defined with a set of processes with related tools that allows us to write scripts, along with its assessment and testing. It also helps with following defined security and compliance metrics.
- **Commit**: This can help us define procedures and its related tools for code assessment, consolidation, and executing it with the main source code repository. This stack also assists in maintaining source control with daily testing, executing on-demand, and the proactive scanning of code.

CI pipeline

The CI pipeline provides processes, practices, and tooling to help with the automated building and testing of every code commit in the source code repository. This includes automated security and compliance testing and logging.

Test processes, practices, and tooling for automated unit, functional, security, and compliance testing, logging results, and gaining approval to promote artifacts to the next stage in the flow.

The artifact repository consists of services and activities that are necessary to achieve the desired end state in terms of maintaining version, promotion, governance, and policy controls that are related deliverable artifacts. Generally stated, such artifacts are those that are converted from sources into binary packages, though other transformations may exist.

We develop and update software continuously so that the software can be released to production on-demand via CD.

The configuration consists of services and activities that are necessary to achieve the desired end state in terms of automating idempotent and expedient deployment of applications to static and on-demand hybrid cloud infrastructures. The design and implementation will be consistent with predefined SDLC process, including proper source artifact management (for example, Puppet modules, Chef cookbooks, deployment blueprints, and so on).

The control stack consists of services that are necessary to achieve the desired end state in terms of managing the tool chains that are recommended to operate the applications that are deployed by this infrastructure. This will also incorporate the SDLC processes, tools, integrations, and actions that are needed to maintain defined service-level agreements for a specific customer.

The feedback stack allows you to get automated feedback such as alerts, audit reports, test reports, and deployment process reports delivered when required.

Planning

To achieve consistently successful business outcomes, VMware collaborates with customers in assessing, recommending, and documenting changes that are necessary to achieve optimal delivery processes. This collaborative effort is based on industry best practices in the following service foundation areas:

- **Software Development Life Cycle (SDLC)**
- **Source code management (SCM)**
- **Continuous integration (CI)**
- **Artifact repository (AR)**
- **Continuous delivery (CD)**
- **Hybrid cloud provisioning (HCP)**
- **Configuration management (CM)**
- **Continuous operational management (COM)**

SDLC

The SDLC foundation consists of services and activities that are necessary to achieve optimally aligned personnel roles, tool chains, and processes to achieve the desired end state of the software delivery life cycle management by the customer.

SCM

The SCM foundation consists of services and activities that are necessary to achieve the desired end state in terms of managing and version-controlling software source artifacts. Source artifacts include, among other sources, application source code, documentation, configuration information, and process control flow configurations.

CI

The CI consists of services and activities that are necessary to achieve the desired end state in terms of automated build, test, and deliverable (that is, binary) artifact creation. The CI process assists in application builds and its verification tests with rapid feedback while developers build software by using tools such as Jenkins, Gerrit Triggers, and vRA.

AR

VMware and customers collaborate to define and refine processes and activities that transform sources into customer deliverable artifacts. This includes assessing and realigning activities and related key accountability roles, responsibilities, and required skillsets, key interactions, and hand-offs related to supporting the service definition process with agreed upon use cases and business outcomes.

The AR foundation consists of services and activities that are necessary to achieve the desired end state in terms of maintaining version, promotion, governance, and policy controls related to deliverable artifacts. Generally stated, such artifacts are those that are converted from sources into binary packages, though other transformations may exist.

Release pipeline automation (CD)

The CD consists of services and activities that are necessary to achieve the desired end state in terms of automating governance and release policies regarding deliverable artifacts. This involves providing the tools and integrations that are necessary to orchestrate manually-gated organizational decision processing and automated delivery processes.

CM

The CM foundation consists of services and activities that are necessary to achieve the desired end state in terms of automated, idempotent, and expedient deployment of applications to a static and on-demand hybrid cloud infrastructure. The design and implementation will be consistent with the agreed upon SDLC process, including proper source artifact management (for example, Puppet modules, Chef cookbooks, deployment blueprints, and so on).

HC

The HC foundation consists of services and activities that are necessary to achieve the desired end state in terms of automating resource provisioning to achieve application deployments to the hybrid cloud. In this context, the hybrid cloud may include the following:

- VMware vCloud Air, Linux containers, AWS, and other heterogeneous cloud platforms
- On-premise virtualized/cloud and physical infrastructures

This foundation service involves providing the tools and integrations that are necessary to automate the provisioning of infrastructure services (that is, compute, network, and storage) for all deliverable artifact deployments. The design and implementation will be consistent with the agreed upon SDLC process, including proper source artifact management (for example, provisioning blueprints, workflow scripts, and so on).

COM

The COM foundation consists of services and activities that are necessary to achieve the desired end state in terms of managing the tool chains that operate the service foundations, as well as the applications that are deployed by that infrastructure. This consists of incorporating processes, tools, integrations, and activities that are necessary to maintain any **service-level agreements** (**SLA**) that the customer is either bound to or reasonably desires.

Feedback

Feedback into the planning stack is necessary as errors occur. This consists of bug reporting and deficiencies in software features, including any change that's required by the operating software and its underlying infrastructure, all of which should be tracked for handling by the coding stack. Then, the cycle continues. This feedback then goes into the planning stack and we start the iteration again. We always want to be ensuring that all of our stacks are working well together and providing us with the desired outcomes. Our various processes can be continually updated an improved to keep pace with changes and updates in the tool chain, in the types of code that the stacks are dealing with, and the infrastructure that the resulting applications are hosted on.

Request fulfillment

vRealize Automation assists users in requesting and managing different kinds of IT services through a unified IT service catalog that spans across the hybrid cloud.

The following is a screenshot of the catalog for software provisioning:

It can provide programmatic access to support the on-demand delivery of software based on the DevOps model.

Change management

vRO has an internal versioning system that automatically keeps track of changes. It has API interfaces to integrate with third-party tools such as Jenkins and also has an audit log that help users to review changes and access. vRA can provide automation for approval processes by integrating with Active Directory and can also be configuring for alternate approvers to ensure that change management and business requirements are met.

Release management

There have been fundamental changes in the application's release process which demands new tooling that can keep up with it. The first change is in the rise of containers and microservices. They enable faster code pushes, but this is at the expense of increased complexity. Instead of the 100 metrics you had for your virtualization environments, now you need to track thousands and at high speed. The old-style tooling cannot keep up with these scale and changes, and they fail over. CD and DevOps are being adopted in larger enterprises, so engineering teams are now pushing code to production many times per day, thus driving the need for continuous monitoring. DevOps is mainstream, even though the tools that the operations teams use are still fragmented and consequentially slowing down troubleshooting services.

Compliance management

Customers expect data centers to be compliant because it is an extension of their IT. Heavily regulated verticals such as the public sector, finance, and healthcare cannot use this infrastructure without compliance certifications. Customers running a hybrid or public cloud infrastructure rely on compliance certifications instead of independent audits to ensure that proper security controls are in place. A number of high profile security breaches, court cases, and global legislative changes have raised awareness of the complexity and risks of running in the cloud. Open a browser and go to `https://marketplace.vmware.com`.

VMware Cloud (VMC) on AWS is working on implementing the compliance certifications and frameworks by targeting **Cloud Security Alliance (CSA)** and **General Data Protection Regulation (GDPR)** first, followed by **International Organization for Standardization (ISO)**, **Security Operations Center (SOC)**, **Health Insurance Portability and Accountability Act (HIPPA)**, **Payment Card Industry (PCI)**, the **Federal Risk Authorization and Management Program (FedRAMP)**, and **Criminal Justice Information Services (CJIS)**. Security certifications that exist today are applicable to cloud computing and should be strongly considered. Cloud services will apply the mandated principles of policy, security, strategy, and compliance, which must be followed even by the lightest requirement use cases.

Incident management

An incident is essentially any issue that, if left unattended, could result in customer escalation. We can avoid many escalations by implementing a customer incident management process. We do not define customer escalation processes in any geographies. Our customer relationship management approach must evolve to emphasize the importance of escalation prevention. In response, we can plan to identify incidents, track them, and resolve them to avoid escalations. Management oversight and guidance during this process should help managers resolve these kinds of situations before they become escalations. Communication is the major focus. Communications protocols must define who, what, and when. The response to the customer must provide a balance between the cost of gained customer satisfaction and the cost of investment. We can do a better job at managing customer expectations and issues before they result in an escalation. The purpose of this process is to highlight issues that could escalate early on so that management and executive oversights can be applied in a timely manner to either prevent escalations from occurring or reduce the severity of an escalation if one does occur. The DevOps team now acts as level 2 support while before they came into action as level 3 support.

Event management

The DevOps team have to monitor and manage all of the applications, as per the customer's requirements, for compute, storage, network, VMs, containers, and so on, by using vRealize tools and get critical alerts for the events related to applications.

Capacity management

Custom profiles allow you to expand the capabilities of capacity planning by automating capacity calculations based on specifications that you create. Choosing a committed project will alter our capacity numbers as it assumes the resource is committed. If we don't want these numbers to change, then we can go back and select a plan from the **Capacity and Utilization** dashboard. Maintenance mode allows us to prevent planned downtime from affecting capacity planning.

The solution must provide the ability to proactively determine capacity issues and risks for the virtual environment. It must provide capacity trending, demand forecasting, and a what-if impact analysis of future projects:

A custom dashboard will be created for use by the test and development team. The intention is to give a specific view of test and dev VMs in the vSphere infrastructure, focusing on workload, capacity remaining, and reclaimable capacity. The following components will make up the test and dev dashboard:

- Dev VMs overview, displaying health, risk, and efficiency for the server and workstation VMs
- VM workload heat map, color-coded to display the selected type VMs
- VMs with the lowest disk space **Capacity Remaining** (%) over the past week:

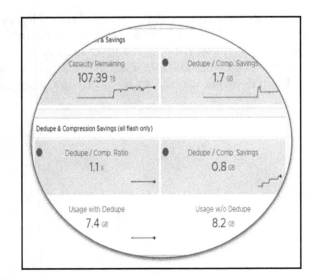

- Idle VMs and VMs with the lowest utilization, flagged as idle if the utilization index becomes 1
- Reclaimable capacity displays the percentage of resources that can be reclaimed
- Powered off VMs and VMs are flagged as powered on

Wavefront dashboard

Wavefront is a metric-driven monitoring and analytics platform. DevOps and developers teams at enterprises that run cloud-native apps such as Box, Lyft, Intuit, and Workday use Wavefront to monitor the performance of cloud applications that reach amazing scale. The Wavefront platform collects and analyzes metrics from distributed applications running on VMware Cloud on AWS, AWS containers, microservices, cloud infrastructure, and even business data. Once metric data is in a Wavefront time-series database, Wavefront customers can apply powerful and flexible analytics in the form of the Wavefront Query Language. Developer teams use this to monitor the performance of their cloud services and distributed applications at unprecedented scale. They can troubleshoot faster and proactively alert and detect the leading indicators of anomalies with instant access, and unified visibility drives accelerate code releases by enabling the same visibility across all cloud services, infrastructures, and tools. Developer teams get instant visibility across all cloud services. Wavefront spreads across hundreds of engineers, enabling a self-service approach and empowering teams to innovate because Wavefront provides visibility in digital environments (digital service is the business). Business decisions are aligned with application code delivery, which helps everyone move faster with unified visibility.

Wavefront offers many ways to ingest data. We can retrieve data from AWS (APIs, CloudWatch, and CloudTrail) directly and can create metrics from logs.

Wavefront's key differentiators from DevOps and developer teams are as follows:

- Wavefront allows you to apply advanced metrics and query-driven analytics. There are over 100 mathematical transformations available for you to work with metrics data. We can troubleshoot issues faster using analytics. Wavefront, as a SaaS analytics platform, offers massive scale and high availability.
- It offers customizable dashboards that help DevOps teams take ownership of code in production. Dashboards can be shared and exported with one click.
- Intelligent alerting and proactive monitoring help detect leading indicators (quickly) or quickly zero-in on an anomaly where we can isolate problems by their desired shape or time, or by any condition we define.

Once Wavefront enters an organization, its adoption spreads across hundreds of developers, enabling a self-service approach and empowering them to innovate in a collaborative fashion. Synchronized business decisions aligned with code releases helps SaaS businesses move faster. Because Wavefront is typically adopted at leading SaaS enterprises, and since their cloud service is their lifeline, it helps business leaders make analytics-driven business decisions. These decisions are synchronized with cloud services code delivery, helping everyone move faster.

Wavefront integrations allow you to collect, analyze, and harness data from any data source, and tier important things to remember. Wavefront integrations help to accelerate this process with full RESTful APIs and user interfaces. Data from individual tools can be correlated with other tiers. Wavefront is unique at a very high scale with these features. Powerful correlations across tiers help us win across point tools and metrics platforms. The Wavefront platform offers RESTful APIs for extensibility. The Wavefront API integrates with any tool of choice for developers or DevOps tooling, and makes integration easy. For example, Lyft wanted to keep their Grafana dashboards and use Wavefront as the most scalable backend time-series database.

Getting insights by monitoring how people work

We have to monitor how people are working and get better insights in to whether the business and operations are going well or not. It is always hard to collect metrics and monitor people, and we can't compel people to generate metrics on their own. So, with the collaborative solutions such as slack and SaaS metrics monitoring solutions such as Wavefront, it becomes easier to track and monitor people's interests and activities, and gain insights from this. Wavefront allows you to apply advanced metrics and query-driven analytics. There are over 100 mathematical transformations available to work with metrics data. We can troubleshoot issues faster with Wavefront, which is a SaaS analytics platform with massive scale and high availability. It offers customizable dashboards, which help DevOps teams to take ownership for code in production. Their dashboards have one-click intelligent alerting and proactive monitoring where we can isolate a problem by its desired shape or time, or any condition that's been defined.

Automation with vRealize

vRA can be designed in a distributed and highly available architecture to provide multi-role services. This highly available architecture with load balancing can be configured from the vRA installation wizard by integrating it with VMware Identity Manager with high availability mode for **Single Sign-On (SSO)**. It will be clustered with embedded vRA appliance PostgreSQL internal databases as the external PostgreSQL option is no longer available. It also has clustered embedded vRO services and high availability for workflows and extensibility. It accesses Microsoft Active Directory servers to perform the authentication of users and Active Directory group membership enumeration. This provides a prescribed reference architecture design that allows for an SDDC content life cycle solution. The solution addresses the following three main objectives:

- Automation of the transfer of vRO and vRA content between different environments
- vRO/vRA content storage and version control, including rollbacks
- Reduction of the time and effort required to test the compliance of the vRO/vRA content using automation

This has been designed to allow authenticated users to achieve the synchronization of content between vRA environments. The services that are defined in the project are as follows:

- Creation of content packages
- Testing packages on a test/validation environment
- Deployment of packages to the deployment's target environment
- Management of endpoints (adding/deleting)

The following diagram shows the **SDDC Content Life cycle**:

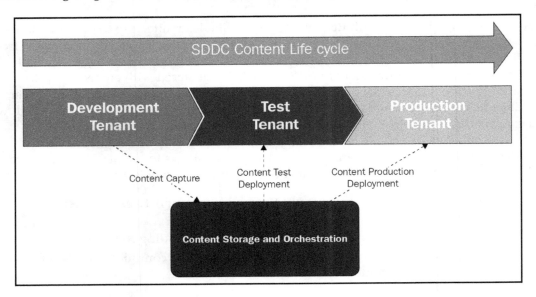

Following are the components:

- The **Production Tenant** is the production vRA tenant endpoint. vRA and vRO content is deployed to this endpoint so that it can be consumed by end users.
- **vRO** provides orchestration capabilities using workflows for capture, test, and release content.
- **Workflows** are organized into a vRCS pipeline that represents the content life cycle, allowing content to flow through development, test, and into production.
- **Xenon** provides the content storage capability. The SDDC content is stored in the repository after it is captured and version controlled throughout its life cycle.
- **Configuration** of the VMs that are used to host the services of the solution is based on the recommendation to deploy an infrastructure that supports up to 100 pipelines and up to 30 simultaneous pipeline executions.

Deploying Infrastructure as Code

We need to configure vRA and NSX, which will allow for an isolated network of VMs to be used from the dev environment.

The network layout of the desired solution is as follows:

```
Dev Machines < --- [Dev Network] ---  NSX Edge < --- [NAT Network] --- Isolated VMs
```

NSX Edge will provide **Source Network Address Translation (SNAT)** routing so that isolated VMs can have access to external dev network resources in this layout. It will also provide **destination NAT (DNAT)** port forwarding so that dev machines are able to access specific services on a target isolated VM by addressing the NSX Edge in this layout. This design will also make use of the vSphere linked clones technology to minimize storage requirements. vRA provisioning will be implemented with the following blueprint structure:

- **Base Windows image**: This will provision a blank Windows image that will become accessible through vRA.
- **Base Linux image**: This will provision a blank Linux image that will be become accessible through vRA.
- **Windows linked clone component**: This will be the linked clone blueprint on top of the VM that was instantiated from the base Windows image and a specific snapshot. This represents the actual isolated VM to be provisioned.
- **Linux linked clone component**: This will be the linked cone blueprint on top of the VM that was instantiated from the base Linux image and a specific snapshot. This represents the actual isolated VM to be provisioned.
- **Multi-machine blueprint**: This will be a collection of the component blueprints that will be provisioned at once:

To provision the machine properly, the following components should be included:

- **External network profile**: This is a definition of the subnet from the external dev network, along with details for routing and DNS resolution:
- **Cluster reservation**: A dedicated reservation is needed to limit resource usage to only a single datastore (so that the linked clone works), as well as to map the network port group to the **External** network profile.

- **NAT network profile**: This is a definition of the subnet that isolated VMs will use behind NSX Edge. This is only a template that will later be copied into the multi-machine blueprint components assignment:

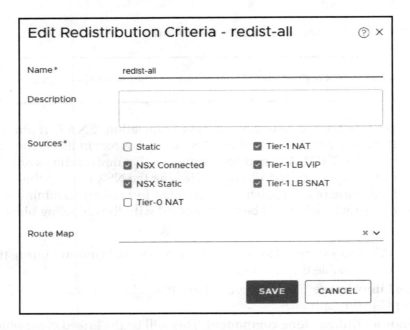

- **Reservation policy**: This will be a dedicated reservation policy that ensures that all blueprints will only address the designated cluster reservation that's created.
- **Machine prefix**: This is only used to distinguish the machines that have been provisioned by the multi-machine blueprint.

vRealize Code Stream

vRealize Application Services is about modeling an application and automating its provisioning. vRCS is about modeling an application release process. The two are complementary: Code Stream relies on integrations with **virtual reality as a service** (**vRAAS**), scripts, Puppet, and so on to deploy code. Code Stream allows us to codify or model the entire release process and promotion of builds across stages and/or environments (functional testing, load testing, systems integration testing, staging, and finally production). This includes not just triggering application deployment (via scripts or other tools) but triggering tests and looking at test results before deciding to promote a build to the next stage.

It also supports creating manual tasks in a stage for operations that are not automated today. It's really a process orchestration tool rather than an app deployment or provisioning solution. Code Stream allows us to trigger the deployment of individual artifacts (`.jar`, `.war`, config files, and so on) as opposed to vRAAS, which forces us to redeploy the entire stack, including the underlying machine. One Code Stream appliance can handle about 100 concurrent pipeline executions. Puppet, Chef, and other configuration management tools are not direct competitors to Code Stream. These tools are often used to configure and deploy software, but Code Stream is all about modeling a release process. The core value of Code Stream is really to tie configuration management and infrastructure provisioning, as well as continuous integration and testing and approval systems together to automate the entire release process.

There are a number of technical advantages of this:

- Code Stream can automate and accelerate the life cycle of any type of software. This includes applications (traditional and cloud-native), as well as infrastructure and IT content (blueprints, workflows, scripts, templates, and so on).
- Code Stream does not prescribe a certain type of release model or toolset. It can model the release process for companies who are just starting out and put a majority of manual tasks to a 100% automated release model. Therefore, it adapts to an organization's maturity level and allows them to gradually move toward a more automated model.
- Code Stream allows teams to provision and deploy code to private as well as public clouds. Code Stream can take advantage of vRA's converged blueprint or work with other provisioning solutions such as Cloud Foundry.
- VMware offers the best full-stack and completely integrated solution from the foundational SDDC to the management/provisioning layer with vRA, and finally release automation capabilities with Code Stream. So, while all products can be used independently (no vendor lock-in), when used together, customers have an unmatched platform to help them become more agile.

We can install Code Stream without vRA as there is definitely value in deploying both products to get benefits from a fully integrated solution for provisioning automation and release automation. Code Stream supports two deployment models:

- Standalone, where only the Code Stream functionality is enabled on the virtual appliance. Admins can then optionally configure Code Stream to provision machines via an external vRA appliance.
- Unified, where both the Code Stream and vRA functionality is enabled on the same appliance. vRA also requires a separate Windows server for IaaS functionality. This configuration is not a supported configuration for production.

Jenkins is a build automation tool that promotes CI, a development practice that requires developers to integrate code into a shared source code repository such as Git several times a day. Each check-in is then verified by an automated build, allowing teams to detect problems early. At the heart of any CI tool is the job that automates a build and build-related activities such as a test that is run pre or post-build.

Release Automation tools such as Code Stream focus on modeling and automating the broader release process, all the way to production, which typically integrates CI and additional categories of tools such as provisioning, change management, and monitoring, and often, people do this for some manual tasks and/or approvals. Companies often use release automation tools to work toward CD, a practice where every good build is potentially pushed to production. CD is a superset of CI, involving more tools and more teams—not just development but operations and release teams as well. At the heart of a release automation or CD tool is the pipeline that models a process, including business constructs such as approvals.

Jenkins is an extensible tool and can be customized to go beyond doing basic builds and testing to orchestrate other activities toward the release process. We can customize vRO workflows to do some of what vRA does, but at some point we end up writing so much logic that the workflow-based solution becomes hard to maintain over time. The same can happen with custom solutions on top of Jenkins: they may work initially but get harder to manage over time, especially as you try to manage more applications. That's the typical drawback of a build versus buy approach. Jenkins Enterprise has a pipeline component to achieve release automation. It's still lacking key capabilities such as manual tasks and approvals and easy passing of variables from one step to the next in the pipeline, which are typically offered by top release automation vendors.

Code Stream is only available as a standalone product because of the following reasons:

- It does not comply with all the requirements and expected capabilities of suites such as vCloud or vRealize. For instance, it does not support localization, HA, or unattended installation.
- It needs to evolve rapidly and follow a more frequent release cadence than existing suites.
- It shares some common services with vRA, but it can be deployed without vRA so that release engineers or DevOps teams who don't use vRA can still have a lightweight continuous delivery solution.

Pipeline automation model – the release process for any kind of software

vRealize Code Stream is used by customers who want to automate their release or CD process. vRealize Code Stream allows developers and operations teams to release software more frequently by reducing operational risk. It is designed based on the principle to integrate and extend rather than rip and replace so that that we can use existing tools alongside the SDLC. This will help developers to use their existing investment in tools and skills. At the time of writing this book, vRealize Code Stream has three main capabilities:

- Pipeline automation
- Artifact management
- Release dashboard

It will provide RESTful APIs and capabilities based on a comprehensive integration framework. Some examples of manual tasks are as follows:

- **Approvals**: Code Stream has its own native approval workflow capability, which is shared with other vRealize products. Approvals can be used to add manual oversight at any stage in the pipeline's execution. In addition, Code Stream can also leverage vRO plugins to call work order ticketing systems to coordinate the approval workflows.
- **Modeling manual tasks**: Tasks that require manual execution usually require some type of notification to the task owner via a work order ticketing system. Code Stream leverages vRO workflows and plugins to integrate with existing systems such as BMC Remedy **IT Service Management** (**ITSM**), HP Service Manager, ServiceNow, and so on.

vRCS deployment architecture

This chapter describes the recommended deployment topologies for vRCS. vRCS can leverage vRA for VM provisioning. There are a couple of possible deployments:

- vRCS and vRA on the same single appliance (recommended for small POCs where vRCS and vRA are both lab/evaluation systems)
- vRCS and vRA on two separate appliances (recommended for large POCs or production)

- vRCS and vRA on two separate appliances where vRA is HA enabled (recommended for large POCs or production)
- Artifactory deployed as an external entity

vRCS does not support connecting to an external vRO and does not support its own HA setup, but it can integrate with an external HA setup of vRA for VM provisioning:

- vRCS and vRA (vRA) on the same single appliance
- vRCS and vRA on two separate appliances
- vRCS and vRA on two separate appliances where vRA is HA enabled
- Artifactory deployed as an external entity

Please be aware of the following when configuring the deployment:

- If the deployment of vRCS and vRA is in same appliance, it can lock up the whole appliance. Since the HA setup of vRA has its own SSO server, and there is no identity federation support, vRCS must use a shared user account to access vRA.
- Please configure the vRA endpoint as a shared account and not per user session. vRCS integrates with **Advanced Service Designer** (**ASD**) forms, and there is a new plugin named ASD that is shipped with vRCS 1.2. This plugin only works with an internal vRA.

System architecture

The vRCS architecture describes the various components that are involved with the system architecture. Both vRCS and vRA can be on the same appliance with the appropriate license. vRCS requires the endpoint to be configured so that it can be integrated with any external product or service deployment. It requires an endpoint from vRA, even though vRA and vRCS are in same appliance for vRCS to communicate with vRA for VM provisioning.

vRCS can interact with vRA in two ways:

- Shared account (using single common user)
- Per user session (SSO):

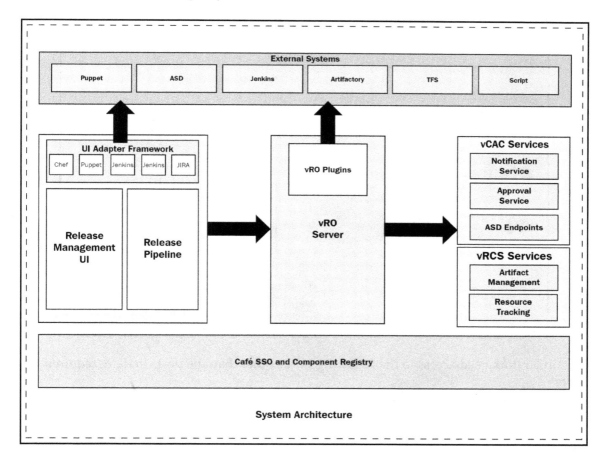

Users have access to the following ports:

Server role	Port
vRCS/vRA appliance	443
vRA identity appliance	7444

The following diagram represents the vRCS communication workflow:

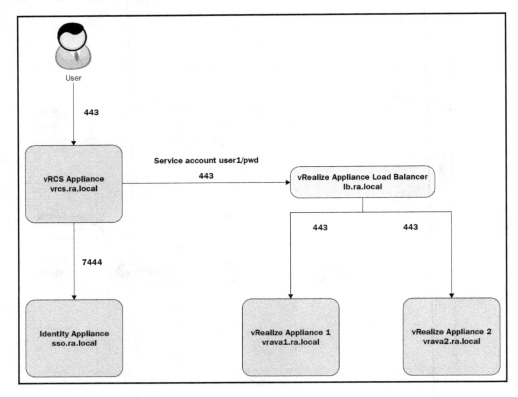

Administrators need access to the following ports, other than the ports that are required by users:

Server role	Port	
vRA identity appliance	5480	
vRCS/vRA appliance	5480	
Server role	**Inbound ports**	**Service/system outbound ports**
vRCS/vRA appliance	443 SSH: 22 VAMI: 5480	Identity VA: 7444
vRA identity appliance	7444 SSH: 22 VAMI: 5480	LDAP: 389 LDAPS: 636

Integrating vRCS with an external, standalone vRA

vRCS can integrate with an existing vRA for VM provisioning. Therefore, an endpoint needs to be created where external vRA endpoint-related details can be specified. This endpoint will be listed under the provisioning category while adding a task in a stage. This endpoint can support both shared account and per user session options. If an external vRA and vRCS links to the same SSO server, both options per user session and shared account are supported. However, if an external vRA has its own SSO server, only the shared account option is supported. This is because the identity federation between two SSO servers is not supported.

The user needs access to the following ports:

Server role	Port
vRCS	443
vRA appliance	443
vRA identity appliance (Code Stream)	7444

Administrators need access to the following ports, in addition to the ports that are required by users:

Server role	Port	
vRCS	5480	
vRA appliance	5480	
Server role	**Inbound ports**	**Service/system outbound ports**
vRCS	443 SSH: 22 VAMI: 5480	Identity CS VA: 7444 vRA VA: 443
vRA appliance	443 SSH: 22 VAMI: 5480	Identity vRA VA: 7444
vRA identity appliance (Code Stream)	7444 SSH: 22 VAMI: 5480	LDAP: 389 LDAPS: 636

Summary

Code Stream provides the ability to model and visualize the release process of any type of software (applications, blueprints, workflows, configuration files, Puppet manifests, Chef recipes, and so on). All stakeholders (devs, operations teams, release engineers, and so on) can go to a central place to track the state of application and software releases. Users can view not just the history but exactly where builds and releases have failed. Code Stream and vRA use the same delivery platform (the same virtual appliance) and share many common services, including capturing release processes that IT is struggling with or spending a lot of time on, and automating those via vRCS and vRA.

As opposed to acquiring, integrating, and managing different solutions for provisioning and release automation, customers can benefit from a single solution. By integrating with artifact repositories such as JFrog Artifactory, Code Stream can manage and track the multiple artifact versions that are generated with new releases, and track their deployment across various environments. As companies release new app versions more often, the risk of deploying the wrong artifact version and breaking production increases significantly. To help customers have visibility into and tie all of their different repositories (Yum, NuGet, Nexus, and so on) into one place for troubleshooting and security auditing, it is important to track which artifacts have been deployed where. Code Stream can work for both Java/Linux and .NET/Windows shops and their respective toolsets. Certain release management tools (for example, Octopus, Microsoft Release Manager, and Chef Delivery) support only one technology or are optimized for one technology or certain toolsets. Code Stream does not prescribe any particular toolset, meaning it can support different teams using different technologies across the enterprise. In fact, it can be even be used for the life cycle of software that is not an application: scripts, workflows, blueprints, and so on.

In the next chapter, `Chapter 10`, *Transforming VMware IT Operations Using ML* we will learn about how to manage different cloud models from a single console and about the phase-wise transformation of data center operations methodologies. We will also learn how to design scalable infrastructure to host both legacy and new cloud native apps on unified platforms using ML-based solutions.

Further reading

- *DevOps and Agile development—VMware,* at `https://www.vmware.com/content/dam/digitalmarketing/vmware/en/pdf/solutionoverview/vmware-devops-agile-development-white-paper.pdf`

- *vRealize Code Stream Management Pack for IT DevOps—VMware,* at `https://www.vmware.com/files/pdf/products/vrealize/vmware-vrealize-code-stream-management-solution-brief.pdf`

- *DevOps-Ready IT: Continuous Delivery of vRealize Automation Blueprints,* at `https://blogs.vmware.com/management/2016/05/devops-ready-it-continuous-delivery-of-vrealize-automation-blueprints.html`

- *vRealize Code Stream | Application Release Automation,* at `https://www.vmware.com/in/products/vrealize-code-stream.html`

- *vRealize Code Stream Documentation—VMware Docs,* at `https://docs.vmware.com/en/vRealize-Code-Stream/index.html`

- *From Zero to DevOps Hero using Cloud Automation,* at `https://blogs.vmware.com/management/2018/10/devops-hero-with-cloud-automation.html`

- *vRealize Code Stream—VMware,* at `https://code.vmware.com/web/sdk/2.2.0/vrealize-code-stream`

- *Overview of vSphere Integrated Containers For DevOps Administrators—VMware vSphere,* at `https://vmware.github.io/vic-product/assets/files/html/1.1/vic_dev_ops/overview_of_vic_devops.html`

10
Transforming VMware IT Operations Using ML

This chapter will help you understand how VMware Operations Transformation for cloud automation creates and implements a life cycle approach for managing and delivering SDDC-based services to help customers transition into a service provider organization. This service focuses on optimizing organizational and process capabilities to support the **Software-Defined Data Center** (**SDDC**) concept to realize the full capabilities of these technologies that are delivered in a modular format and to deliver real business benefits through the integration of the technology, people, and processes.

This service-based approach targets both new and existing VMware customers who have prior experience with VMware infrastructures, but might not have experience with the products that are part of the cloud automation solution or who have no experience in delivering SDDC-based services. An operations transformation for a cloud automation service is often a critical step in large projects.

In this chapter, we will learn how to manage a cloud model from a single console and transform data center operations in different phases by designing the scalable infrastructure to run both legacy and new cloud native apps from a unified platform. We will leverage ML techniques in the SDDC approach to do this.

In this chapter, we will cover the following topics:

- Overview on business and operations challenges
- Transforming VMware technical support operations
- Virtual data centers

Overview on business and operations challenges

We're trying to drive application management transformation to make life easier with VMware solutions. We may be experiencing many of the issues that come with managing apps, such as legacy provisioning, complex and lengthy updates, and having to manage separate solutions for app delivery. VMware is taking a different approach to managing applications. We have methods where we can provision one app to many desktops, thereby saving considerable time and storage costs. We can deliver apps in seconds and at scale. We can isolate apps to remove the app conflict barrier. Apps can then be consumed on any device and on one portal. We can even transform the way you monitor your applications for better performance.

VMware Cloud operations and stakeholders want to analyze the consumption of the on-premise private cloud infrastructure services in relation to their customer's different functional groups to determine the current trend, future demand, and budget compliance. A customer's cloud operations and stakeholders have to charge the customers for the consumed resources. The customer's stakeholders want a precise view of the costs that are required to provide a unit of IaaS resource, gain better visibility into the loaded costs of components it is comprised of, and provide **total cost of ownership** (**TCO**) to run the IaaS. The customer gets the total capital expenses and operating expenses for running the IaaS infrastructure, so they want to allocate these costs to the underlying resources that constitute the services. These resources are CPU, RAM, storage, operating systems, license, and labor. The customer's operation team for private cloud operations, cloud administrators, and designated business owners must make cost-based analyses and decisions by achieving an in-depth understanding of how the cloud infrastructure is being provisioned to business units, and what the allocated and unallocated costs of provisioned resources, such as CPU, RAM, and storage are. They want to analyze the allocated and unallocated costs of infrastructure by resource type. Cloud administrators also want to determine whether there is hardware available to run VMs on the existing infrastructure, create reports on groups of old servers nearing expiry or end-of-support, and also create automatic reports to show stakeholders that new infrastructure might need to be procured.

Cloud operations and business owners want to analyze the consumption of the on-premise private cloud infrastructure services in relation to the customer's business functional groups to determine the current trend, future demand, and budget compliance. The cloud operations team want to charge the customers for the consumed resources. They want to provide private cloud services to consumers using vRA software. The private cloud resources are hosted in the customer's data center, which is why the business stakeholders are asking for the optimum pricing policy to measure the business value of the private cloud resources in terms of return on investment.

An IT development and operations team is required to rapidly provision new applications and their continuous updates almost every year. These applications have fully functional applications such as Oracle enterprise resource planning and home-grown apps such as the My VMware portal being integrated with various SaaS applications. Modification and testing of new software instances was slow and mostly prone to errors with manual processes. The development team normally needs an application development instance and an application test instance during any project for a few weeks. They need another one week for correction, even after application deployment to get the applications into production. This will make the business wait for new applications.

Cloud admin is responsible to the customer for the definition, design, deployment, and ongoing maintenance and support of a particular service, and work with the architects and developers to maximize the level of automation to support the service and manage its performance. He is also accountable for the service management delivery of the service.

The challenges of not having services owners for the operations team

We lack a single point of contact for customers, which creates different, individual channels for contacting IT and can affect customer experience. It also isn't able to provide an overall, end-to-end vision of the service, resulting in a lack of understanding of the service by customers and an alignment to the customer's needs. This way, ownership is diffused among different people, creating possible breakdowns between service life cycle stages or among different stakeholders, and things may fall between different people or create duplicacy. It also creates a tendency toward finger-pointing due to a lack of single point of accountability, which ultimately leads to reactive management with a lack of explicit commitment to evolve the service and promote the cloud more broadly. It will also lack overall vision as the same service may be delivered differently across the enterprise, making standardization harder to shift to proactive management of the service.

A solution with service owners

Once service owners are nominated, then we will have clear ownership with a single point of accountability. It will transform into a consistent approach for the consistent delivery of the services across the organization by facilitating between IT and customers with the accountability of ongoing delivery and continuous improvement of the service so that they can focus on the end-to-end quality of a service, its alignment to a customer's needs and IT strategy, and its future evolution. It will also drive the proactive management and optimization of the service.

Responsibilities of the service owner

Service owners are responsible for the overall service definition and the delivery of the following cloud service offerings:

- Gathers together all necessary stakeholders in IT to define the service scope, objectives, SLA, and so on upon the customer's new service requirement
- Manages development and enhancement efforts and works with cloud service architects
- Improves the services as well as expanding the demand due to an overarching vision of the service
- Continuous monitoring and reports on service-level attainment for their cloud service offerings
- Defines KPIs and reporting, which is necessary to manage the live services
- Maintains an active dialog with customers regarding service performance to anticipate and take required actions
- Responsible for service desk training to put the new or changed services into production based on their knowledge of the service and customer goals
- Works closely with support teams to define best processes and ensures that the support team is enabled
- Accountable for managing the service portal information, parameters, and characteristics for their services
- Ensures that customers have the right information in the portal and can understand the service they receive in case of a new service or a change
- Assists in service costs and financial models for cloud service offerings, for which they are accountable for the service costs
- Builds the right cost models with the right stakeholders, including finance and customers, and also educates customers on driving a customer's consumption behavior

Transforming VMware technical support operations

VMware is innovating smart capabilities in Workspace One to get customer insights and enhance security. Identity management will monitor a user's behavior, software performance, and hardware information by using ML. Business applications are coming with AI capabilities. VMware Skyline will help save time as collecting product data, events and conditions, and identifying issues will be quicker, allowing for faster **time to resolution** (**TTR**). The largest areas of influence to start with will be around problem identification, and the time it takes for support engineers to find answers to the problems that are reported along with also sending product data, which is utilized in support investigations. VMware Skyline will ensure that **VMware Validated Designs** (**VVDs**) should be followed. All support engineers associated with a premier support services team will be responsible for understanding the value and benefits of VMware Skyline and including it in daily conversations to drive customer adoption by encouraging customers to download and install the collector. As the viewer is made available, support engineers will also need to actively use it as they work on support requests for VMware Skyline customers. **Support Account Engineers** (**SAEs**) and **Support Account Managers** (**SAMs**) can use the **Operational Summary Report** (**OSR**) to have more impactful conversations that enhance and broaden the focus of these calls to be more proactive. It will help summarize the changes that are identified and the recommendations to fix any potential issues that have been identified. There will be a compilation of relevant **Knowledge Base** (**KB**) articles, field alerts, and security issues to review with the customer.

Customer success dashboards will use VMware Skyline data to highlight opportunities for customers to realize the maximum value from VMware products and services. The customer success team members will be responsible for understanding the value and benefits of VMware Skyline and including it in daily conversations to drive customer adoption. The customer success team can leverage VMware Skyline data as it will provide product usage data that will be a key input into the customer health score. It will provide both purchased versus deployed data (app adoption) and also provide health information through the customer health check report which can be used by the services team. This report is available to **Cloud Service Managers** (**CSMs**) as input to better plan for future. This report should be run quarterly for now.

Skyline will also provide key information regarding the product version to ensure the compatibility of products prior to an upgrade. It will also provide hardware information to show current state compatibility with the VMware product, as well as a site profile which will provide a topology view of the customer environment for VMware products. It is a tool that allows the consultant to engage with customers and give them recommendations so that the implementation team will continue to drive all execution planning and implementation of these recommendations.

The implementation team will be able to view the incoming data in the VMware Analytics Cloud that customers send back, but the services team must complete the Data Privacy training before requesting access to the data in a raw format. VMware Skyline should be seamless for customers, and there is no additional cost to customers as it's included in their support subscription. Customers on VMware Skyline will have their reactive support cases resolved more quickly, allowing them to get back to business faster. Reactive support issues can be resolved more quickly with proactive, predictive, and prescriptive recommendations, which will improve the environment's overall performance and health. This overall environment health will include improved reliability, scalability, configuration, design compliance, and cross-product recommendations.

Many customers rely on partnerships with VMware's authorized service providers to manage and support their VMware deployments, so partners should be included in the VMware Skyline program to leverage this technology in joint support processes. vSAN support analytics build a scalable support mechanism to leverage the CEIP framework. The wide variety of data that's collected allows the health check team to rapidly test improvements on existing health checks as well as new ones for accuracy. The vSAN compatibility guide team identifies common causes for problems, and the engineering team fixes issues that have not yet been reported or escalated.

The support team can quickly resolve issues by reducing the overall resolution time and enhancing the customer support experience. The product management team is able to better prioritize features by better understanding how customers have configured their environments, while product development need to prioritize additional configuration assist functionality to fix the most common configuration issues. This is leveraged for customers with production support and is integrated for reactive support purposes. vSAN CEIP data is transferred using the SSL (HTTPS) protocol from the vCenter Server. This will leverage a proxy that's configured for the vCenter Server. CEIP data is transferred to `https://vcsa.vmware.com`. vSAN is currently using the CEIP data for configuration, health, and performance telemetry, since unique information is complicated.

SDDC services

SDDC is achieved through a series of modular service components that progressively build organizational capabilities to define, design, develop, and release cloud services, and to manage the service catalog through which they are published. These modular services can be delivered individually, or as a program of sequential modules that gradually build on outcomes from each other. These components begin with requirement identification and then the development of repeatable processes with validation of these against the use cases.

Service catalog management

This service increases predictability in publishing cloud services for user and business self-services so that the customer's cloud service catalog is designed, managed, and operated to meet business requirements of availability, service publication, and self-service. It also provides the publication of the agreed-to service use cases to the cloud service catalog to validate the correct operational process, which supports delivery of the catalog with a service/tenant focused role, responsibility, and a skill-set enablement guidance to allow customers to manage and deliver the service catalog's capability.

Service design, development, and release

This improves the operational ability to build and release cloud services efficiently with a process for the design, development, and release of a customer's cloud services into a cloud-based infrastructure. The instantiation of the agreed-to service use cases to validate and refine the service design, development, and release process. The process is designed for sprint-based Agile service development, but the process can still be used for a traditional waterfall service development methodology by assuming a single development cycle.

Cloud business management operations

A cloud business management service can be enabled for better TCO and ROI with detail reporting to make rapid business decisions that assist cloud service owners in finding out the overall end-to-end specific cloud service per unit costs, including the following:

- Cloud services costing
- Pricing
- Showback reporting

Service definition and automation

This is a comprehensive approach to defining a customer's cloud service automation and provisioning roadmap by using a proven approach to discover, assess, and develop a service automation roadmap. This service provides customers with a clear and actionable roadmap to implement automated provisioning and deployment capabilities in their cloud environment. It provides a service definition framework, process, and a set of reusable templates to enable a comprehensive definition of a customer's cloud services for the agreed service use cases and provides a service/tenant-focused role.

NSX for vSphere

We have to first know about our current deployment and future expectations, along with all the information related to the applications (along with subscriptions details) that are hosted in the public cloud in different regions. We should collect information regarding virtual networks/**Virtual Private Clouds** (**VPCs**) with all of the VMs that are spawned in each VPC/VNET. We have to design a network with NSX for PaaS offerings such as API managers, along with an on-premise environment, and can't manage on-premise separately from the public cloud environment. We have to suggest hosting applications, databases, and web UIs across both environments, and connectivity to the public cloud through a dedicated express route/direct connect connection.

The **Virtual Cloud Network** (**VCN**) is the network model for the digital era. It is also the vision of VMware for the future of networking to empower customers to connect and protect applications and data from edge to edge, regardless of where they reside. It allows customers to embrace a cloud networking fabric as the software-defined architecture for connecting everything in a distributed world. It is a ubiquitous software layer that provides customers with the maximum visibility of, and context for, the interaction among users, applications, and data. Virtual cloud networking is the category of next-generation networking service consumption technology that's increasingly being adopted across IT to provide the digital fabric that helps unify a hyper-distributed world.

ESXi hosts are prepared for NSX for vSphere with the following values:

MTU	9000
Segment IDs	5000–7999
Teaming mode	Source MAC
Transport zones	1—encompassing all clusters

NSX is extending from the data center out to the edge, since delivering on the VCN requires a pretty robust portfolio. NSX Data Center is the best end-to-end consistent platform for data center networking. NSX Cloud is extending the data center network into the public cloud, along with VMC on AWS, native Azure support, and containers/Kubernetes support with **Pivotal Container Service** (**PKS**). We intend to deliver controls, policy, and automation that sits in the data center with consistency to deliver to the cloud environments that customers are running.

NSX Hybrid Connect will help in delivering application and network hybridity and mobility. Powerful network insights and discovery through **vRealize Network Insight** (**vRNI**) will drive improved security and network optimization across physical, virtual, and cloud environments. The following diagram depicts a traditional VMware vSphere-based infrastructure and a **VMware Cloud Foundation** (**VCF**) (HCI/VSAN)-based virtual infrastructure, both of which are integrated with **NFS Storage**:

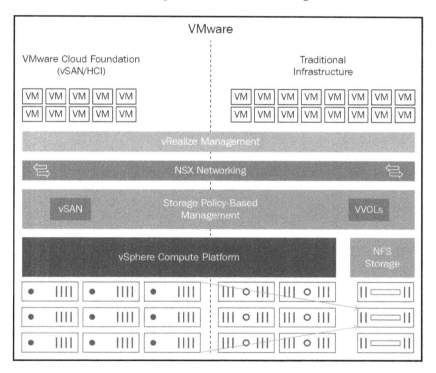

Layered approach in SDDC

If we are using NSX for on-premise, we can use switch port analyzer, **IP flow information export (IPFIX)** on-premise, and so on. Here, we can use Traceflow and get a peek into how the packets are flowing. This becomes complicated once we start moving to the cloud. This is because there is an underlay network that is not operated by the customer. The backbone network belongs to AWS or Azure, so what we want from a tool like this is end-to-end, real-time operational visibility across all cloud accounts and users.

Each public cloud provider has a different way of creating and instantiating security groups, and it can get hard to manage all of this. Customers operate the cloud today since every team creates its own VNET and the security policies for that VNET are discussed manually upfront before deployment. A ticket is raised every time when something new needs to be run. They generally create security groups that they attach to VMs in an on-premises environment.

Whenever a new VM is created, the VM inherits a bunch of restrictions based on the security group associated with it. In the following diagram, we can see how a four-node VSAN-based cluster has been configured with a distributed switch to host all management VMs such as **SDDC Manager**, **vCenter**, **NSX Manager**, **vRealize Log Insight** appliance, **PSC** controller, and **NSX** controllers:

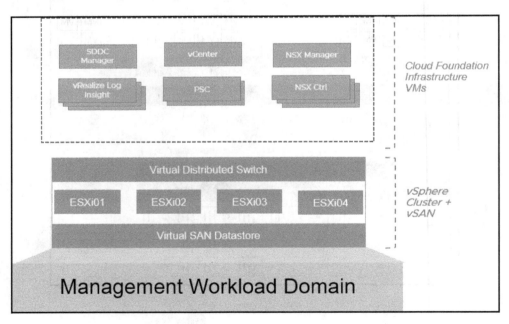

Workload clusters

vRA streamlines the application deployment process which consumes that network and contains blueprints with definitions, which allows new networks to be provisioned automatically. NSX is the future of networking and we are ready to help customers move forward in their digital transformation. We have a powerful technology for the way we can believe that networking is moving forward in the digital era. VMware is solving key customer needs around multi-cloud, multi-application framework, and modern application constructs, and is enabling consistent networking and security policies to follow the apps and data across the entire IT environment. NSX is the future of networking and we are excited to help our customers move forward in their digital transformation. vCenter Server and Active Directory servers are added to the exclusion list to avoid any human error and are available all the time. The following security groups, policies, and rules were created for the environment.

Recommendations with priority

The physical configuration specifications of the ESXi host list the characteristics of the ESXi hosts, and can be used during deployment and testing as per VMware best practices. The configuration and assembly process for each system is standardized, with all of the components installed in the same manner on each ESXi host. Standardizing the entire physical configuration of the ESXi hosts is critical to providing an easily manageable and supportable infrastructure because standardization eliminates variability. You can deploy ESXi hosts with identical configuration, including identical storage, and networking configurations, across all cluster members. For example, consistent PCI card slot placement, especially for network controllers, is essential for the accurate alignment of physical to virtual I/O resources. Identical configurations ensure an even balance of VM storage components across storage and compute resources. The following are the recommendations that we've mentioned, along with their priorities.

Recommendations with priority 1

The following constraints fall under recommendations with priority 1:

- Enable HA admission control on all clusters. Reason: protect the running workloads at all times.
- Increase the number of hosts in certain clusters to analyze the various scenarios. Reason: there won't be enough ESXi hosts in some clusters to be able to run all of the existing VMs in the event of hardware failure.
- Use resource pools both to reserve resources for **Site Recovery Manager (SRM)** failed over VMs and to ensure fair access to resources during contention events. Reason: protect the workloads.

- Remove CPU reservations from VMs in the cluster. Reason: potential for a VM restart failure in the event of ESXi host failure. Configuration isn't providing any genuine benefit.
- Ensure that the **network time protocol** (**NTP**) is configured correctly and that the NTP server has started on all ESXi hosts. Reason: having accurate timekeeping is essential in any IT environment.
- Use the route based on the physical NIC load-balancing algorithm for VM networking. Reason: make the most efficient use of available network bandwidth. Protect the workload.
- Investigate all level 3 recommendations in the vSphere 5.1 Hardening Guide. Unless there is a specific reason not to apply a security recommendation, then all recommendations should be applied. Reason: improved security.
- For the specific cases where VMs have RDMs, place the VM configuration files and `.vmdk` files on their own datastore and create SRM protection groups containing the datastore and RDMs. Reason: ensure that these specific VMs can be recovered successfully and independently of other VMs.
- Gain a thorough understanding of the recovery priorities and dependencies of VMs and configure SRM as appropriate. Reason: increase confidence that, in the event of disaster recovery, VMs can be recovered correctly and in the expected time frame. Services often have a preferred order of startup, which should still be adhered to during disaster recovery failover.
- Within SRM, configure a 1:1 datastore to protect group mapping where appropriate. Reason: this removes current issues with adding new LUNs to ESXi hosts and having situations whereby disaster recovery may not be possible during consistency group re-synchronization. It will allow multiple recovery groups to be initiated simultaneously and also allow for the testing or failover of specific services as opposed to every single protected VM. It adds complexity but introduces a substantial amount of intelligence and awareness to the disaster recovery plan.
- Have a pre-identified list of the 50% of silver VMs that would be recovered in the event of disaster recovery. Reason: this removes confusion during a disaster recovery event and allows a disaster recovery plan to be tested under controlled conditions.
- Introduce a service-based approach to recovery plans so that individual services can be tested and recovered as necessary. Reason: this brings a service orientated approach to disaster recovery and allows for the testing or failover of specific services as opposed to every single protected VM. It adds complexity but introduces a substantial amount of intelligence and awareness to the disaster recovery plan.

- Perform test recovery on a regular basis to increase confidence that disaster recovery would run as intended. Reason: increase confidence so that, in the event of a disaster recovery, VMs can be recovered correctly and in the expected time frame.
- Configure all virtualized Microsoft SQL Server clusters with best practice recommendations. Reason: ensure the stability of the cluster and remove performance inhibiting configurations.

Recommendations with priority 2

The following constraints fall under recommendations with priority 2:

- CPU utilization is generally low, so consider increasing the amount of RAM per ESXi host. Reason: this leads to greater consolidation ratio without impacting CPU performance.
- Determine whether strict enforcement of the 1vCPU: 4 GB RAM RU model is necessary. Reason: potential waste of compute resources. May lead to greater consolidation ratios.
- Don't have full backup jobs overlapping with antivirus scanning to limit the impact on ESXi host CPU utilization. Reason: lessen the CPU load requirements on ESXi hosts, which may otherwise lead to performance reduction within the VMs and the services running on them.
- Spread antivirus scanning of VMs across multiple time windows to limit the impact on ESXi host CPU utilization. Reason: lessen the CPU load requirements on ESXi hosts, which may otherwise lead to performance reduction within the VMs and the services running on them.
- Configure DRS rules for each vCenter Server. Reason: protect the vCenter Server VMs at all times.
- Configure each vCenter Server with memory reservations. Reason: protect the vCenter Server virtual machines at all times.
- Configure the HA restart priority of High for each vCenter Server. Reason: protect the vCenter Server VMs at all times.
- Identify and configure a secondary NTP server for all ESXi hosts. Reason: the current implementation contains a single point of failure. Accurate timekeeping is an essential part of any vSphere implementation.
- Investigate the use of host profiles or a PowerShell script to check for and remediate differences in ESXi host configuration. Once a solution has been identified, make regular checks to ensure ESXi host configuration consistency. Reason: this ensures a standard build and configuration for all ESXi hosts, which makes troubleshooting easier.

- Automate resource pool reservations for failover VMs and automate resource pool shares to ensure fair sharing of cluster resources during contention. Reason: protect the workloads.
- Modify vCenter Server settings so that tasks and events are truncated after 180 days (or however long tasks and events need to be retained within a virtual application appliance). Reason: this prevents the SQL Server database from growing too large, which may lead to performance problems.
- Use **vSphere Distributed Switch** (**VDS**) for all ESXi host networking. Reason: it's easier and simpler to configure. Provides a more consistent networking configuration across all ESXi hosts.
- Modify network bandwidth configuration for the **virtual network interface cards** (**vNICs**) within the HP Virtual Connect environment to maximize the overall use of network bandwidth. Reason: to use all available network bandwidth more efficiently.
- Configure multi-NIC vMotion. Reasons: this enables faster vMotion events by utilizing network bandwidth more efficiently.
- Identify all VMs that require a specific Mac address for licensing purposes. Hardcode this Mac address into the VM configuration. Modify all distributed port groups so that **Forged Transmits** and **MAC Address Changes** are set to **Reject**. Reason: this improves security within the vSphere environment.
- Configure SSO administrator groups and populate them with the appropriate Active Directory accounts. Reason: improved security and auditability.
- Remove the privileges from the `admin@system` domain account in vCenter Server. Reason: improved security and auditability.
- Modify the password expiry timeout within SSO to meet local security policies. Reason: improved security.
- Add all ESXi hosts to Active Directory. Use the `ESX Admins` group (or create your own and configure as appropriate) and populate with Active Directory user accounts. Configure appropriate SSH and ESXi shell timeouts. Modify the root passwords for all ESXi hosts so that it is long and complex. Store the password(s) in a safe location. Train staff to connect to ESXi hosts using their Active Directory accounts and not the root account. Reason: improved security and auditability.
- Create datastore clusters and add the appropriate datastores. Configure **Storage DRS settings** in **Manual Mode** with I/O measurement disabled. Reason: makes the placement of VMs a less complex task.
- Enable storage I/O control on all datastores and undertake a thorough analysis of all VMs and the workloads running on them. Configure VMs with specific best practices for the hosted application. Reason: to protect the workloads.

- Ensure that the most recent version of VMware tools is installed and running on all VMs. Reason: improved performance, security, compatibility, and manageability.
- Identify all VMs that have been configured with more than 4 GB RAM running an operating system that doesn't support using in excess of 4 GB. Reason: reduces compute resource wastage. Allows for greater consolidation ratios.
- Upgrade to a more recent version of vSphere. Reason: takes advantage of new software features, improves performance levels, and includes newer hardware support.
- Upgrade to **vRealize Operations Manager** (**vROP**) 6.7. Reason: to take advantage of significantly improved architecture.
- Identify and implement use cases for vROP dashboards. Reason: to take advantage of a large number of metrics that are available within vROP to provide deep visibility into the vSphere platform and visualize this in an easy to consume manner.
- Identify how vRealize Operations Manage can be integrated into the overall monitoring solution. Reasons: to improve the monitoring of the vSphere environment. Removes the need to use vCenter Server alarms, which are less capable than the features that are available in vROP.

Recommendations with priority 3

The following constraints fall under recommendations with priority 3:

- Only use VMs with a large number of vCPUs where it is absolutely necessary. Reason: reduces consolidation ratios, adds complexity when VMs are larger than the **non-uniform memory access** (**NUMA**) boundary, and may impact performance.
- Use HA restart priorities to bring important VMs back online first in the event of physical host failure. Reason: smart restarting of VMs is generally preferred.
- Alter the way that host capacity calculations are done. Reason: the existing method is complex and prone to error, and could be automated and presented in a dashboard format via vROP.
- Reduce the number of virtual data centers per vCenter Server. Reason: removes unnecessary complexity.
- Investigate combining bronze and silver clusters. Reason: may provide a greater consolidation ratio and also reduces the complexity of the environment.

- Add the server OEM **vSphere Installation Bundle** (**VIB**) depot to vCenter Update Manager so that the server OEM-specific software and drivers can be updated via vCenter Update Manager. Reason: this adds additional patching capabilities to vCenter Update Manager.
- Configure jumbo frames to enable faster vMotion events. Reason: to enable faster and more efficient vMotion events, which allows ESXi hosts to be evacuated more quickly.
- Ensure that all ESXi hosts are correctly licensed. Reason: this reduces the need to license hosts in the event of a DR scenario and ensures that the ESXi hosts are connected to vCenter Server with the appropriate configuration when needed.
- Configure the SSO default domain configuration feature to permit simpler sign-on. Reason: simplifies user login.
- Remove the local operating system as an identity source within SSO. Reason: improved security and auditability.
- Create dedicated datastores for templates and ISOs. Reason: remove the potential for performance issues during VM deployment or when accessing ISO images.
- Remove mismatches in configured and running OS types. Reason: improve compatibility between VM and VMware Tools.

Virtual data centers

There will be four virtual data centers per vCenter Server that relate to the various networking zones. The virtual data center construct is an administrative boundary, but it is not necessary to create multiple instances whereby there isn't a requirement to completely segregate the various vCenter constructs from a privileges perspective. Four virtual data centers are used solely for the purpose of placing the **vSphere Distributed Switches** (**VDS**). ESXi hosts and networks would need to be recreated in a new single virtual data center. This activity should only be undertaken with extensive research and planning.

The following are the configuration recommendations for virtual resources:

- **VM density per host**: The operation team ensures that they run all required VMs on different clusters and that the RAM will not be overcommitted. It can also decide to use up to 90% available RAM capacity of each host. They use the concept of resource units while scaling their VMs, and each RU is the equivalent of 1 vCPU and 4 GB RAM.

- **Consolidation ratio recommendation**: They have a general rule regarding that the vCPU to pCPU ratio should be less than 3:1. This is this ratio that normally assists the RU limits on the ESXi host. The ratio should be guided by a combination of the specific applications of each VM, the CPU configuration and utilization of the VMs, and the performance metrics of the ESXi hosts on which the VMs are residing. Consolidation ratios and vCPU:pCPU ratios can be influenced by the following parameters:

    - **Workload awareness**: Not all workloads are equal; a 4vCPU VM will not have identical performance characteristics to another equally configured 4vCPU VM.

    - **Virtual machine configuration**: Due to the constraints to the RU model, there may be unnecessary additional overhead that impacts the overall consolidation ratio. It is generally a best practice that VMs should only be configured with the resources they require so as to reduce the negative impacts of symmetric multiprocessing of VMs that have more than one vCPU. As the RU model is a fixed model, VMs with increased RAM demands must have more vCPUs configured, even if these are not needed.

    - **ESXi performance metrics**: Having a fixed CPU consolidation ratio is not generally recommended. Instead, taking into account the preceding detailed considerations with two important ESXi host metrics will permit a greater understanding of the potential consolidation ratios.

    - **CPU ready%**: The percentage of time the VM was ready to run but no physical CPUs were available to schedule the request. A value higher than 10 should generally be avoided.

    - **Dashboards and supermetrics**: vROPs can be utilized to create powerful and informative dashboards. Use cases always need to be identified as the following:

        - **Capacity planning dashboard**: RU calculations are done through a combination of getting numbers from individual clusters and using these with a spreadsheet to determine capacity. Creating a dashboard and using metric/supermetrics to determine what *full* looks like to a customer will reduce the manual tasks that are required. This could also be used in conjunction with alerts to provide proactive warnings in regards to the cluster capacity.

- **RU model dashboard**: A dashboard containing metrics that are affected by the RU model; under-utilization of CPU or memory, and ESXi host metrics affected by **symmetric multi-processing (SMP)**. We can identify use cases for dashboards and create them as required.

vROPs has a powerful alerting engine, which can be based of dynamic or static symptom thresholds. There are many out-of-the-box alerts from both VMware and third-party partners that have created solution adapters for vROPS. It will be always a task to resolve the initial number of alerts that are spawned by vROPS as this is an opportunity to identify and fix the issues that are identified, as well as to tune the existing alerts and symptoms and/or create new symptoms and alerts that fit the environment better. Custom groups and profiles can be used to create a granular approach to monitoring. The metrics for a production SQL cluster may be vastly different from a non-production file server. Using custom groups and profiles allows the alerts to be fine-tuned for the specific environment. This can identify how alerting from the vSphere environment should be achieved, and can determine whether vROPS can meet these requirements and, if so, configure them as required.

IaaS solution using vRealize Suite

vRA includes a number of grouping mechanisms. Administrators can use these grouping constructs to organize the compute fabric as well as create business-level grouping to partition services, resources, and users.

Today, applications are running across the globe in hybrid IT infrastructure. We have to extend the private data center into the public cloud as well as with containers. It can also be extended by connecting IoT service providers. NSX is a unified networking and security platform for all preceding technologies or infrastructure that allows customers to connect, secure, and operate to deliver services wherever applications may hosted. It has an embedded security engine segmenting the network through micro-segmentation and encrypting data in motion.

When we talk about the cloud, we basically want to configure and manage a hybrid network environment through just one tool. We don't want each cloud management system operating in a silo, and the same holds for on-premise, which should be oblivious to where the workload is currently hosted and where it will be moving to in the future. We should be able to port security policies along with workloads, immaterial of where they are hosted.

A developer doesn't want us to be in the development path, but we can't leave developers with these new technologies. Operations team has to help development team to get familiar with these new tools. The IT admin has the onus of setting up the firewall and not making sure there are any security vulnerabilities. The developer is not tasked with creating the security policies, they should just consume security groups that are designed by the IT admin. The goal is to have a cloud provisioning solution that has minimal work for the Devops team to do. We have to provide consistent networking and security for applications.

NSX Cloud is an extension of NSX features for public cloud and is not a separate product. When we have NSX loaded for our on-premise environment, we already have 90% of what we need for NSX Cloud. NSX has already abstracted the physical/on-premise network through our logical networking constructs. Now, it comes down to replicating the same for public cloud with NSX Cloud by providing visibility across all clouds for all traffic flows. We can't secure what we can't see. A new VM is created by a developer while the IT admin needs to have a dashboard and some kind of a UI that will make that visible to them. We have to design a unified consistent security policy across on-premise and the public cloud so that we can provide advanced L2/L3 networking capabilities, or if we are creating logical topologies for our on-premise network, then there can be APIs to port network topology from on-premise to the cloud. Management/operation need a single pane of glass for management, since that is at the heart of what we want to do for NSX Cloud. The deployment process or workloads that we use, such as Ansible or whatever else we're using for the deployment workflow for the developer, won't change because we are using NSX. This is one of the key value propositions as we see these options in Azure and AWS—and every public cloud provider, for that matter. However, they come with a bunch of limitations (especially in scale), and that is where NSX differentiates itself. We obviously don't want to get locked into the offerings of one public cloud provider.

Business-level administration and organizational grouping

NSX assists customers in configuring multi-layered security. An NSX firewall will provide primary security, and AWS security groups that are managed by NSX will provide a second layer of security. It is fully configurable to each VPC with exclusion lists. It enables agility for VM deploy/tear-down in test-dev while maintaining the structural integrity of production VPCs to get the best of both worlds.

There are environments where we would say VPCs need to be fully onboarded. It is okay to have some VMs that have an agent and some that won't have an agent in some environments. This is a typical test and dev environment, or a brownfield environment, that already has VMs running so we may not want to install an agent on all of them, but it doesn't mean that they can be quarantined.

If we have production VPC and it has a VM running in there with an agent installed and somehow someone manages to get in and install a rogue VM, then it is possible to detect it and quarantine it.

We have the gateway sitting in there and it is constantly polling for new resources that are being spun off inside a VPC/VNET. The gateway expects the agent in a VM to come and register itself, and if it doesn't, the gateway will move the VM to a quarantine security group. We can do this by using a default quarantine policy setup. Since the agent is not there, NSX **Public Cloud Gateway** (**PCG**) can't push any policies there, which doesn't mean that NSX doesn't have control over the VM itself. NSX can speak with the cloud provider and move this VM to a quarantine state. This is like adding another level of security and if we have an agent running, the PCG can push policies and manage the VM. If the agent is absent, PCG can move the entire VM to a quarantine state. Since PCG is the one doing this task, we don't have to worry about losing connectivity with on-premises systems. PCG has **Identity and Access Management** (**IAM**) roles assigned to it, which lets it talk to the cloud inventory. This is patented and we don't ask for admin privileges to do any of this. We can provide our customers with a cloud permission template, wherein they can assign roles and permissions to every component in NSX Cloud. PCG will be given the necessary roles to be able to talk to the cloud inventory manager and move a particular resource into a quarantine state.

We need an agent with a native security group to get an agentless solution. If AWS, Azure, and on-premises all worked the same way, then we could have done this easily. One single policy would have been good enough for all of these environments, which is not the actual scenario. We can apply one security group per VM in Azure and we can have five security groups that are nested in AWS. There is no way we can nest security groups in Azure as we will have to write a third security group for VNET in Azure. We are now talking about security group explosion, but we don't have any of these problems with NSX Cloud. We can't have a *deny* rule in AWS as we can only have an *allow* rule. If we say don't allow web-web tier communication for a particular instance, it doesn't take it. Anything that is not part of the *allow* rule is implicitly denied.

We have not seen any strong use case for doing encryption on the agent, but we do have the following defined role-based users for all tasks:

- VPC should be managed (cloud admin)
- Tagging the VM (developer)
- Adding the agent (developer)

However, if we need to provide additional isolation between different groups or divisions within companies or need tenant-specific branding, a number of tenants can be configured. Each tenant can have dedicated fabric groups, or shared fabric group resources if necessary. They have two or three subscriptions and a lot of VMs in these subscriptions, while other scenarios may have multiple subscriptions. The VMware IT job is to manage AWS and Azure accounts. Each employee here has their own AWS/Azure account, but the onus is on IT to make sure that we come from a secure interface by removing multiple security touch points. The problem with assigning security groups to VPCs and VNETs is that this has to be manually/statically done for every VPC/VNET. As an IT admin, we have two ways to go about this: by users creating VPCs for the workload or to impose security restrictions on them. But here, security is more like an afterthought. If we are looking for a consolidation of security groups for all VPCs and VNETs, then we need some level of abstraction. If we want a security group that can span across env, then we need a tool such as NSX. We can create NSX security policies using NSGroups in our NSX-T environment. NSGroups can be created with dynamic attributes such an VM name, location of the VM, which VNET it is running in, what region it is running in, and so on. It can also be based on user-defined custom tags, such as what the application is running in, and so on. NSX can learn about the tags, bring them back into NSX Manager, and based on these tags, can create some security groups and apply them to NSX Manager.

Azure has other limitations, such as we can have only one NSG per VM, but we wouldn't have any such problems with NSX Cloud. We can have any superset of NSGs with NSX. VM can be part of multiple SGs based on metadata and VM names. The policy can be based on attributes and not on a VM or interface VM, and there are no limitations on how many security groups can be stacked. Policies can be more dynamically defined instead of being statically defined to a particular VM, an in-bound or outbound access list, and so on.

vRA deployment

The vRA virtual appliance is SUSE Linux-based. This appliance runs the common services, such as authorization, approvals, notifications, and the component registry service, which allows all the other services in the distributed system to be discovered. The appliance also has several integration points that interface to **Lightweight Directory Access Protocol (LDAP)** and vCenter Orchestrator. The vRA appliance also contains an embedded Postgres database.

The service catalog holds all the configured services and catalog items. This is a common catalog and can be used by vRA and other solutions such as the application director to populate items and services, such as machine blueprints, application services, and services based on vRealize Orchestrator workflows. The most common services are hosted by the vRA virtual appliance. The advanced service designer (custom service designer) exposes vCenter Orchestrator workflows as catalog items, and the IaaS component is the Windows component, which handles the functionality related to reservations, blueprints, endpoints, workflows, and so on. The following configuration will be initiated in a vRA virtual appliance:

- Component registry-service, which allows other services to be discovered
- Authentication-user authentication
- Authorization-controls access
- Approvals-approval policy

vRA appliance communication

The following is a list of incoming ports through which vRealize Components listen :

Port	Protocol	Comments
22	TCP	SSH
80	TCP	Redirects to 443
111	TCP, UDP	RPC
443	TCP	Access to vRealize Automation console and API
5480	TCP	Access to web management UI
5488, 5489	TCP	Management
7444	TCP	SSO over HTTPS
8230, 8280, 8281	TCP	Internal vRealize Orchestrator instance

The following table shows the list of outgoing ports:

Port	Protocol	Comments
25, 587	TCP, UDP	SMTP for sending notification emails
53	TCP, UDP	DNS
67, 68, 546, 547	TCP, UDP	DHCP
80	TCP	Optional for fetching updates
110, 995	TCP, UDP	POP for receiving notification email
143, 993	TCP, UDP	IMAP for receiving notification email
123	TCP, UDP	NTP sync directly instead of using host time
443	TCP	IaaS manager service over HTTPS

IaaS components are installed onto a Windows host and include the model manager, the management interface, execution managers, and the database. The model manager that's installed with vRA includes all of the default models that are available from VMware.

A model is a collection of elements that make up a provisioning process and includes a data model, logic, event definitions, security, and the specification of how a **Distributed Execution Manager** (DEM) communicates with an external system. The database holds the configuration, workflows, and information about all of the objects in a vRA environment.

vRA has a vRA appliance and an IaaS component. The identity appliance is a Linux-based virtual appliance that provides single sign-on capabilities to vRA. vRA VA is also Linux-based and provides the user interface and several common services. The IaaS component is installed onto a Windows host and contains the management services, agents, model manager, and execution managers that process and execute the requested workflows.

Services running as part of the identity service

The following are the services that are running as part of the identity service:

- **VMware directory service**: Since the VMware directory service is a part of the **Single Sign-On** (**SSO**) installation itself, this service will always run on the same machine as the rest of the SSO services. There is no option to run it as a remote service. vmdir is the VMware directory service.

- **VMware KDC service**: This is a Kerberos KDC that can help in ticket generation for the **VMware Certificate Authority** (**VMCA**) service, which is an x.509 compliant certificate authority. The VMCA service depends on it to operate correctly. It also supports the issuing and revocation of certificates. The identity management service is accountable for incoming authentication requests and routes them to the defined directory or identity source. This is an important step so that the Global Support Service knows that any error during authentication will mostly occur here.
- **VMware Secure Token Service**: The **Secure Token Service** (**STS**) is responsible for issuing security tokens once the user's identity is verified. This service runs the Tomcat server. This service is responsible for issuing tokens once the user is authenticated. All logs associated with these services are located in the `/storage/log/vmware` directory on the identified appliance.

The API interface that's used to communicate with the components of vRA are interfaced with the identity management service and the **simple object access protocol** (**SOAP**). The interfaces to both the vRA VA and the IaaS component use **Representational State Transfer** (**REST**) of HTTPS. Customers can use the APIs to build their own interface to vRA.

Resource reservations can further divide the resources that are allocated to a specific group by creating different service tiers of resources using reservation policies. Multiple business groups can be created within each tenant. Business groups can share resources from the same fabric group, or utilize different fabric groups for greater isolation of resources between groups. If we need to provide additional isolation between different groups or divisions within companies, or need tenant-specific branding, then a number of tenants can be configured. Each tenant can have dedicated fabric groups, or shared fabric group resources if required. vRA supports time zones, European date formats, and major currencies.

Part of the real beauty of CF is the automation it provides around workload domains and how it makes deploying and extending workload domains very easy. In addition, it makes it very easy to reclaim capacity by deleting workload domains. Everything is done, from configuring the physical servers to configuring VLANs and IP addresses on the switches to deploying vSphere, setting up vSAN, and deploying and configuring NSX. There are some shared aspects between workload domains, an example of which is that we have a management domain running with two user-defined VI workload domains.

It is a good idea to review the global settings for the **virtual desktop infrastructure** (**VDI**) within the SDDC Manager prior to provisioning a VDI workload domain. These settings allow the administrator to define naming, sizing, and AD placement for desktops and Horizon servers. NSX also provides micro-segmentation for VDI workload domains. The 26 rulesets have been automatically created to provide the micro-segmentation of VDI components.

A complete solution with the desired result

There will be major efforts involved for operations teams in creating new VMs, as well as deploying applications manually with the risk of human error. We have to move the entire infrastructure to the private cloud and automate end-to-end processes to improve the resolution time of the operations team.

The operations team utilized the VMware internal private cloud that's powered by the vRealize suite to provide IaaS, including compute, storage, and networking resources for delivering all applications on top of these services. They are able to achieve fully automated management functionalities to control their application development life cycle process. The vRealize solution is extensible and can leverage automation scripts to integrate third-party tools such as load balancers, monitoring agents, and code repositories.

Previously, developers used to call the operations team for new application entities and would take weeks of provisioning, but now developers and testers can get a new, or manage their, application landscape with a self-service portal to customize their requirements. After the environment has been provisioned and tested, developers will get a link for their application entities with login details and a web console that's used to monitor the different metrics of the environment. They will now get fully operated and tested services in a few hours.

Summary

 The VMware operation team have created templates for all of their applications, alongside their configurations, through vRA. This automation tool minimizes the end-to end application provisioning time from a few weeks down to 36 hours. We are able to enhance the whole cycle to less than 24 hours after the first year. Automation will help not only in quick provisioning but also in maintaining consistency in repeated tasks. We can build development and test labs rapidly with automated, predefined policies, and so we avoid any human errors. VMware engineers can now use their time for new developments and help their operation team to be more agile. Employees can initiate and execute their tasks through a self-service portal. This means that applications are provisioned in a few hours and so the development team have more time for new projects. This enhances the efficiency of VMware developers and also reduces the security risk which comes as malicious codes, and backlogged jobs. VMware private cloud-based IaaS will also help in annual savings of both CapEx and OpEx costs. VMware is able to minimize the cost as well as enhance the services to their end customers. They have focused more on output and quick response to achieve agility in services to improve customer experiences. We are happy with our automated delivery process, but we can also develop other processes based on VMware software-defined services by using the hybrid cloud model. We have to be competitive in this market by regularly upgrading IT services as per business demands.

In the next chapter, Chapter 11, *Network Transformation with IoT*, we will learn about VMware Pulse IoT use cases in different domains such as health, research, science, and retail. We will learn about the application and data utilization from the data center to cloud to edge devices by transforming a network for IoT and understanding how to manage and process massive amounts of data across edge devices.

3
Section 3: Dealing with Big Data, HPC , IoT, and Coud Application Scalability through ML

The new vSphere Scale-Out edition is specifically designed for running **high-performance computing** (**HPC**) and big data workloads. We have to ensure that HPC and big data performance and other requirements can be met either by development or by fine-tuning guidelines with our mainstream products. This vSphere edition comes with a feature set that has been adjusted to align with these two Scale-Out workload types, HPC and big data, and at a competitive cost. It packages all the core vSphere features required for big data and HPC workloads and is sold in packs of 8 CPUs. Key features included in the vSphere Scale-Out edition include ESXi hypervisor, vMotion, Storage vMotion, Host Profiles, Auto Deploy, and Distributed Switch.

This section contains the following chapters:

- Chapter 11, *Network Transformation with IoT*
- Chapter 12, *Virtualizing Big Data on vSphere*
- Chapter 13, *Cloud Application Scaling*
- Chapter 14, *High-Performance Computing*

Network Transformation with IoT

11

This chapter will brief you about how **Software-defined Data Centers** (**SDDC**) can span across multiple data centers and into hybrid service providers, independent of physical infrastructure with distributed data and applications. Digital transformation is changing the mode of business, and the **Internet of Things** (**IoT**) plays a critical part in this transformation. Business growth is accelerating and exploring better ways to bring new products and services to market quickly with a modern data center that can provide the agility, security, and scalability required to power innovation and growth. We will learn about the core requirements that customers are looking for in IoT implementation.

We will learn about why IoT is so critical for health, research, science, and retail customers as their application and data will be utilized from data center to cloud to edge devices. We will also look at the transformation of networking for IoT by understanding how to manage/process massive data across edge devices, along with VMware Pulse IoT use cases across different verticals.

We will cover the following topics:

- IoT and ML
- IoT need hybrid cloud to be managed beyond regional boundaries
- Distributed networking
- Security with the virtual cloud network
- VMware Pulse IoT Center

Technical requirements

You can download VMware Pulse IoT Center 1.1.0 from `https://my.vmware.com/web/vmware/details?downloadGroup=PULSE_IOT_110productId=751rPId=23122` and VMware NSX-T Data Center from `https://my.vmware.com/en/web/vmware/info/slug/networking_security/vmware_nsx_t_data_center/2_x`.

IoT

IoT use cases exist in most industries. They may not be apparent to us, and they may not even be apparent to customers. IoT is a tool, and businesses use this tool to achieve better outcomes. They are consistent when dealing with outcomes which depend on the IoT tool as the pattern: *Ingest, analyze,* and *engage.* An IoT solution *ingests* data from sensors and devices, the analytics component then uses this data to arrive at conclusions (*analyze*), and the results trigger actions that allow the business to *engage* with the infrastructure or their customer.

Ingest, analyze, engage is used by businesses to constantly improve their products and services; this active or passive feedback could be coming from humans, computers, trucks, or assembly lines. IoT use cases observed in the market can be divided into three high-level IT value-management goals:

- Continuous customer engagement
- Digital engagement
- New business model

Let's go through some of these use cases:

- Treatment adherence would allow care facilities to monitor whether patients are following their treatment plans by using smart pill boxes
- Smart inspections in insurance allows the inspection of damages using drones and image recognition
- Mining companies use of predictive maintenance to schedule preventative maintenance of heavy infrastructure, since maintenance impacts productivity immediately
- Imagine getting a new sports driving mode for your car, just like you can buy an app in the Apple Store or Google Play Store—that's what software feature delivery can enable in the automotive space

- Driving risk-based pricing for automobile insurance enables an insurance company to price insurance per individual driving habits, as measured by devices tethered to the car's onboard computer
- Automated checkouts, as being trialed by Amazon and Wal-Mart, allows customers to shop without the lines
- Smart cities have been in the news in the recent past. These enable efficient energy consumption and safer roads

Ingest, analyze, engage is evident in every use case.

VMware Pulse

VMware Pulse IoT Center is a secure, enterprise-grade IoT device-management and monitoring solution. You can onboard, manage, monitor, and secure IoT use cases from the edge to the cloud, bridge the gap between IT and **Operational Technology** (**OT**) organizations, and simplify IoT device management with Pulse IoT Center. Liota Agent, on edge systems, enables data orchestration, automatically detects edge systems, and onboards and provisions **Over-the-Air** (**OTA**) by mapping edge systems to connected devices. It collects telemetry data about infrastructure health and detects anomalies in real-time with high accuracy. It manages software OTA of any edge type along with connected end points, by configuring rules to upgrade in flexible package combination.

It provides security across IoT things, network, data, and people by creating segmented data flows with network virtualization that offers a complete visibility of all things. We have to first discover customer pain points which create hindrance in their business growth and also slow down their overall process.

The queries that arise related to VMware Pulse

The following are the queries that arise regarding VMware Pulse.

Discover customer pain points with the below probing questions which fits for most of the customers:

- Struggle with securing IoT devices OTA with firmware/software updates
- Looking for onboarding remote, unmanned IoT devices, for example, an oil rig in the middle of the ocean
- Struggling to go from test to company-wide implementation

- Looking for the option to host an IoT management solution on-premise and have more control of data privacy
- New end points are rapidly getting added to the network
- IT has no visibility or control on IoT deployments
- Struggle with compliance for IoT devices
- Have too many different proprietary management tools
- Challenges to get metrics out of connected things/hardware
- IT needs a solution that allows to make changes in coordination with OT

Discovery questions for cities going with IoT solution:

- What does a smart city or municipal IoT project encompass?
- Do we have plans to increase camera surveillance to protect citizens?
- How are we planning to monitor, manage, and secure the devices, such as cameras and road sensors?

Here are some probing queries for hospitals adopting an IoT project:

- How much medical equipment gets lost every year? (Statistically, about 30%)
- Do we know about all the things (Hardware) connected to our network and whether they are secure?
- Have we thought about tracking our equipment? Would that solve some pain points in knowing where they are and their status?
- If we could monitor the whereabouts of our patients and doctors, could we use this information to improve the quality of patient care?
- How is preventive maintenance on medical equipment done today?

Here are some probing queries for equipment-manufacturing companies adopting IoT technology:

- Are we providing a preventive maintenance service today? How are we doing it?
- How do we ensure that the technology we are using inside the machine (vehicle, and so on) is working accurately and reports the correct data? How are we securing it?

- Can we update the software equipment OTA for our customers? Do you give our customers the ability to do this themselves?
- Do we have a smart factory or Industry 4.0 (the current trend of automation and data exchange in manufacturing technologies is referred to as the fourth industrial revolution) project?
- What are the biggest road blocks in implementing Industry 4.0?
- What if we could help monitor, manage, and secure heterogeneous IoT environments?
- What if we could collaborate with OT to ensure IoT projects are managed and secure?

Pulse IoT Center infrastructure management blueprint

The OVA is basically a vApp that contains three **virtual machines** (**VMs**) that run the Ubuntu server. The VMs are named, by default, as follows:

- `mqttbroker`: This has the EMQTT broker from `http://emqtt.io` installed
- `iceapi`: This has the VWware Pulse IoT API and PostgreSQL pre-installed
- `iceconsole`: This has VMware Pulse IoT Console with all dependencies

During deployment, the OVAs will need some application-specific properties to help initialize itself. These properties are basically used to configure the applications in each of the VMs.

Deploying and configuring the OVA

The OVA can be deployed through vSphere using the **Deploy OVF Template** from the vSphere UI or using the OVF Tool from the command line. Before powering on the VM for the first time, make sure that Guest OS Customization is enabled for the host to inject the right system and network settings for each of the guest OSes.

The Guest OS Customization Wizard is shown here:

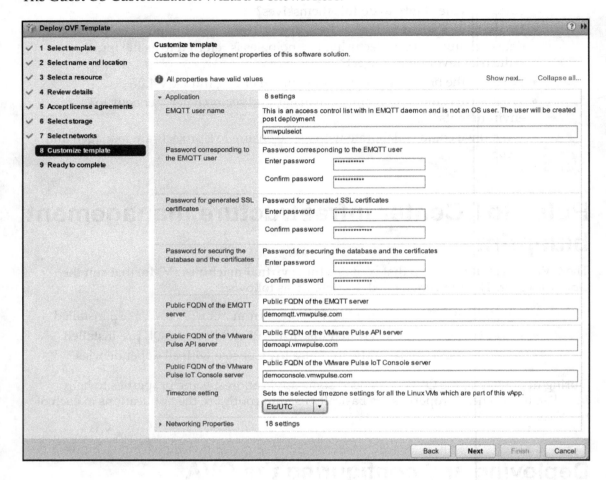

The deployment will also ask for a few properties to help the appliance configure itself to a certain extent. Add an EMQTT credential (username, password) so that the broker starts up with this pre-staged user once the VM starts up for the very first time. This is not a system user but an EMQTT user that the clients can use to connect to the broker. Only one username and password can be configured over this option. Any additional users will have to be created from the command line after logging into the `mqttbroker` VM. The username and password should be between 8 and 64 characters. It is advised you keep the username purely alphanumeric. This password is not used for any built-in Linux user accounts.

Similarly, the wizard asks for passwords for the IoT API and IoT Console. The password for the IoT API will be used to secure the DB and the generated certificates. The password for the IoT Console is used for the generated certificates alone. The username and password should be between 8 and 64 characters. It is advised you keep the username purely alphanumeric. This password is not used to for any built-in Linux user accounts.

We can use VMWare Pulse IoT API and Console as input to generate SSL certificates by taking the public DNS name for the MQTT broker. These values are used during certificate generation. The name goes into both the CN and SAN sections of the generated SSL certificate. Therefore, it is necessary to freeze the domain names before proceeding with the deployment in case you need to continue using the server with a self-signed certificate.

As an example, here are the features of the following deployment:

- The **EMQTT user name** and password are `vmwareiot` and `vmwareiot`
- The IoT API password for the DB and certificates
- The IoT Console password for the certificates
- **Public FQDN of the EMQTT server**: `demoemqtt.vmwpulse.com`
- **Public FQDN of the VMware Pulse API server**: `demoapi.vmwpulse.com`
- **Public FQDN of the VMware Pulse IoT Console server**: `democonsole.vmwpulse.com`
- The time zone settings can be left as the default

The configuration settings through the **Import Wizard** are shown here:

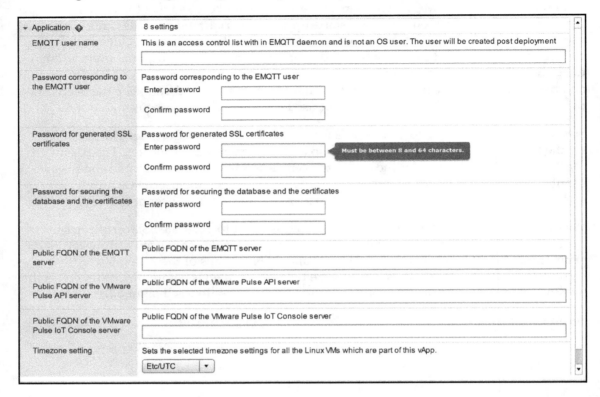

We will learn about the installation and configuration of products specific to the Pulse IoT Center. The deployment would need to be done in the following order to address dependencies:

- VMware Pulse Device Management Suite
- VROPs Suite with Helix Adapter Support
- EMQTT broker
- VMware Pulse IoT Center Console (UI)
- VMware Pulse IoT Center API server
- vIDM for **Single Sign-On** (**SSO**) support

Before the VMware Pulse IoT Center components are deployed, make sure all computing and networking resources are available in the deployment infrastructure, be it VMware OneCloud or the VMware vCenter. The OVAs do not have the firewalls or iptables rules enabled by default, and are left to the deployment team in case additional security reinforcements or hardenings are needed.

Configuring IoT support

`projectice` is a standard Linux user with no `sudo` privileges and is used to run the VMware Pulse IoT Center components. The VMware Pulse IoT Center console, Hazelcast, and VMware Pulse IoT Center API server run as system services under this account. The service runs as a daemon to support an automatic restart in the event of a system reboot. No password has been set for this account and, hence, a local login is only possible using `sudo` or `su` through another logged-in session. This user is limited to the VMs of the Pulse IoT API and the VMs of Pulse IoT Console. The EMQTT broker VM doesn't have this user. The root account exists as well, for which the default password is `vmware`. All default passwords will need to be changed on the first login.

The following prerequisites are required prior to installation:

- SSL certificates.
- Valid domain names for the API, console servers, and EMQTT broker. The name should be reflected in the common name and SAN of the SSL certificate.
- Enable **Guest OS Customization** on the VMs before starting the VM to ensure that the VM is configured with the right hostname and network settings.
- VM hosting environments, such as vCloud or vSphere.

Virtual machines in the OVA

`iceadmin` is an admin user that has `sudo` privileges and is mainly meant for configuration and management of VMware Pulse IoT Center components. The VMware Pulse IoT Center components are generally system services and the `iceadmin` account will be used to install/start/stop/restart the services as the situation demands. This service management requires a user with admin privileges. The default password for this account is `vmware` without the quotes.

After installation, the IoT support needs to be enabled in **Settings** | **Device & Users** | **Advanced** | **IOT Support**:

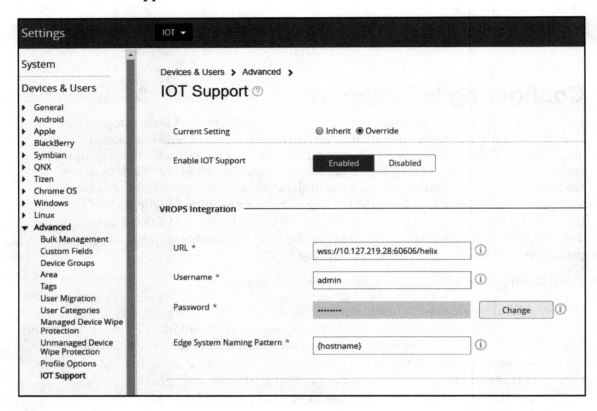

This section should be configured only after the IoT API server has been installed. The VMware Pulse IoT API registers for notifications from VMware Pulse Device Management Suite to speed up refreshing the resources, rather than relying on the sync interval. This helps the Pulse IoT API to maintain resources to a reasonable accuracy. These notifications are sent from VMware Pulse Device Management Suite to the Pulse IoT API whenever one of the following events happens:

- A new device is enrolled
- A device is unenrolled
- A device changes its organization group

VMware Pulse Device Management Suite and the Pulse IoT API honor the device's attribute change notification, such as asset number, device-friendly name, organization group ID, user email address, ownership, OS, phone number, or device MCC, only when the device's attribute-change flag is enabled in the events section. VMware Pulse Device Management Suite only supports organization group changes, which is done within the same OG tree, that is, in its child OGs. The event for the same is notified to the listener after some time.

While installing the Pulse Device Management Suite console in a Windows server, the VMware Pulse Device Management Suite installer suggests you enable TLSv1.2. Make sure to enable TLSv1.2, or, if the step is missed, perform the manual steps as outlined previously. Always confirm the following key is persisted in the registry. This is a mandatory registry entry for the device notifications to be notified to the VMware Pulse IoT API server.

Check out the following registry keys in the Pulse Device Management Suite physical server:

```
"HKEY_LOCAL_MACHINE\\SYSTEM\\CurrentControlSet\\Control\\SecurityProviders\
\SCHANNEL\\Protocols
 TLS 1.2 Client"
 Value name : DisabledByDefault
 Type : DWORD (32-bit) value
 Value : 0
 Value name : Enabled
 Type : DWORD (32-bit) value
 Value : 1
```

Use this registry file to create the settings in the registry if they are missing. Just right-click the file on the Windows server as an admin user and choose merge. If the Pulse IoT API is installed using a self-signed certificate, make sure to add the root CA certificate of the self-signed certificate in the **Windows System Certificate** stored under **Trusted Root Certificates** on the machine where Pulse Device Management Suite is installed as per the following steps:

1. Choose **Add/Remove Snap-in...** from the **File** menu:

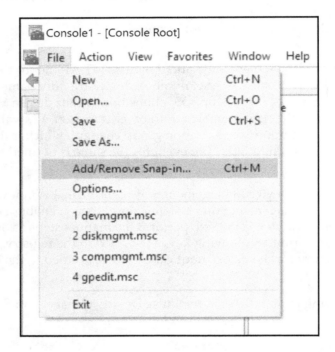

2. Choose **Certificates** from the **Available snap-ins**, then click **Add>**:

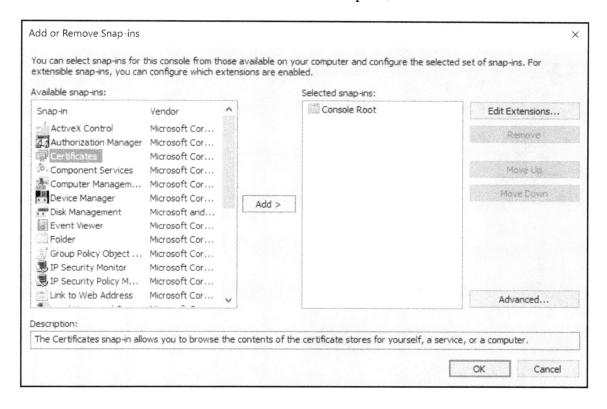

3. Choose **Computer account** and hit **Next**:

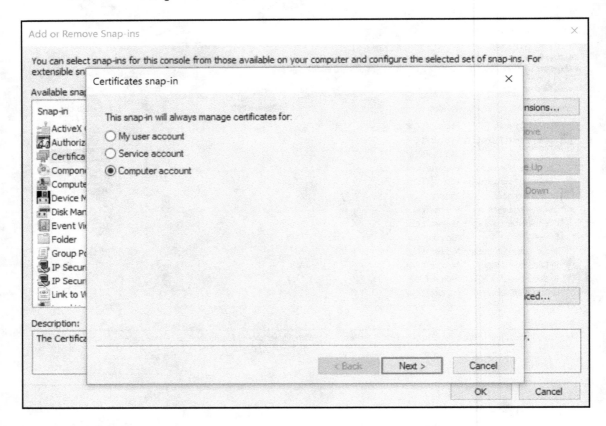

4. Make sure **Local computer** is selected. Click **Finish** and hit **OK**:

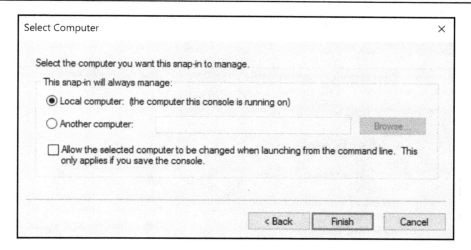

5. Go to the **Certificates** node under **Third-party Trusted Root Certificates Authority** and right-click to import the certificate:

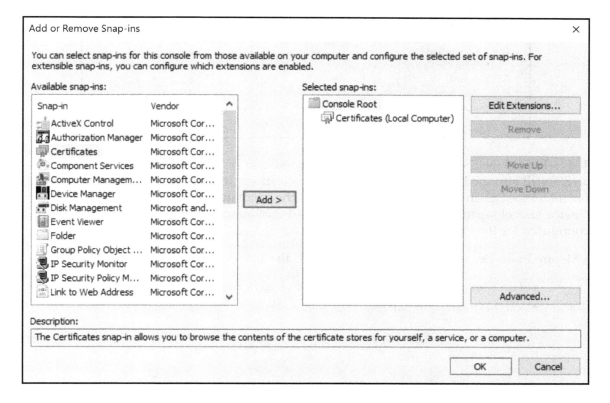

6. Follow the import wizard to save the private CA certificate that was saved from the browser:

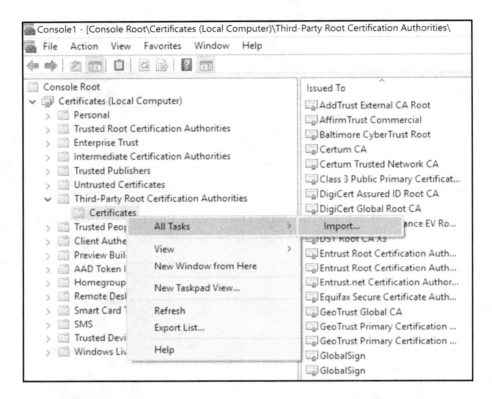

This will help the SSL validation to succeed when Pulse Device Management Suite makes an SSL call into the Pulse IoT API to deliver notifications. Just adding the certificates will not allow the SSL invocation to succeed, unless the hostname used by the VMware Pulse Device Management Suite API to reach Pulse IoT API matches with the actual certificate configured for the Pulse IoT API service.

VMware Pulse Device Management Suite needs to reach out to the following:

- The VMware Pulse IoT API server, to send notifications
- VIDM (if configured)

VMware Pulse system, if available through an internal route from the Windows VM, adds an alias in the `%SystemRoot%\drivers\etc\hosts` file to either of the machines that are using the external DNS name to avoid a round trip. The DNS name is important for the SSL validation to happen, as each of these servers is invoked over HTTPS.

A custom-built version of the VMware Pulse operational analytics backend, based on VROPs 6.6, can be downloaded from the link in the IOT release artifacts. To log into the VM, the default password for the root user will be empty. Hence, just press *Enter* and set a new password on first login. This login should happen from the Terminal console where the OVA is deployed. SSH is disabled by default. Once deployed and powered on, access the vROPs instance web UI at `https://<IP-address>`, which will guide you through the basic installation steps of vROps. You can select **Install/ Express Installation** and provide a password for the vROps instance. You will need to obtain a license key to use vROPs.

IoT use cases with VMware Pulse

The primary motivation for businesses to consider and implement IoT solutions is to improve business productivity and internal efficiency by identifying customer-specific IoT use cases. When considering IoT use cases, we focus on quantifiable goals to show an improvement in productivity and efficiency. Anywhere we notice data being produced, we have the capacity for data ingestion. This may be a problem that hasn't yet been addressed and, therefore, the business hasn't done anything with the data. However, when we observe an opportunity to ingest data, we should think about analyzing that data and engaging using results from that with customers or with infrastructure.

Onboard the Liota agent on edge systems to enable data orchestration, automatically detect edge systems and onboard and provision OTA, and map edge systems to connected devices. We can monitor and collect telemetry data about infrastructure health, detect anomalies in real-time with high accuracy, and set rules to automatically fix OTA whenever possible.

We can also manage software OTA of any edge type and connected end points, set rules to automatically upgrade/fix in flexible package combination, and set rules to automatically fix OTA . We can secure across IoT—things, network, data, people, create segmented data flows with network virtualization, and have complete visibility of all things.

Choose the gateway/server based on use case needs, environment, and desired rugged ability; we have the flexibility to choose what hardware VMware IoT edge runs on.

VMware Pulse IoT edge supports the new distributed IoT architecture by enabling analytics at the edge using technologies we trust. Next, we will deep dive into some of the use cases.

Powering the connected car (automotive industry)

- **Business problem**: Customer is struggling with the rising costs of software-related recalls for connected cars.
- **Use case**: OTA updates, operational analytics.
- **Customer benefits**: Manage the head unit and ECUs of these cars by deploying security patches, component upgrades, and new services OTA and in real time. Collect telemetry from vehicle components and analyze it in real-time to detect anomalies and deliver corresponding admin-defined commands and alerts. Reduce the recall rate and increase the warranty of the cars to enhance customer satisfaction and loyalty in the long term.

Entertainment, parks, and resorts

- **Business problem**: Customer has deployed wearables and other sensors across all their properties to better track customer behavior, reduce wait times, and optimize customer experience. However, they are finding it hard to cope with the fragmented heterogeneous ecosystem of their IoT deployments, which is leading to rising costs of management and operations.
- **Use case**: Asset tracking, OTA updates.
- **Customer benefits**: Reduce the cost of maintaining these connected devices and infrastructures by providing a method to monitor devices remotely and deliver OTA updates. Ensure all connected devices are up to date with security patches and firmware updates. Achieve the gold standard of guest experience for all their visitors, maximize sustainability, and improve the productivity of the workforce and operations overall.

Smart hospitals (medical)

Doctors want to collect key info and provide real-time access to patient vitals, diagnostics, and imaging at the point-of-care by interpreting data and proactively to detect and treat medical problems.

- **Business Problem**: Customer's goal is to improve efficiency and eliminate mistakes in the management of patients, staff, and equipment. This can be achieved by implementing RFID tracking, which will enable locational identification of all parties and equipment.

- **Use case**: Asset tracking, OTA updates to RFID infrastructure, operational analytics.
- **Customer Benefits**: Manage, monitor, and secure the gateways that serve as the connection point for RFID tags. Provide OTA security patches in real-time. Help gain insight into the device life cycle with real-time operational analytics. Improve efficiency and eliminate mistakes in the management of patients, staff, and equipment, and enable improvements in processing, resourcing, and equipment usage.

Smart surveillance (higher education)

- **Business problem**: University wants to amp up security for students and staff for the university campus. University plans to deploy V5 systems smart cameras that detect gunshots, smell sulphur, and so on to preemptively detect public disturbances, such as shootings and riots, in real-time.
- **Use case**: Operational analytics, asset tracking, OTA updates.
- **Customer benefits**: Manage, monitor, and secure the gateways that serve as the connection point for RFID tags. Provide OTA security patches in real-time. Help gain insight into the smart camera device life cycle with real-time operational analytics. Make campuses safer for staff and students and vastly improve emergency response.

Smart warehouse (retail industry)

Customers want to give workers real-time, hands-free access to complex assembly instructions by automating process control to eliminate downtime with increased visibility and quickly sort out inbound materials with suppliers.

- **Business problem**: Customer wants to create efficiencies in their distribution and shipping processes in store by employing robots to reduce failure due to human error and fatigue. They are starting with managing robots for their distribution centers and retail stores, where one robot is used to scan shelves and identify out-of-stock items, and the other robot is used to find in-store pick-ups for customers.
- **Use case**: Asset tracking.
- **Customer benefits**: Manage, monitor, and secure all the deployed robots to provide a single-point solution for all IoT projects across all business units. Manage all IoT use cases within a single pane of glass and have a consistent way of managing and monitoring all connected devices.

The internet of trains (transportation and logistics)

- **Business problem**: Customer is looking to eliminate/reduce downtime by being able to maintain their equipment.
- **Use case**: Real-time device monitoring, OTA updates.
- **Customer benefits**: Monitor IoT gateways and connected air compressors in real-time to determine whether devices go offline. Deliver OS and software updates to the partner's gateways.

Customer will have a system to monitor air compressors and other equipment remotely, which will create efficiencies and reduce costs by partnering with VMware.

The financial industry

- **Business problem**: Create the bank of the future and improve customer experience at hundreds of retail banks, such as identifying customers as they arrive and anticipating services they might need. In addition, the branch manager has a series of tasks that must be performed each day before the bank can close (vault, teller drawers, and so on), but there is no reliable method to confirm each step was completed.
- **Use case**: Real-time device monitoring, OTA updates.
- **Customer benefits**: Remotely managing and monitoring the IoT infrastructure (gateways, sensors, beacons, cameras, and so on) to ensure devices are online and secure. Pulse provides a single console to manage the various IoT devices required to enable the bank of the future and ensure bank operations are not interrupted.

Smart weather forecasting

- **Business problem**: Customer wants to use IoT to deploy sensors to get richer data on weather and seasonal patterns to inform the general public as well as for research. The bureau is deploying thousands of weather-monitoring sites with multiple sensors that cannot be centrally managed or secured easily since they are in remote, unmanned sites.
- **Use case**: Single-point management, monitoring/alerting, OTA updates.

- **Customer benefits**: Provide a secure central control point for gateway devices and respective sensors that exist across multiple weather-monitoring sites. Provide OTA security patches in real-time. Help gain insight into the smart camera device life cycle with real-time operational analytics. Be able to successfully get standardized images and centralized data from all sensors to provide weather monitoring, forecasting, trending, and alerting to the public, weather scientists, and international partners.

IoT data center network security

IoT traffic differs and data centers network traffic as communication becomes digital and control instances become communication hubs from from on-premise data center to clouds.

There are three new areas of massive horizontal (east/west) traffic:

- **On-edge**: That is, a LAN connecting vending machines
- **Intra-DCs**: Between different apps, storage, and DBs for various purposes (billing, analytics, control)
- **Inter-DCs**: Interaction between apps of different customers in data centers (order, manufacture, ship)

Traffic with new paths and new content has massive east/west sensitive private data, and today's applications are dispersed to hundreds of either identical (load sharing) or complementary (process chain) instances while every set of data collections will be processed multiple times (over time) by different applications across the data centers. Their east/west traffic is highly dynamic as app instances come and go. These apps get frequently updated with most of the sensitive data processed and stored. We should prepare ourselves to prevent, detect, and contain breaches in a highly dynamic environment.

We can apply below policies and proactive actions to avoid any security breaches :

- **Distributed firewall (DFW)**: Micro segmentation to protect and filter every instance individually at its interface. People can't harm what they can't touch.
- **Guest introspection**: Observe data and behavior in every instance to detect data leakage or dormant malware by spotting the symptoms and preventing its execution.

- **Network introspection**: Observe network traffic on layer 7 in mid-air to protect valuable data, and protect instances by turning out pockets when crossing levels. As we are evolving our data center from a shopping mall into a jail, we have to automate or fail the whole process with automation by one engine to gain and sustain coherence.
- **Automate remediation**: We find breached instance and distributed firewall quarantines it immediately by doing guest introspection.
- **Automate coherent perspective**: Allow OPS to have holistic views across silos from declarative perspectives.

NSX distributed firewall

We can deploy logical firewall at every vNIC by decoupling network and security. Firewall instances at every vNIC to any kind of vSwitch embedded in the hypervisor as close as possible to the guest VM but not part of the guest VM. We won't move the traffic from the source to an inspection point, but instead move the inspection point to the source of the traffic with network infrastructure irrelevant to the granular protection of servers.

Distributed Firewall at vNIC is the right spot, and fully integrated to apply policies most effectively. Integrated means that it doesn't matter where we are or where we go—even if we are off the track or change direction—it still works because it is built into hypervisor. Integrated also means that it is not our responsibility as a driver or passenger to put on our protection, we can't forget or avoid it because it is built into hypervisor. Integrated also means it is physically and functionally integrated with some sensors and will set off the air-bags at the right time. NSX DFW define automation with Service Composer by abstracting and automating based on vCenter/active directory rulesets.

Prerequisites to any automation

Dynamic sources of data represent conditions and changes of the system and abstraction layer will define on a higher level to respond to conditions and changes. We use vCenter and active directory to represent information about the servers and users in a specific solution. Service Composer in the NSX manager dynamically translates service definitions and FW rules into interface rule sets and pushes them down.

We own the vCenter with the necessary data for abstraction. NSX DFW Service Composer helps customers react immediately to changes and declares the strategy with every imperative, tactical move. The admin cannot remotely control the actions of each individual component, but instead they define a strategy—a set of abstract rules and measures—to control and follow the compliance policy:

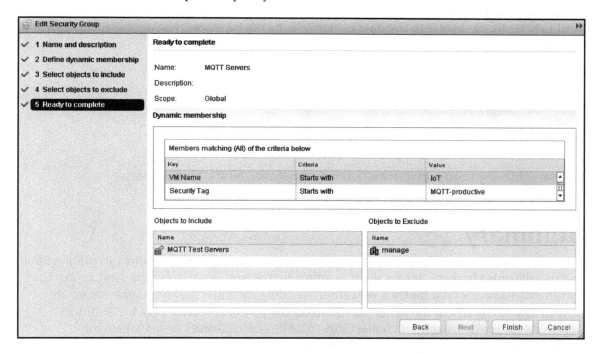

The controller in turn is responsible for translating the strategy into tactical moves and orchestrating them and keeping oversight as they are especially responsible for changing tactics immediately when the situation changes. Each component in the data center plays its individual role, which is assigned by the controller. We should automate inter-data-center traffic and all N/S traffic as well, from the perspective of the local data center or, inter-data-center traffic which is N/S traffic.

Automating the local data center is pointless if deployments or changes are kept from going live ASAP by the necessary changes of N/S FW ruleset. The N/S Firewall could consume the VMware objects in their rules, as these objects would be dynamic and wouldn't touch the ruleset of the N/S firewall for daily changes when an instance comes or goes. NSX security groups can be dynamically consumed by third-party firewalls that automate changes to their ruleset objects.

Hybrid cloud for scale and distribution

Physical perspective is hard to manage and needs logical, coherent operations across DCs. The local feed of on-premise data centers is probably not big and redundant enough to scale compute which we can spread out across multiple data centers.

IoT-ready data centers must follow specific security and scalability practices as more N/S (and E/W) traffic comes into the data center. We also need more inter-data-center traffic for third party tool integration to achieve the below objectives:

- Micro-segmentation
- Declarative management
- Integrated automation
- Distributed scaling
- SDDC for coherent management

We can achieve end-to-end automation by virtualizing all the moving parts.

Summary

The IoT space opens many new doors to places where federation solutions can offer unique value. IoT comes in many forms, such as smart thermostat, a wearable medical device that monitors a patient's vital metrics, or a smart vending machine that remembers favorite drinks. The IoT is where the cyber world meets the physical world. Any IoT solution requires some combination of connectivity, mobile communication, management, infrastructure, and security with an application's life cycle.

Customers need an infrastructure on which they can build an IoT solution; then they need to provision and manage millions of things on that infrastructure. Those things spit out massive data, so customers also need to collect, store, and analyze data, gain meaningful insights from it, and then translate those insights into worthwhile actions. We do this by providing the IoT essentials, which enable us to achieve three top-line business outcomes.

Following are the three business objectives :

- Manage millions of things as easily as managing one
- Use things related data into action
- Make IoT a business reality

In the next chapter, we will learn how to leverage shared storage in modern big data platforms by evaluating current in-memory big data platforms. We will explore how Big Data application (such as Hadoop) fits for virtualization as an in-memory feature of these platforms, to make them less dependent on I/O and storage protocols, so we can leverage virtualized shared storage and the basic VMware vSphere features to design a highly-available and performance-oriented architecture for big data platforms.

12
Virtualizing Big Data on vSphere

In this chapter, you will learn to leverage shared storage in modern big data platforms. We'll evaluate current in-memory big data apps on vSphere virtualization platform. The in-memory feature of these platforms makes them less dependent on I/O and storage protocols. We will go through with administrator productivity and his control while creation of a Hadoop cluster and show the use of a Hadoop management tool for installation of software onto virtual machines. Further, we will learn about the ability to scale in and out, such that any workloads on the platform can expand to utilize all available cluster resources by pooling of resources to be shared by multiple virtual Hadoop clusters, resulting in higher average resource utilization.

We will cover the following topics in detail:

- Big data infrastructure
- Open source software

Technical requirements

You can download VMware vSphere Big Data Extensions 2.3.2 from `https://my.vmware.com/web/vmware/details?downloadGroup=BDE_232productId=676rPId=28154`.

Big data infrastructure

A cloud implementation always has a service catalog with all the services that are available for consumption. It also has service-design, catalog-management, and knowledge-management systems. These services will provide an organization with the ability to accelerate the operations and build an agile cloud services framework. We have to define some roles, responsibilities, and functionalities to manage the process:

- **Service owner**: Responsible for the value of a service and managing the service backlog
- **Service backlog manager**: Responsible for defining the service's priority with all backlogs, including functional, non-functional, and technical requirements
- **Service release manager**: Responsible for planning, scheduling and controlling the builds, tests, and releases by delivering new features as well as taking care of existing services

Hadoop as a service

VMware vSphere **Big Data Extensions** (**BDE**) is the platform that runs scale-out clustered Hadoop applications. It provides the agility to change the configuration through a single console and the flexibility to scale up and out for both compute and storage resources with better reliability and security on the vSphere platform:

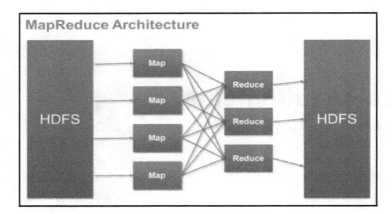

We categorize the Hadoop journey in three stages:

- **Stage 1**: This is what we call the piloting stage; typically the size of the cluster we see is under 20 nodes. In this stage, the customer is dabbling with Hadoop, trying to understand the value of Hadoop, and in many cases, prove the value of Hadoop in providing new business insights. Usually, the journey starts with a line of business, where someone wants to apply Hadoop on one or two use cases, often on data the enterprise is collecting but not doing much with. For example, one of the oil and gas companies we spoke with was collecting all these sensor data from oil wells and drill platforms. With Hadoop, they were to do some interesting analyses and get some very interesting insights.

- **Stage 2**: Once the initial value is proven for Hadoop on big data, enterprises typically move into codifying these use cases and running them regularly as a production workload. One common phenomenon we see at this stage is that, as people hear about this production Hadoop cluster, they want to leverage it to explore their data; more and more jobs are added to the cluster, and the cluster starts to expand and grow. Another common thing we see is that it's not just about core Hadoop components of MapReduce and **Hadoop Distributed File System** (**HDFS**). The other non-core Hadoop components of Hive, Pig, HBase, and others are often added to the cluster. Typically, we see the production cluster ranging from dozens of nodes to hundreds of nodes, and it may grow very rapidly. Here, there are typically dedicated Hadoop administrators to ensure the health of the system.

- **Stage 3**: At this stage, customers are using Hadoop extensively throughout their organization, and have built mission-critical business workflows around it. For example, for an e-commerce retailer, the recommendation engine is now a critical part of their business, and Hadoop is a critical part of the workflow. Often, at this stage, we see enterprises expanding beyond Hadoop, and adding other big data technology and services into the mix. Often, **massively-parallel processing** (**MPP**) databases, NoSQL databases, and more non-core Hadoop components are part of the big data production system. In terms of Hadoop nodes, typically we see hundreds to thousands of nodes. On the extreme end, companies such as Yahoo and Facebook have several thousands of nodes.

Deploying the BDE appliance

VMware enables you to easily and efficiently deploy and use Hadoop on existing virtual infrastructure through vSphere BDE. BDE makes Hadoop virtualization-aware, improves performance in virtual environments, and enables the deployment of highly-available Hadoop clusters in minutes. vSphere BDE automates the deployment of a Hadoop cluster, and thus provides better Hadoop manageability and usability.

Let's get started with these steps:

1. Select **File** in the VMware vSphere Client and go to **Deploy VMware-BigDataExtensions-x.x_OVF10.ova**.

2. In the **Select the source location** dialog box, click the **Local file** radio button, click **Browse...**, browse to the location of the identity appliance, click **Open**, and then click **Next**:

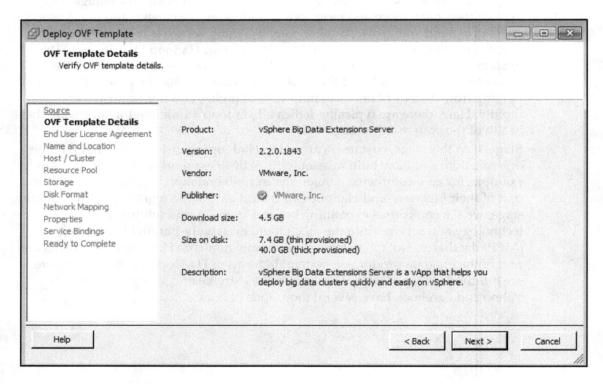

3. In the **Review details** dialog box, review the summary details and click **Next**.

4. In the **Accept EULAs** dialog box, accept the license agreement by clicking the **Accept** button and then click **Next**.

5. In the **Select name and folder** dialog box, enter a unique name for the virtual appliance in the **Name** text box.

6. Select the folder or data center location where we have to deploy virtual appliances and then click **Next**. For QA deployment, **East FP** | **Pumulus** | QA folder is selected.

7. In the **Select a resource** dialog box, select the cluster where you want to deploy the virtual appliance and click **Next**. For QA deployment, the **ECHADMIN01** cluster is selected.

8. Select the required resource pool in the **Resource Pool** dialog box.

9. Select the **QumulusQA VMs** resource group.

10. In the **Select storage** dialog box, select the disk format that you want to use for the virtual appliance from the **Select virtual disk format** drop-down list.

11. Select the datastore you wish to place the virtual appliance on by clicking on it in the list. Click **Next**. For QA deployment, the **ECHADMIN01-DEV and QA-VMX** datastore cluster is selected.

12. In the **Disk Format** dialog box, select **Thin Provision** and click **Next**.

13. In the **Setup networks** dialog box, select the network that you want to connect the virtual appliance to using the **Destination** drop-down list and then click **Next**.

14. For **QA deployment**, **xx.xxx.0.0/22** is selected.

15. In the **Ready to complete** dialog box, select the **Power on after deployment** check box and click **Finish**.

Configuring the VMware BDE

We will deploy the vApp, power on, and then browse the console of the management server. There are four Hadoop clusters configured in this vSphere environment. The columnar view on the right indicates each cluster's name, status, which Hadoop distribution is running, the resource pool it belongs to, and the list of nodes. Resource pools manage how Hadoop consumes the underlying physical resources.

Steps to configure BDE on vSphere are given below :

1. Log in as Serengeti and change the Serengeti user password with the following command:

   ```
   run sudo /opt/serengeti/sbin/set-password -u
   ```

2. Close the management console and SSH with the serengeti user. Configure the YUM repository by running the following commands:

   ```
   # cd /opt/serengeti/www/yum/repos/centos/6/base/RPMS/
   wget
   http://mirror.centos.org/centos/6/os/x86_64/Packages/mailx-12.4-7.e
   16.x86_64.rpm
   wget
   http://mirror.centos.org/centos/6/os/x86_64/Packages/wsdl4j-1.5.2-7
   .8.el6.noarch.rpm
   ```

3. If we can't connect using `wget`, download `.rpm` and then winscp (open source tool) them over. To create the repo, run the following command:

   ```
   createrepo ..
   ```

The BDE plugin

We will get to the BDE plugin by clicking the Home icon and then choosing **Big Data Extensions**:

1. Open a web browser and navigate to `https://xx.xxx.x.xx:8443/register-plugin`. Remember that the IP address will be user-specific.

2. Select the **Install** radial button, fill out the form with vCenter information, and click **Submit**:

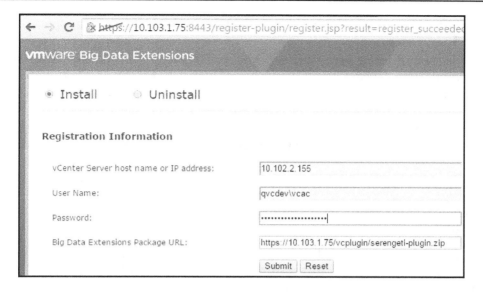

3. Click on **Big Data Extensions** in the vSphere Web Client, then click on the **Connect Server...** hyperlink in the **Summary** tab and navigate through the inventory tree to find the management server:

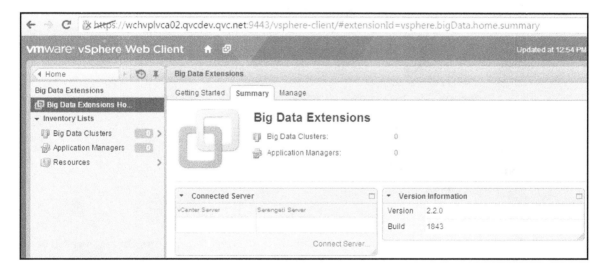

4. Click on **OK** to accept the certificate. The server is now connected in the **Summary** tab.

5. To set up the Hadoop YUM repository, SSH into the YUM repo server as the root user. Type the commands shown in the VMware KB article (`https://kb.vmware.com/s/article/2091054`) to configure **Hortonworks Data Platform** (**HDP**) 2 YUM.

6. Browse to the new repo at `http://puppet2.qvcdev.qvc.net/hdp/2/`. We will utilize an existing YUM repo server for this environment.

Configuring distributions on BDE

We will now log in through SSH into the Serengeti Management Server with the Serengeti user account:

1. Use PuTTY to SSH to the management server, then double-click the **PuTTY** icon on the desktop

2. Click the **SerengetiCLI** session and then click **Open**

3. Run the following commands:

```
# navigating to the scripts directory

cd /opt/serengeti/sbin
[root@10 sbin]# ./config-dist
ro.rb \
> --name qumulusqahdp \
> --vendor HDP \
> --version 2.x.x \
> --repos http://puppet2.qvcdev.qvc.net/hdp/2/hortonworks-hdp2.repo
```

The `qumulushdp` distro is added into `/opt/erengeti/www/distros/manifest` successfully.

The old manifest is backed up to `/opt/serengeti/www/distros/manifest.bak`.

```
[root@10 sbin]# sudo service tomcat restart
```

4. Log into the vCenter Web Client and click on **Big Data Extension** from the tree on the left

5. Click on **Big Data Clusters** and then click the icon to add a new cluster (a green +)

We can see the name of the new HDP distro now in the Hadoop distribution. Keep in mind that the name will match the parameter specified when we ran `./config-distro.rb` (`pumulushdp`).

The Hadoop plugin in vRO

We can now see how vRO integrates the BDE plugin and runs the workflow:

1. Log into the vRO configuration page at `https://xx.xxx.x.xx:8283/config_general/General.action`:

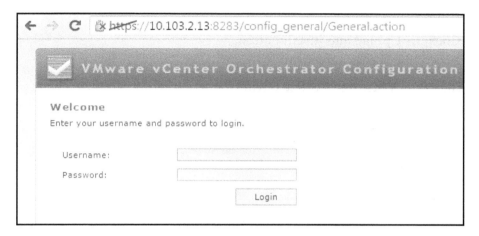

2. Click on the **Plug-ins** tab on the left:

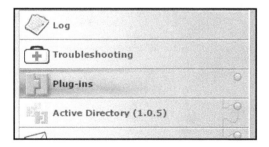

3. Scroll toward the bottom and click the magnifying glass. Look for the magnifying glass and select the required plugin file:

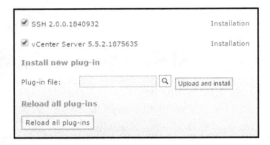

4. Click the **Upload and install** button.
5. Accept the license agreement.

   This is the **VMware vRealize Orchestrator** console through which we can manage tasks:

6. Click **Startup Options** to restart the vRO service and restart the vRO configuration server.

7. Log into the vRO client, and, under **Run**, select **Workflows**.

8. Under **Library**, you should see **Hadoop Cluster As A Service**.

9. Expand **Hadoop Cluster As A Service** and then expand **Configuration**. Right-click **Configure The Serengeti Host** and click **Start Workflow**:

10. Type in the URL for the Serengeti Management Server as `https://xx.xxx.x.xx:8443/serengeti`.

11. Enter the username for an administrative user on vCenter in UPN format (for example, `user@domain.com`). Enter the password for the administrative user and click **Submit**:

   - **Connection url for a Serengeti host**: For example, `https://10103.3.18:8443/serengeti`

- **vCenter Server username**: For example, `vrasvcqa@qvcdev.qvc.net`:

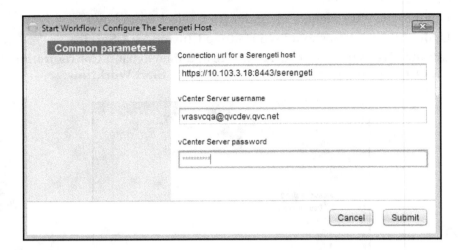

12. We get a question about importing the certificate. On the last page of the form, select **Install certificate...** from the dropdown:

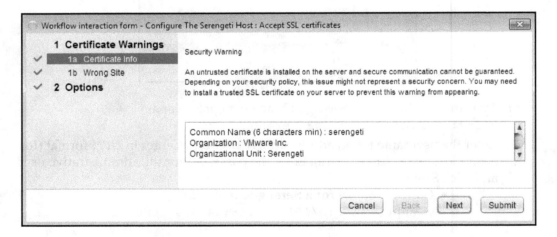

13. Click **Next** and then click **Submit**:

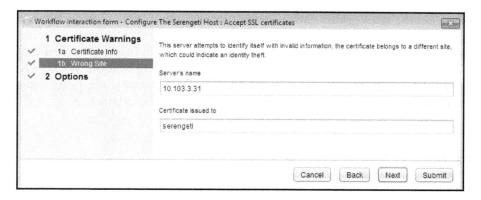

The Serengeti host is now fully configured.

We can provision the cluster using VRO as the workflow "**Configure The Serengeti Host** " has rest host connection and operation timeout value hardcoded as 30.

The following screenshot shows the **Workflow** creation settings; the user can create different workflows as per their requirements:

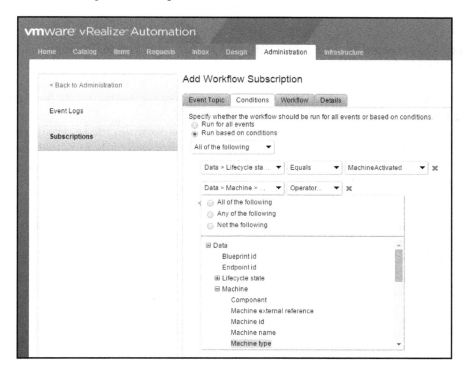

We have to select the network or datastore resource option in BDE Cluster Blueprint in vRA. There should be a drop-down option to select a certain BDE Resource on the Web Client side. This needs to be customized on the vRA blueprint forms. Configure the Serengeti host to add a timeout value for the connection and operation. We also have an option to select BDE cluster sizes (**Small**, **Medium**, **Large**) from the vSphere web console. This needs to be customized on the blueprint side from vRA Blueprint.

Open source software

Organizations need great skill sets to accept open source compared to traditional proprietary solutions as there's a big difference between building a solution from scratch with all integrated support and utilizing tried-and-tested vendor solutions. For many enterprises, these challenges are too daunting, and erode the value of the open source choice for them. Business strategies, investments, and many other factors come into play. In these situations, enterprises find that a commercially-supported distribution of open source solutions, or a proprietary solution, better supports their strategy. Customers build digital and online selling channels as a pillar of their go to market strategy, develop their own proprietary implementation of OpenStack aligned to the unique demands of their business use cases.

Customers have invested in the time, talent, and resources to refine OpenStack to meet their specific needs. A major sports retailer had chosen open source based solution rather then to implement a commercial distribution of OpenStack .VMware Integrated OpenStack help customers to save their time and resources, investing their technical talent in refining the outbound customer-facing portions of their strategy. Open source is undeniably a strategic part of every company's software portfolio today. While open source software has its strong suits, being production-ready is not one of its top attributes. There's still a lot of work to do: getting that code to meet the standards of a commercial, sold product is not an insignificant investment, and requires specialized skills.

From selection to testing, integration, and security, some assembly is required. For most enterprises, that's not an investment they want to make; they are better served investing in their core competence, not in becoming an expert in a single implementation of an open source project. That's where commercial providers, such as VMware, step in to provide the pragmatic, practical open-source-based software that enterprises can rely on.

Open vSwitch (**OVS**) is another example of VMware's contributions. The code was transferred to the Linux Foundation collaborative projects for ongoing community support with VMware, and continues to play an active role as VMware engineers are responsible for as much as 70% of the active commits to OVS. These contributions are considered personal, and community support across the industry continues to grow. VMware is making strategic investments in the IoT space with EdgeX and **network functions virtualization** (**NFV**) with expertise in the **open network automation platform** (**ONAP**).

Clarity is an excellent example of creating software internally and choosing to open source it to benefit a broader community. Clarity is a UX/UI design framework as it helps both developers and designers with the visual aspects of applications. Clarity was developed internally in VMware to meet the UI/UX needs of products but it's not contingent upon VMware products to work or to deliver value. It can be applied and used in nearly any environment, so the choice was made to open source it. Clarity has taken off as it has an active community, has been downloaded more than 100,000 times, and has nearly 1,000,000 views on its homepage. Our open source projects also include tools and kits that help a developer to be more efficient.

Challenge handshake authentication protocol (CHAP) is a tool that analyzes un-instrumented ELF core files for leaks, memory growth, and corruption.

VMware products are based in open source, which we support and contribute to but we are not an open source software company. VMware software, whether propriety or based on open source, is production-ready: it is fully supported, fully tested, and optimized—it's secure and ready to deploy.

Considering solutions with CapEx and OpEx

We can see with open source solution that CapEx cost reduces as license costs potentially diminish, while OpEx cost rises as
the support and skilled technical manpower required to deploy and maintain the open source solution. We see CapEx rise in popularity, which reflects the license and support contract costs for a **commercial off-the-shelf** (**COTS**) software solution, while OpEx falls as the burden for patching, upgrading, enhancing, and securing the software rests with the vendor, not the enterprise IT department.

This is not a 1:1 tradeoff, but something you must consider across your enterprise and it's not a short-term decision; it has long-term, structural, and strategic implications. If you are struggling to hire or retain staff, converting to an open source solution where you are relying on your intellectual property and technical prowess to make the solution work could put you in a very precarious situation. You may be held captive by consultants or outsourcing companies that promise to *hold your hand* as you approach production operations. Those costs rarely fall over time. Another option to consider is a hybrid solution: commercially-supported open source distributions or commercialized versions of open source projects. Another option to explore is the two-tiered option: some companies offer a *community version*, which is their open source project offered at no cost, and offer a second version, typically labeled *enterprise,* which is a sold product that offers a more robust version of the software and is fully supported. We can go with open source to build our strategy and make the right decisions for business. Therefore, to start with the basics, we must know where and how our application developers or IT staff are leveraging open source and understand the decisions behind their choice, including the benefits as well as the gaps.

As our team starts to engage in open source projects, arm them with guidelines so that they feel confident in their contributions. We should have a single point of contact for questions about IP, license types and compliance, and best practices with a safety first option. If we want to create a new open source project or engage at a deeper level in an existing project, be sure to understand the strategic intent. This is a long-term commitment and requires an investment in talent and time, or our efforts will flounder as they're time-consuming, distracting, cost money, and can be annoying. We have to evaluate the choice between an open source solution and a proprietary, vendor-backed and -sold solution, as it is a strategic choice, not just a purchasing decision. We need to weigh the pros and cons of CapEx and OpEx, and carefully evaluate our long-term commitment and ability to hire staff. We can discuss to understand the costs and benefits along with the technology curve.

Benefits of virtualizing Hadoop

The benefits of virtualizing Hadoop are as follows:

- **On-demand provisioning**: Automate the cluster-deployment process as per the defined policy
- **Continuous availability**: vSphere's built-in HA protection protects the single point of failure
- **Flexibility**: Resources (CPU, memory, network, and storage) can be scaled up and down on demand as per your requirements
- **Multi-tenant environment**: Different tenants running Hadoop can be isolated within a shared infrastructure as per security compliance

Use case – security and configuration isolation

The Hadoop authentication and authorization model is weak. Sensitive data is hard to protect. It has multiple MapReduce workloads for production batch analysis, ad hoc analysis, and experiment tasks with different SLAs for different jobs.

We need to take the following into consideration:

- Where it makes sense, HDFS is consolidated to minimize data duplication
- High-priority jobs get more resources to ensure they are completed on time
- Each type of job can get as many resources as possible at any time
- Avoid CPU and memory contention so better utilize resources to get a job done on time

Our objective is to integrate Hadoop workloads and other workloads by having a big data shared infrastructure. The Hadoop MapReduce framework uses HDFS as an underlying filesystem to process large sets of data and use their own storage mechanism. We also have other technologies, such as HBase and Pivotal.

Case study – automating application delivery for a major media provider

The following are the challenges:

- Customer had a mandate that any application must be deployable to any number of backend infrastructures, spanning multiple private clouds
- A specific application (with a footprint of over 10,000 servers) needed better provisioning procedures and tools to ensure the mandated goal was met
- Customer's current provisioning model required an extensive overhaul, as spin-up time was several weeks if not months, largely consisting of manual procedures

The following is the solution:

- Implemented an automated workflow-based approach using a version-controlled, software-defined infrastructure via the **Business Process Management** (**BPM**) platform/workflow engine and underlying Java services
- Leveraged Puppet architecture for build processes and packaging, and bakery workflow for images
- Provided insight into the operations via a Ruby-based console and reporting UX

- Integrating Jira into the provisioning workflow will make delivery ease-of-use from familiar tools
- Provisioned application servers and requisite number of Memcached and related instances
- The new system validates a newly-provisioned infrastructure, provides an automated cleanup of any failures, and automatically switches routing rules to serve up the new infrastructure
- Provided customer with tools and patterns necessary for repeatable operation
- Created better build procedures and processes, which yield more stable infrastructure changes
- Deployment time for the target infrastructure was decreased from weeks/months to 90 minutes for 270 servers

Summary

Hadoop is still quite new for many enterprises, and different companies are at different stages in their Hadoop adoption journey. Having worked with several customers on this, it's evident that, depending on the stage the customer is at, there are distinct Hadoop use cases and requirements. Virtualization can help to address all the key requirements of each stages. Multiple Hadoop clusters can be used by different departments within a company.

It is difficult to manage multiple clusters for different departments in a company and keep them all running well. We have multiple use cases running data mining, recommendation engines, and for our online service, we have one shared dataset, rather than duplicated data everywhere. We are now managing a single cluster rather than multiple clusters.

In the next chapter, we will learn how to support cloud-native application development by providing developers with access to traditional and modern application-development frameworks and resources, including container services and open APIs, on a common vSphere platform. This enables microservice-based architectures for faster and frequent development without compromising security, reliability, or governance.

Further reading

Check out the following resources for more information on the topics covered in this chapter:

- *Adobe Deploys Hadoop as a Service on VMware vSphere* at `http://www.vmware.com/files/pdf/products/vsphere/VMware-vSphere-Adobe-Deploys-HAAS-CS.pdf`

- *Virtualizing Hadoop in Large-Scale Infrastructures, technical white paper by EMC* at `https://community.emc.com/docs/DOC-41473`

- *Virtualized Hadoop Performance with VMware vSphere 6 on High-Performance Servers* at `http://www.vmware.com/resources/techresources/10452`

- *A Benchmarking Case Study of Virtualized Hadoop Performance on vSphere* at `http://www.vmware.com/resources/techresources/10222`

- *Transaction Processing Council—TPCx-HS Benchmark Results (Cloudera on VMware performance, submitted by Dell)* at `http://www.tpc.org/tpcx-hs/results/tpcxhs_results.asp`

- *ESG Lab Review: VCE vBlock/systems with EMC Isilon for Enterprise Hadoop* at `http://www.esg-global.com/lab-reports/esg-lab-review-vce-vblock-systems-with-emc-isilon-for-enterprise-hadoop/`

- *VMware BDE Documentation site: vSphere Big Data Extensions (BDE)* at `https://www.vmware.com/support/pubs/vsphere-big-data-extensions-pubs.html`

- *VMware vSphere Big Data Extensions—Administrator's and User's Guide and Command-line Interface User's Guide* at `https://www.vmware.com/support/pubs/vsphere-big-data-extensions-pubs.html`

- *Blog articles on BDE Version 2.1* at `http://blogs.vmware.com/vsphere/2014/10/whats-new-vsphere-big-data-extensions-version-2-1.html`

- *VMware Big Data Extensions (BDE) Community Discussion* at `https://communities.vmware.com/message/2308400`

- *Apache Hadoop Storage Provisioning Using VMware vSphere Big Data Extensions* at `https://www.vmware.com/files/pdf/VMware-vSphere-BDE-Storage-Provisioning.pdf`

- *Hadoop Virtualization Extensions* at `http://www.vmware.com/files/pdf/Hadoop-Virtualization-Extensions-on-VMware-vSphere-5.pdf`

- *Container Orchestration on vSphere with Big Data Extensions* at `https://labs.vmware.com/flings/big-data-extensions-for-vsphere-standard-edition`

13
Cloud Application Scaling

This chapter will guide you through how to support next-gen cloud app development by providing developers with access to traditional, cloud-native, and modern application development frameworks and resources, including production-grade container services and open APIs. These will be used on a common vSphere platform and will also support legacy or traditional applications side by side with cloud-native and containerized apps, across a virtualized environment.

You will learn how to optimize resources to get maximum output by defining parameters and what-if scenarios. These will be considered for future scalability, so that we can configure and autoscale parameters across different clouds.

In this chapter, we will cover the following topics:

- Cloud-native applications
- The **Pivotal Container Service (PKS)** on vSphere

Technical requirements

You can download VMware Enterprise PKS from `https://cloud.vmware.com/vmware-enterprise-pks/resources`.

Cloud-native applications

Digital technologies are always changing, due to today's dynamic business objectives. Everything is connected via mobile, social networks, wearable devices, connected cars, and so on, and they are all influencing the way that we behave and engage with technologies today. Customers are demanding more innovative, flexible, and fast ways to experience products and services, due to this innovation in technology.

Let's look at the systems operating in isolation from each other, responsibility, and skills set. We are going through a digital transformation and need all of these operations across various segments. Digital transformation redesigns organizational structures in many environments, so that they're collaborative. Technology can enhance performance and an organization's reach across the globe.

Cloud-native applications have four characteristics:

- **Cloud-native apps are composed of microservices**: Cloud-native apps adopt a microservices architecture, where each application is a collection of small services that can be operated independent of one another. Microservices are often owned by individual development teams that operate on their own schedules to develop, deploy, scale, and upgrade their services.
- **Cloud-native apps are packaged in containers**: Containers provide isolation contexts for microservices. They are highly accessible, scalable, easily portable from one environment to another, and fast to create or tear down, making them ideal for building and running applications that are composed of microservices.
- **Cloud-native apps are running in a continuous delivery model**: Software developers and IT operations teams collaborate under this model to build, test, and release software updates as soon as they are ready, without affecting end users or developers on other teams.
- **Cloud-native applications are dynamically managed in the cloud**: They are often built and run on modern cloud-native platforms, which offer easy scale-out and hardware decoupling, helping in terms of the orchestration, management, and automation of the application.

Automation with containers

Customers who have a substantial deployment of the VMware automation tools can easily drive agility and streamline the consumption of IT services. VMware will help customers to deliver both application and container services. This platform will extend the benefits of BOSH (autoscaling, self-healing, load balancing, and so on) to **container as a service** (**CaaS**) solutions (PKS). BOSH is an open source tool which helps in deployment and life cycle management of distributed systems. PKS is the only CaaS solution that can deliver fully managed Kubernetes clusters on premise, as well as a public **Infrastructure as a Service** (**IaaS**). This platform will also include **functions as a service** (**FaaS**). This will allow organizations to secure their abstraction planning, regardless of IaaS, by providing application deployment and runtime constructs on one platform. Because of this, we have to plan with various teams that are responsible for the app's rationalization and subsequent migration related to business and technical requirements, in detail.

The **Pivotal Cloud Foundry** (**PCF**) includes both **Pivotal Application Service** (**PAS**) and PKS as critical components. PAS is the cloud-native platform for deploying and operating modern applications. PKS enables customers and service providers to deliver a production-ready Kubernetes on a VMware SDDC and other public cloud environments.

As an example, if we have a system of 10 apps running in containers, those 10 apps will have 10 instances of isolated user spaces. Imagine that two applications are installed on the same operating system, but each needs a different version of that file. We can manage this condition with containers by using a common shared library file. Containers (more specifically, Linux containers) have been around for a while, and companies such as Oracle, HP, and IBM have been using containers for decades. However, Docker has become more popular among users.

Easy-to-use API and CLI tools for deploying apps that support namespace and resource limits reduce the complexity involved in deploying and managing containers. A container is a running instance of an image that runs a container. We need to download an image to use this. An image is a layered filesystem, where each layer has its own filesystem.

When you want to make changes, there's no need to crack open a single, large, monolithic application and shove new changes in. If we have to make changes, then we can just add them to a new layer.

Containers are doing to operating systems what VMs did to server hardware. Tools and organizational processes that are required to run and operate containers are generally not defined. VMware and Pivotal are in a unique position to solve these new challenges and become the **incumbent**. Containers virtualize the operating system by limiting the number of application dependencies that we need to install on the OS.

Container use cases

The following are the use cases for containers:

- **The need for a developer sandbox**: Developers often want access to a cluster of machines running a particular framework to build or quickly test and validate their applications. Provisioning such environments is time-consuming and often involves tickets and approvals. As a result, developers either request VMs and customize them to their needs, creating snowflake deployments, or they never give up these resources, because they are worried about obtaining a new one, which could be a tedious process.

- **Application repackaging**: Customers can take their existing applications and package them as a container. You don't need to refractor code or make changes to the architecture. While this forms the first logical step in a customer's containerization journey, it allows customers to derive certain benefits. Patching and maintaining the application is one primary benefit, where updates can be restricted to just the individual layers of the image. This ensures that other layers are intact, reducing errors and configuration issues that could arise.

- **Portability**: Packaging an application as a container enables portability. The container image, by virtue of packaging not just the application code but also all of its dependencies, is guaranteed to work anywhere. We are now able to move this image from a developer's laptop to your test/dev or production environment without having to invest time and resources in getting the target environments to exactly mimic the dev environment (or vice versa) as a result.

Challenges with containers

We focus on enabling developer code to instantiate all the resources developers need, even for legacy systems, to provide high levels of automation during the waterfall approach and to enable the customers to self-serve their resource requirements.

Traditional model uses traditional application architectures, tooling, and processes, where developers have to raise tickets for resources in cloud delivery models. Resources are provided through self-service. Cloud-native applications initiate these requests through code and provide service **infrastructure as code (IaC)**.

Code replaces the service tickets, and APIs play a critical role. A developer-ready infrastructure can be achieved with automated VMware SDDC tool by providing APIs that assist in running containers, such as OpenStack, PCF, and so on, as normal VM environments. Containers can be managed from existing operating models, since developers get all of the benefits. This is because IT has to manage the underlying resources in a consistent way.

The globally consistent infrastructure layer has benefits in the microservices architecture, as each service defines its relationship to other microservices. This can be broken if the underlying network is complex and doesn't have visibility. The network should be wide open to avoid this problem. Pivotal value VMware NSX and developer-ready infrastructure have the same code, which defines the relationships between microservices and instantiates secure micro-segmented network connectivity. Even serverless architectures can have an Internal Server Error message.

PKS on vSphere

vSphere cluster groups are sets of ESXi hosts that have a common compute entity; there are from 2 to 64 hosts per vSphere cluster when vSphere HA and DRS are activated at the cluster level. Resource pools are created under a vSphere cluster instance, and vCenter is able to manage multiple vSphere clusters instances, as there is no hard limit to the number of vSphere clusters. We can create different types of vSphere clusters, such as management clusters, compute clusters, and Edge clusters, since PKS fully leverages the vSphere cluster construct.

The following vSphere clusters are recommended in a typical PKS deployment:

- **Management cluster**:
  - **Hosted components**: vCenter, NSX manager, and controller VMs
  - vSphere HA and DRS enabled
  - ESXi hosts need to be NSX prepared, as micro-segmentation is enforced on the hosted VMs
- **Compute cluster(s)**:
  - **Hosted components**: Kubernetes (K8s) clusters nodes VMs
  - vSphere HA and DRS should be enabled, as BOSH will check whether DRS is turned on
  - ESXi hosts need to be NSX prepared
- **Edge cluster**:
  - **Hosted components**: NSX Edge Nodes VMs
  - vSphere HA and DRS enabled
  - ESXi hosts don't need to be NSX prepared

The PKS Management Plane can reside on the management cluster or compute cluster, depending on the selected design scenario. PKS Management Plane VMs are the Ops Manager, BOSH, the PKS control plane, and Harbor.

The PKS data plane (or compute plane) will only reside in a compute cluster. Up to three K8s master nodes and 50 worker nodes are allowed per K8s cluster, and many K8s clusters can be created in the same PKS environment.

The K8s master node also hosts the etcd component. vSphere DRS and HA must be enabled on the vSphere compute cluster. vSphere **DRS Automation** has to be set to **Partially Automated** or **Fully Automated**. vSphere HA is set with **Host failure = Restart VMs**.

The following are the compute and storage requirements for the PKS component:

PKS Component	CPU	RAM (GB)	Storage (GB)
Ops Manager	1	8	HD1: 160
PKS Control Plane VM	2	8	HD1: 3 HD2: 16 HD3: 10
BOSH	2	8	HD1: 3 HD2: 50 HD3: 50
Harbor	2	8	HD1: 3 HD2: 64 HD3: 30
K8s master node	Configurable per PKS plan	Configurable per PKS plan	Ephemeral disk: 8 to 256 GB Persistent disk: 1 GB to 32 TB (Configurable per PKS plan)
K8s worker node	Configurable per PKS plan	Configurable per PKS plan	Ephemeral disk: 8 to 256 GB Persistent disk: 1 GB to 32 TB (Configurable per PKS plan)

PKS availability zone

PKS supports the concept of an **availability zone (AZ)**, that is, *AZ = vSphere cluster + resource pool*. The AZ dictates the placement of a VM that's created by BOSH/PKS into the corresponding vSphere cluster/resource pool.

There are two types of AZ:

- **Management AZ**: Used for BOSH, PKS control plane, and Harbor VMs
- **Compute AZ**: Used for K8s master and worker node VMs

PKS supports multiple compute availability zones, and each PKS plan supports up to three distinct ones. Each K8s master node (for a max of three) will land in one separate AZ. K8s worker nodes will be dispatched across the three zones.

Three PKS plans are allowed (for a total of nine distinct compute zones). Each PKS plan can use the same three zones or a completely different set of three AZs. An AZ is commonly used to set the locality of a VM against different locations; or, we can say that AZ = physical rack (or room).

Following are the PKS design topologies:

- **Physical topologies (integration with vSphere)**: Multiple topologies can be deployed with PKS/NSX-T integration
- **PKS Management Plane in the management cluster**: Multi-compute clusters:
    - The PKS Management Plane is hosted in a management cluster and connected to a DVS virtual switch
    - Multiple compute clusters, to support K8s cluster nodes
    - Each AZ is mapped to a different vSphere cluster (with 1:1 mapping between the AZ and vSphere cluster).
    - **AZ can represent a physical location**: Each compute cluster can be in a dedicated rack or room
- **PKS Management Plane in the management cluster for a single compute cluster**:
    - The PKS Management Plane is hosted in a management cluster and connected to a DVS virtual switch
    - Single Compute Clusters to support K8s cluster nodes
    - Each AZ is mapped to a unique vSphere cluster/different resource pool
    - AZs can be used to limit the CPU/memory per PKS plan

- **PKS Management Plane in the compute cluster for multi-compute clusters**:
  - The PKS Management Plane is hosted in a compute cluster and connected to an NSX-T logical switch
  - Multiple compute clusters, to support K8s cluster nodes
  - Each AZ is mapped to a different vSphere cluster (with 1:1 mapping between AZs and vSphere clusters)
  - **An AZ can represent a physical location**: Each compute cluster can be in a dedicated rack or room
- **PKS Management Plane in a compute cluster, or a single compute cluster**:
  - The PKS Management Plane is hosted in a compute cluster and connected to an NSX-T logical switch
  - Single compute clusters, to support K8s cluster nodes
  - Each AZ is mapped to a unique vSphere cluster/different resource pool:
  - An AZ can be used to the limit CPU/memory per PKS plan
- **PKS AZ (Single/multiple Compute and Management Clusters) design model**:
  - **PKS AZ with single vSphere compute cluster**: By default, there is no guarantee that K8s master nodes land on different ESXi hosts. A workaround is to create a DRS affinity rule on the vSphere Compute Cluster.
  - **Type**: Separate VMs.
  - **Members**: All K8s master node VMs.
  - The vSphere cluster must have a minimum of three ESXi hosts (this is a vSAN prerequisite). However, to protect against one host failure (and to make sure that the DRS affinity rule will operate properly), a recommendation is to start with four ESXi hosts in the cluster.
  - NSX-T 2.2 supports all types of traffic on N-VDS. This means that an ESXi host in the compute cluster can start with two physical NICs.

The minimum vSphere cluster configuration for a production environment is as follows:

- **Management cluster**:
  - **Non-vSAN**: Min hosts: Two
  - **vSAN**: Min hosts: Three (To guarantee data protection for vSAN objects, you must have two replicas and one witness)

- **Compute cluster(s)**:
    - **Single compute cluster topology**:
        - **Non-vSAN**: Min hosts: Three (To guarantee one K8s master node VM per ESXi host by using a DRS affinity rule)
        - **vSAN**: Min hosts: Three (To guarantee data protection for vSAN objects, you must have two replicas and one witness)
    - **Multiple compute clusters topology**:
        - **Non-vSAN**: Min hosts: Two per AZ, with three AZs in total (The K8s master node is instantiated across different compute clusters. Each compute cluster is 1:1 mapped with one AZ)
        - **vSAN**: Min hosts: Three per AZ, with three AZs in total (To guarantee data protection for vSAN objects, you must use two replicas and one witness)
- **Edge Cluster**:
    - **Non-vSAN**: Min hosts: Two.
    - **vSAN**: Min hosts: Three (To guarantee data protection for vSAN objects, you must use two replicas and one witness.) Note: An Edge Cluster can be collapsed with a compute cluster (or even a management cluster) if you need to lower the number of starting ESXi hosts.

The following table gives information about PKS/NSX-T networks:

Network	Description	CIDR
PKS Management Network	• This network hosts the Ops Manager, BOSH, the PKS control plane, and Harbor • Can be co-located with vCenter, NSX-T management, and the control plane, if desired • PKS Management Network is routable or non-routable, depending on NO-NAT or NAT topology	192.168.1.0/28 (for instance) CIDR with /28 is a good starting point.

Nodes IP Block	• This block will be carved to create a network that will host K8s cluster node VMs • Each K8s cluster will be allocated a /24 portion of the block • The nodes IP block is routable or non-routable, depending on NO-NAT or NAT topology	Depends on the NAT or NO-NAT topology. 172.23.0.0/16 (for instance)
Pods IP Block	• This block will be carved to create a network that will host K8s pods belonging to the same K8s namespace • Each k8s namespace will be allocated a /24 portion of the block • The pods IP block is always non-routable	172.16.0.0/16 (for instance)

Floating IP Pool	• This pool will be used for two purposes:
	  ○ SNAT rules for each K8s namespace on T0 (for pods networking)
	  ○ LB virtual servers IP allocation
	• The floating IP pool is always routable
		192.168.20.2-192.168.20.254 (for instance)

CIDR for nodes IP block:

- Must be unique in the case of a routable scenario (NO-NAT topology)
- Can be duplicated in the case of a non-routable scenario (NAT topology)

The `172.17.0.0/16` CIDR must not be used in all cases, as Docker on the K8s worker node is using the subnet.

If PKS is deployed with Harbor, then the following CIDR must not be used, as Harbor is leveraging it for its internal Docker bridges:

```
172.18.0.0/16 ;172.19.0.0/16 ;172.20.0.0/16 ;172.21.0.0/16 ;172.22.0.0/16
```

Each K8s cluster uses the following IP block for Kubernetes services, so avoid using it for a nodes IP block: `10.100.200.0/24`.

PKS/NSX-T logical topologies

PKS supports two types of topologies when it's integrated with NSX-T. NAT and NO-NAT topology selection is done in the **PKS tile | Networking** section. NAT topology is the default, but you can uncheck NAT mode to go with the NO-NAT topology. The NAT and NO-NAT terminology essentially applies to the PKS Management Network and the K8s cluster nodes network (that is, whether to use routable subnets). Irrespective of the NAT or NO-NAT topology, the same procedure is used to access the K8s API.

A virtual server on the NSX-T LB instance that's allocated to the K8s cluster is created for the following purpose:

- One IP from the PKS Floating IP Pool is extracted (`1x.x0.1x.1xx` here), and the port is `8443`
- The same IP address is shown from the output of the `pks cluster <cluster name>` command

Following are the objectives with different NAT topologies:

- **NAT topology**: For customers with a limited amount of available routable IP addresses in their DC and who want to automate PKS deployment using a concourse pipeline (for instance)
- **NO-NAT topology**: For customers who avoid NAT as NATs break full path visibility and having plenty of routable IP address resources

Use cases with different configurations

The following are the use cases with different configurations:

- Access to PKS Management Plane components (Ops Manager, BOSH, PKS control plane VM, Harbor) from the corporate network:
    - **NO-NAT topology**: No action is required as those components use routable IP addresses
    - **NAT topology**: User needs to create DNAT rules on T0
- Access to K8s API (using a kubectl CLI, for instance):
    - **NO-NAT topology**: 1 virtual server (on the NSX-T LB instance that's dedicated to the K8s cluster) is automatically created using 1 routable IP from the PKS Floating IP block
    - **NAT topology**: The user needs to point to this IP to access K8s API

- One virtual server (on the NSX-T LB instance that's dedicated to the K8s cluster) is automatically created using one routable IP from the PKS floating IP block:
    - **NO-NAT topology**: The user needs to point to this IP to access the K8s API
    - **NAT topology**: The user needs access to the K8s nodes VM (like BOSH SSH, for instance)
- Components using routable IP addresses:
    - **NO-NAT topology**: The user needs to SSH to the Ops Manager to perform BOSH commands against the K8s nodes VM
    - **NAT topology**: An alternative is to install a jumpbox server on the same subnet, instead of the PKS Management Plane components
- Using the K8s nodes VM to access the corporate network (or internet):
    - **NO-NAT topology**: No action is required, as those components use routable IP addresses
    - **NAT topology**: PKS automatically creates a SNAT rule on T0 for each K8s cluster, using one IP address from the PKS Floating IP Pool

PKS and NSX-T Edge Nodes and Edge Cluster

PKS only supports NSX-T Edge Node VM configurations that are large in size. PKS only supports one Edge Cluster instance of T0 (8 vCPU, 16 GB RAM). The T0 router must be configured in Active/Standby mode, as SNAT rules will be applied there by PKS. An NSX-T Edge Cluster can contain up to eight Edge **Transport Nodes** (TN). You can add new Edge Nodes (up to eight) in the Edge Cluster to increase the overall capacity (LB, for instance) and provide scalability to the NSX-T Edge Cluster. You can use two different Edge Nodes for the T0 uplinks IP addresses (two IPs in total) to provide HA to NSX-T T0 in an Edge Cluster. We should enable HA VIP on T0 so that it's always operational, even if one T0 uplink is down. The physical router will only interoperate with the T0 HA VIP.

The following are the NSX-T and load balancer scale numbers:

	LB small		LB medium		LB large		Pool members	
NSX-T release	2.1	2.2	2.1	2.2	2.1	2.2	2.1	2.2
Edge VM: Small	-	-	-	-	-	-	-	-
Edge VM: Medium	1	1	-	-	-	-	30	30
Edge VM: Large	4	40	1	1	-	-	120	1,200
Edge: Bare Metal	100	750	10	100	1	1	3,000	22,500

PKS and NSX-T communications

Multiple PKS components need to communicate with the NSX-T manager. A PKS control plane VM using an NSX-T superuser principal identity certificate as an authentication mechanism is needed to create a T1/LS for each K8s cluster node network and an LB instance for each K8s cluster.

BOSH uses credentials as an authentication mechanism to tag all of a VM's logical ports with a special BOSH ID tag and NCP pod. It uses the NSX-T superuser principal identity certificate as an authentication mechanism to create T1/LS for each namespace, a SNAT rule on T0 for each namespace, and an LB virtual server for each K8s service of the type LB.

The following is a list of the NSX-T objects that are created, for each K8s cluster.

When a new K8s cluster is created, the following NSX-T objects are created by default:

- **NSX-T LS**:
    - One LS for K8s master and worker nodes
    - One LS for each K8s namespace, that is, kube-public, kube-system, and pks-infrastructure
    - One LS for the NSX-T LB associated with the K8s cluster
- **NSX-T T1**:
    - One T1 for K8s master and worker nodes (called cluster-router)
    - One T1 for each K8s namespace (default, kube-public, kube-system, and pks-infrastructure)
    - One T1 for the NSX-T LB associated with the K8s cluster
- **NSX-T LB**:
    - One NSX-T LB small instance, containing the following objects:
        - One virtual server to access the K8s control plane API (with port 8443)
        - One server pool containing the three K8s master nodes
        - One virtual server for the ingress controller (HTTP)
        - One virtual server for the ingress controller (HTTPS)
        - Each virtual server is allocated an IP address derived from the PKS Floating IP Pool

When a new K8s cluster is created, the following NSX-T objects are created, by default:

- **NSX-T DDI/IPAM**: A /24 subnet from the nodes IP block will be extracted and allocated for the K8s master and worker nodes.
- **NSX-T DDI/IPAM**: A /24 subnet from the PODs IP Block will be extracted and allocated for each K8s namespace (default, kube-public, kube-system, and pks-infrastructure).
  - **NSX-T T0 router**:
    - One SNAT rule created for each K8s namespace (default, kube-public, kube-system, pks-infrastructure), using one IP from the Floating IP Pool as the translated IP address.
    - One SNAT rule created for each K8s cluster (in the case that NAT topology is used), using 1 IP from the Floating IP Pool as the translated IP address. The K8s cluster subnet is derived from the nodes IP block, using a /24 netmask.
  - **NSX-T DFW**:
    - One DFW rule for kubernetes-dashboard: Source=K8s worker node (hosting the dashboard POD/Destination= dashboard POD IP/Port: TCP/8443/Action: allow
    - One DFW rule for kube-dns: Source=K8s worker node (hosting the DNS POD)/ Destination = DNS POD IP/Port: TCP/8081 and TCP/10054/Action: allow

Storage for K8s cluster node VMs

You can provide storage for K8s PODs by using **persistent volumes** (**PV**). A PV can be mapped to a **virtual machine disk** (**VMDK**) file on vSphere by using the **vCP** (short for **Cloud Provider**) plugin. A VMDK file will then be attached to the worker node VM as a disk. We can then POD mount the volume from that disk.

Datastores

The following is a table of information regarding datastores:

Deployment topology/storage technology	vSAN datastores	VMFS over NFS/iSCSI/FC datastores
Single vSphere compute cluster (single AZ, or multiple AZs if using RPs) with a datastore local to a single vSphere compute cluster	• **Static PV provisioning**: Yes • **Dynamic PV provisioning**: Yes	• **Static PV provisioning**: Yes • **Dynamic PV provisioning**: Yes
Multi-vSphere compute clusters (multiple AZs) with datastore(s) local to each vSphere compute cluster	• **Static PV provisioning**: No* • **Dynamic PV provisioning**: No*	• **Static PV provisioning**: No* • **Dynamic PV provisioning**: No*
Multi-vSphere compute clusters (multiple AZs) with datastore(s) shared across all vSphere compute clusters	• N/A • vSAN does not support shared datastores across vSphere clusters	• **Static PV provisioning**: Yes • **Dynamic PV provisioning**: Yes

Following are the steps to provision Static PV:

1. Manually create a VMDK file
2. Create a PV referencing the aforementioned VMDK file
3. Create a PVC
4. Deploy a stateful POD or StatefulSets by using a reference to the PVC

Following are the steps for Dynamic PV provisioning:

1. Create a PVC (vCP K8s storage plugin; a hatchway will automatically create PV and VMDK files)
2. Deploy stateful POD or StatefulSets using a reference to PVC

The following are some vSAN considerations in regards to PKS/NSX-T:

- Using vSAN, a vSphere cluster must start with a minimum of three ESXi hosts to guarantee data protection (in this case, for RAID1 with failure to tolerate set to 1)
- A PKS AZ does not map with the vSAN fault domain
- A PKS with a single compute cluster is currently supported with vSAN (all ESXi hosts are located in the same site)
- **Caution**: A PKS with a vSAN stretched cluster is not a supported configuration, as of right now (no mapping of AZs with the vSAN fault domain)

- A PKS with multiple compute clusters is not a supported configuration with a vSAN-only datastore
- Master and worker nodes can be created across the different ESXi clusters (BOSH tile allows you to specify multiple persistent and ephemeral datastores for the VMs)
- PV VMDK disks are created for only one vSAN datastore (and no replication across the different vSAN datastores will be performed automatically)

Data centers maintain independent PKS instances, NSX deployments, Kubernetes (K8s) clusters, and vSphere infrastructures. A **Global Server Load Balancer** (**GSLB**), which is available through a third party, monitors the availability of the sites' K8s cluster API and PKS controller API. Operations and development direct API requests to the GSLB virtual server URL for creating and managing K8s clusters and deploying apps. Manually deployed apps (through kubectl, for instance) are not automatically replicated between environments and need to be redeployed following a failover to site B.

You can configure a CI/CD automation server to execute build pipelines against the K8s' URL in each environment or single builds against the GSLB virtual server URL. Harbor policy based replication, a built-in feature, manages cloning images to the standby location. You can replicate the datastore(s) between environments to support PV. Following a site A failure, the pods are redeployed at site B, mounting the original persistent volume's VMDK file.

Summary

There is a new IT approach called cloud-native behind this digitalization trend, which is one of the driving forces of business digitalization. The cloud-native methodology allows enterprises to greatly increase developer productivity, allowing them to deliver new apps and services to the market much more quickly than before; they can therefore improve customer experience and satisfaction. If adopted successfully, the cloud-native methodology can also help to cut operations and infrastructure costs, as well as to enhance app security.

In the next chapter, Chapter 14, *High Performance Computing for Machine Learning,* you will learn about the specific aspects of virtualization that can enhance the productivity of a **high-performance computing** (**HPC**) environment. We will explore the capabilities which are enabled by VMware vSphere to meet the requirements for researching computing, academic, scientific, and engineering HPC workloads.

High-Performance Computing 14

In this chapter, we will learn about the specific aspects of virtualization that can enhance the productivity of a **High Performance Computing** (**HPC**) environment. We will focus on the capabilities provided by VMware vSphere, and how virtualization improves scientific productivity.

We will explore vSphere features, such as **Single Root I/O Virtualization** (**SR-IOV**), **remote direct memory access** (**RDMA**), and vGPU, to architect and meet the requirements for research, computing, academic, scientific, and engineering workloads.

This chapter covers the following topics:

- Virtualizing HPC applications
- Multi-tenancy with guaranteed resources

Technical requirements

You can download vSphere Scale-Out from `https://my.vmware.com/en/web/vmware/info/slug/datacenter_cloud_infrastructure/vmware_vsphere/6_7`.

Virtualizing HPC applications

This chapter describes our work at VMware to support HPC applications. The first section describes in detail many of the values identified by customers of using virtualization in HPC environments. The second section shows a few examples of how virtualization is deployed in an HPC environment, and the third discusses various aspects of performance, starting with an examination of some core aspects of performance, and then turning to throughput applications and performance for parallel-distributed **Message Passing Interface** (**MPI**) applications. It also includes pointers to several technical publications that will be of interest to those considering virtualizing their HPC workloads.

The majority of HPC systems are clusters, which are aggregations of compute nodes connected via some interconnect, such as Ethernet or **InfiniBand** (**IB**). Clusters can range in size from a small handful of nodes to tens of thousands of nodes. HPC clusters exist to run HPC jobs, and the placement of those jobs in the cluster is handled by a **distributed resource manager** (**DRM**). DRM is the middleware that provides the ability for HPC users to launch their HPC jobs onto an HPC cluster in a load-balanced fashion.

Users typically use command-line interfaces to specify the characteristics of the job or jobs they want to run, the DRM then enqueues those requests and schedules the jobs to run on the least loaded, appropriately configured nodes in the cluster. There are many DRMs available, both open source and commercial. Examples include Grid Engine (Univa), LSF (IBM), Torque, **Portable Batch System** (**PBS**), and Slurm. DRMs are also called batch schedulers. IB is a high-bandwidth, low-latency interconnect, commonly used in HPC environments to boost the performance of code/applications/jobs and to increase filesystem performance. IB is not Ethernet, it does not use TCP or any of the standard networking stack, and it is currently usable in a virtual environment only via VM direct path I/O (passthrough mode).

The purpose of this chapter is not to explain how virtualization works. x86 virtualization has evolved from its invention at Stanford in the late 1990s using a purely software-based approach to the current situation in which both Intel and AMD have added successively more hardware support for virtualization, such as CPU, memory, and I/O. These hardware enhancements, along with increasingly sophisticated virtualization software, have greatly improved the performance for an ever-growing number of workloads. This is an important point to make because HPC people have often heard that the performance of HPC applications is very poor when they get virtualized with some cases but run extremely well, even very close to native performance, in most of the cases. Massive consolidation isn't appropriate for HPC environments, so the values of virtualization for HPC can be utilized elsewhere.

We will now learn the use cases for virtualization in HPC that have been identified by customers and through our own research. Because HPC includes such a wide variety of workloads and environments, some of these will resonate more with specific customers than others. HPC clusters host a single, standard OS and application stack across all hosts as uniformity enables us to schedule jobs easily by limiting the options in these environments for different use cases, such as multiple user groups needing to be served from a single shared resource. Because these traditional clusters can't satisfy the needs of multiple groups, they encourage the creation of specialized *islands of compute* scattered across an organization, which is inefficient and expensive.

Multi-tenancy with guaranteed resources

Customers want to utilize existing investments in hardware and software such as in hypervisors or physical hardware along with the feasibility to provision directly into the public cloud. We can address this landscape, along with related services, through a service-automation solution that can manage across many platforms and many clouds. This solution can automate all manual processes of the provisioning services by abstracting the core tasks with its automation tool and then managing the access and control of these automations. Automation is very useful only if we link it with policy. Policy-based control and governance provides us with the ability to control the application of the automations that drive the cloud solution. The cloud service portal and catalog give end users self-service, on-demand access to authorized services.

All modern x86 systems are **non-uniform memory access** (**NUMA**) systems, which means that memory is attached directly to individual CPU sockets in the system. This means that access to memory from the local socket can be very fast, but access to memory that is attached to another socket will be slower because the request and data have to transit the communication pathway between the sockets. That's why it is called non-uniform memory access. Sometimes workloads can run a little faster in virtual environments than on bare metal. This is true especially of throughput workloads and is often the result of NUMA effects. The point isn't so much that virtualized can run faster than bare metal, but that virtualized's performance can be nearly identical to the bare-metal performance for some HPC workloads. Live migration can be used to increase the efficiency and flexibility of HPC environments. It can also be used to increase resiliency. In traditional bare-metal HPC environments, jobs are placed statically. Consider the scenario in which Application C must be scheduled, but there is currently no node with enough resources available to run it.

There are a two choices in a bare-metal environment:

- Application C can wait in the queue until Application A or B finishes
- Application A or B could be killed to make room for Application C

Either of these options reduces the cluster's job throughput. And in the case of killing jobs, the loss of work can be very expensive if the running applications are costly Independent Software Vendors' application. The solution in the virtual environment is to use live migration to move the workload to make room for Application C. This approach is relevant primarily in environments where these jobs are relatively long-running.

Let's look at another use of live migration: to increase overall throughput on a cluster. Consider the bare-metal environment with two jobs running. As the third job is started, it may consume more memory than expected by the user. This will bound other jobs on the system to swap, which will affect the overall performance of these jobs in negative way. **Dynamic Resource Scheduler** (**DRS**) can address these kind of situations in a virtual environment: as the third job starts to consume all available memory, DRS can shift the overloaded VM to another machine with few workloads and help the jobs to continue running with the desired performance.

This lack of guaranteed resource use for specific groups or departments is another barrier to the centralization of bare-metal environments. For example, an owner of a large island of compute will often be unwilling to donate their hardware resources to a shared pool if they cannot be guaranteed access to at least those resources when required. DRS provides the ability to address this need. Snapshots can be used to save the state of a running VM to protect against hardware failures; when a machine fails, the VM is restored and the application continues the execution from the point at which the snapshot was taken.

This is similar in concept to checkpoint mechanisms used in HPC, except that, rather than extracting the state of a process from a running OS, which is often subject to various limitations, we take advantage of the clean abstract that exists between the VM and the underlying virtual platform. A more advanced resiliency scheme (Proactive HA Policy) would use telemetry from the underlying system to predict upcoming hardware failures and then proactively migrate the workload from the questionable host to avoid application interruption. Examples include a fan failure on a system running an important job or an increase in the rate of detected soft memory errors, which could indicate increased probability of an upcoming hard memory error.

While such an approach would not likely remove the need for checkpointing, it may reduce the need. Less frequent checkpoint operations and less frequent restorations from checkpoints can increase overall job throughput on the cluster.

Critical use case – unification

The desire of some administrators is to treat their HPC jobs as *just another workload* and move away from a partially virtual and partially physical infrastructure to an all-virtual infrastructure with more flexibility and manageability. This is a simple example of a deployment done by one of our financial services customers. In this case, the central IT department created a shared compute resource that could rent out virtual clusters to the different lines of business within the organization. Groups that need access to a cluster for some period of time would receive a set of VMs rather than a physical machine to be used for some specified time period.

The benefits to the organization are as follows:

- **Lines-of-business** (**LOBs**) get the resources they need when they need them
- Clusters and the cluster nodes can be sized to the LOBs' application requirements (for example, most process runs consume only a single CPU per job; they are serial (not parallel) jobs)
- A central IT team can extract maximum from the available hardware
- Hardware is flexible enough to be shared among various jobs with security compliance between users/workloads
- Relative priorities between LOBs can be enforced by policy to ensure (for example) that groups with hard deadlines receive a higher *fairshare* of the underlying hardware resources:

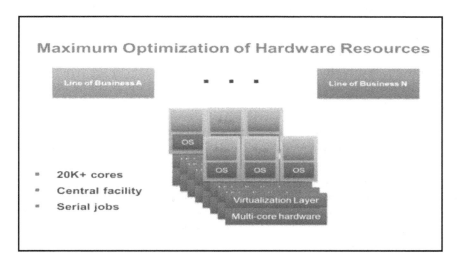

There are certain benefits of configuring platform-level (and sometimes guest-level) tuning in order to achieve best performance for HPC applications on vSphere. Tuning is needed because HPC applications (unlike most Enterprise applications) are latency-sensitive. The sensitivity might be in storage, in networking, or in the communication interconnect.

While VMware's goal is excellent out-of-the-box performance for any application, the HPC workloads are relatively new to us, so some tuning is required. We have begun setting some of these tunables automatically by configuring vCenter advanced VM parameters where we intend to run latency-sensitive workloads in a VM. This auto-tuning will become more comprehensive over time.

The customer's initial **Network Filesystem Storage** (**NFS**) benchmark experience pointed directly to storage latencies in some cases. By tuning the networking stack that underlies any NFS data transfers, we were able to bring application performance directly in line, as seen in bare-metal environments. The network is by default tuned for throughput by moving large amounts of data through the network efficiently in an enterprise environment. This means that, as data packets arrive, they may not be processed immediately.

Typically, a small number of messages are allowed to accumulate before the system wakes up and processes the entire batch. This reduces the load on the CPU, but it slows down message delivery. It makes much more sense to spend more CPU cycles to process the packets promptly as each packet arrives in situations where the arrival of the data is a gating factor on performance. This is often the case with HPC workloads. Both the virtual and physical network devices should have coalescing turned off to make this change.

There is another level of coalescing, which happens at a higher level in the **transmission control protocol** (**TCP**) stack (disable **Large Receive Offload** (**LRO**) within the guest)—it should be turned off. We evaluate results of some experiments to see whether the additional level of memory abstraction which is introduced by virtualization, has any effect on HPC application performance or not.

The special circumstance is applications that have little or no spatial data locality. This includes applications that can't effectively use their caches because they don't access memory in regular ways, such as the random-access benchmark. It doesn't affect except in a special circumstance where the overhead can be greatly reduced by using large pages within the guest operating system. Turning off EPT (RVI on AMD) and reverting to a software-based page-table approach can also help in this special circumstance. Created by the **National Security Agency** (**NSA**), it has no locality even updating random memory locations one after another.

These workloads incur a very large number of **translation look-aside buffer** (**TLB**) misses. Because misses in this page-table cache are frequent, the application can be slowed down if that operation is slow. Indeed, it turns out that the EPT and RVI technologies created by Intel and RVI, although implemented in hardware, are slower at handling TLB misses than the older *shadow page table* approach developed by VMware. TLB misses can be reduced by using larger pages, so turning off EPT or RVI can help in these situations.

The fact is that EPT and RVI perform very well in the vast majority of cases, but it pays to keep the issue in mind. **High-performance LINPACK** (**HPL**) uses caches very nicely like other HPC applications and get better performance. We can see that performance is uniformly excellent for this application type.

This is an important aspect of our virtualization platform for HPC customers who run applications that require large numbers of threads, and, therefore, VMs that would span multiple CPU sockets within a host.

ESXi has been *NUMA-aware* for many releases, which means that when it runs a VM, it is careful to place the executing thread on the same socket that is hosting the VM's memory so all memory accesses are local. When a VM spans the two sockets, we distribute similar threads across both sockets and then allocate memory on the local socket to deliver the best performance. So, even if the VM were big enough to span multiple sockets, it would not see the NUMA-ness of the underlying hardware. We introduced vNUMA to make the NUMA topology visible to the guest OS, which can then make its own optimizations based on this information. This can matter a lot from a performance perspective.

High-performance computing cluster performances

Standard Performance Evaluation Corporation OpenMP (**SPECOMP**) is a well known HPC benchmark suite for multi-threaded applications running on multiple nodes. Each benchmark (for example, Swim) is listed along with the *x* axis.

For each benchmark, there are three pairs of comparisons: one for a 16-vCPU VM, one for a 32-vCPU VM, and one for a 64-way VM. Default-16 means performance for a 16-way VM with no vNUMA support and vNUMA-16 means the same 16-way VM, but with vNUMA enabled.

Ratio to Native, lower is better:

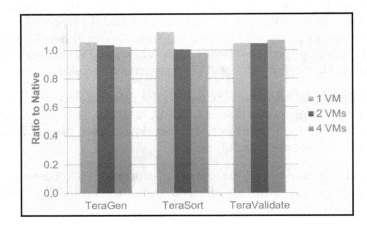

The chart shows run-times, so lower is better. We can see significant run-time drops in virtually all cases when moving from default to vNUMA. This is a hugely important feature for HPC users with a need for wide VMs. These charts show published performance results for a variety of life sciences workloads running on ESXi.

They show that these throughput-oriented applications run with generally under a 5% penalty when virtualized. More recent reports from customers indicate that this entire class of applications (throughput), which includes not just life sciences, but financial services, **electronic design automation** (**EDA**) chip designers, and digital content creation (movie rendering, and so on), run with well under a 5% performance degradation. Platform tuning, not application tuning, is required to achieve these results.

We have results reported by one of EDA (chip designer) customers who ran first a single instance of one of their EDA jobs on a bare-metal Linux node. They then ran the same Linux and the same job on ESXi and compared the results. They saw a 6% performance degradation. We believe this would be lower with additional platform tuning.

They then ran the second test with four instances of the application running in a single Linux instance versus four VMs running the same jobs. So, we have the same workload running in both cases. In this configuration, they discovered that the virtual jobs completed 2% sooner than the bare-metal jobs.

HPCC performance ratios (lower is better):

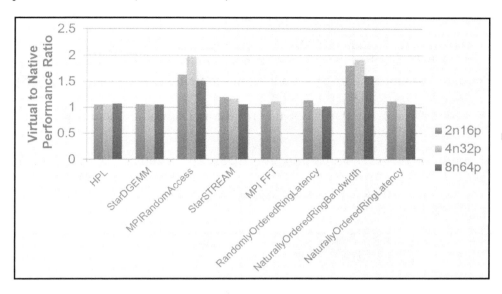

This speedup usually results from a NUMA effect and an OS scheduling effect. The Linux instance must do resource balancing between the four job instances and it must also handle the NUMA issues related to this being a multi-socket system.

Virtualization will help us with the following advantages:

- Each Linux instance must handle only one job
- Because of the ESXi scheduler's NUMA awareness, each VM would be scheduled onto a socket so none of the Linux instances needs to suffer the potential inefficiencies of dealing with NUMA issues

We don't have to worry about multiple Linux instances and VMs consuming more memory: **transparent page sharing** (**TPS**) can mitigate this as the hypervisor will find common pages between VMs and share them where possible.

A standard Hadoop architecture

Let's understand a standard Hadoop architecture:

- **Hadoop File System** (**HDFS**): A distributed filesystem instantiated across a set of local disks attached to the compute nodes in the Hadoop cluster
- **Map**: The embarrassingly parallel computation that is applied to every chunk of data read from HDFS (in parallel)
- **Reduce**: The phase that takes map results and combines them to perform the final computation

The final results are typically stored back into HDFS. The benefits of Serengeti (open source project) provide ease of provisioning, multi-tenancy, and flexibility to scale up or out. BDE allows Serengeti to be triggered from a vRealize blueprint, making it easy to self-provision a Hadoop cluster of a given size:

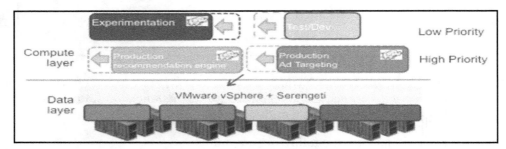

The preceding diagram shows a virtualized Hadoop environment. Local disks are made available as VMDKs to the guest, Map, and Reduce tasks running in VMs on each Hadoop cluster node.

The next generation of our approach is one in which there are two types of VMs: Compute nodes and Data nodes. The Data node is responsible for managing the physical disks attached to the host and for HDFS. The Compute nodes run the Map and Reduce tasks. Communication between the Compute node and Data node happens through fast VM-VM communication.

Standard tests

These tests were run on a 32-node (host) cluster with local disks and 10 Gigabit Ethernet interconnect. The most important point is that four configurations were run, each solving the same problem:

- **Configuration 1**: A 32-host physical cluster
- **Configuration 2**: A 32-VM virtual cluster
- **Configuration 3**: A 64-VM virtual cluster (two VMs per host, each using half the hardware)
- **Configuration 4**: A 128-VM virtual cluster (four VMs per host, with two on each socket, each with one quarter of the hardware resources)

We used common benchmarks to evaluate various aspects of Hadoop performance. Here is the ratio of virtual run-time to native/physical/bare-metal run-time:

- **TeraGen**: 6%, 4%, 3%
- **TeraSort**: 13%, 1%, -1%
- **TeraValidate**: 5%, 5%, 7%

Generally, breaking the problem into smaller pieces and running more VMs results in performance closer to native.

There is a wide range of latency sensitivities found in MPI applications. The application on the **Particle Mesh Ewald Molecular Dynamics (PMEMD)** is a molecular dynamics code with more than 40% MPI data transfers involving messages that are a single byte long. Contrast this with **Lattice Boltzmann Magneto-Hydrodynamics (LBMHD)** code, all of whose messages are greater than 1 MB in size. The first application is critically sensitive to interconnect latencies, while the second is insensitive and is instead bandwidth-bound.

Each application has its own communication patterns about its process flow with each other. The process/processor number is shown on both the x and y axis. The darker the data point at (x, y), the more data is transferred between the x and y processes. The PMEMD pattern shows that each process communicates across the range of available processes, but significantly more communication happens with nearby/neighbor processes. There are algorithms where the displayed pattern would be a dark expanse across the entire pattern, indicating intense communication between all processes.

It is common in HPC bare-metal environments to bypass the kernel to get optimum bandwidth with lowest latency, as this is important for many MPI applications. Rather than using a standard TCP networking stack (which adds overhead), **remote direct memory access** (**RDMA**) devices, such as IB, allow transfers to be initiated directly to and from the application without using the host CPU to transfer the data:

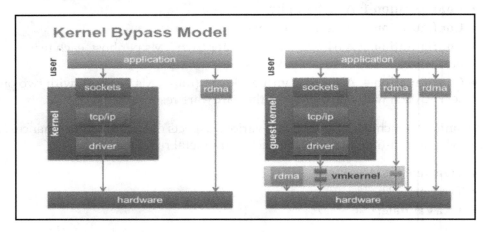

We can opt for the analog way for our virtual environment. We can make the hardware device, such as IB, directly visible to the guest (rightmost **rdma** box in the preceding diagram) using the VM direct path I/O. It will allow the application to get direct access to the hardware, as in the bare-metal case, by using ESXi. The **rdma** box to the left of the VM direct path I/O case represents ongoing work within VMware to develop a vRDMA device, which is a paravirtualized RDMA device.

This device will continue to allow direct application hardware access for data transfers, while also continuing to support the ability to perform snapshots and to use vMotion. This represents ongoing work that will make the RDMA approach available for use by ESXi itself and by ESXi services such as vMotion, vSAN, and FT. We've shown very large performance gains for vMotion using an RDMA transport.

Intel tested a variety of HPC benchmarks

High-performance computing cluster (HPCC):

HPC challenge benchmarks are combination of multiple benchmarks to test various attributes along with their performance of HPC systems. STAR-CD is a **computational fluid dynamics (CFD)** code used for in-cylinder analysis. These are **Message Passing Interface (MPI)** codes responsible for multi-process running on multiple nodes. The results are for a small cluster in several configurations: 2-node, 16 processes; 4-node, 32 processes; 8-node, 64 processes (*node* means *host* in HPC circles). We show excellent parity with native, even for this old configuration. Intel should turn off EPT or use large page sizes for better MPIRandomAccess. We have not explored naturally-ordered ring bandwidth to understand the issue there.

HPCC represents a set application, such as benchmarks over a range of HPC needs. It is very positive that we do so well, even if this is admittedly at very low scale. Before we look at the STAR-CD results, it is useful to look at the messaging characteristics of the application.

MPI applications perform two kinds of communication between processes:

- **P2P**: Individual processes send or receive data from another process
- **Collective operations**: Many processes participate together to transfer data in one of a set of patterns

This majority of P2P messages exchanged by STAR-CD are in the 1 KB - 8 KB range. We would characterize these as medium-sized messages. As the node count is increased, more of these messages move into the 128 B-1 KB range. This means that interconnect latency becomes more of a factor as the number of nodes increases. For collective operations, there is a very clear latency-sensitivity in Star-CD since virtually all messages fall into the 0 - 128 B range.

The *y* axes on these two charts are different. Star-CD uses P2P messages much more often than collectives. Thus, while the collective operations are very latency-sensitive, the overall effect of latency overheads may be reduced since the collectives don't represent the majority of messages transferred by Star-CD. The results show a 15% slowdown running an A-class model (a Mercedes car body) with STAR-CD using 8 nodes and 32 processes on 2-socket nodes.

This is a significant slowdown for many HPC users, which is why we continue to work on characterizing and reducing latency overheads in the platform. The next set of our results is using the VM direct path I/O with QDR (40 Gigabits per second) IB and ESXi.

The bare-metal and VM over a wide range of message sizes use two different transfer mechanisms send and RDMA read respectively. We deliver equivalent bandwidth in the virtual case.

The **hybrid run time** (HRT, runtimes which run as kernel) latencies over a wide range of message sizes for bare-metal and virtual environment are different and depend on many factors. These results are generated using RDMA read operations. Using **quad data rate (QDR)** (40 gigabits per second) IB and ESXi, virtualization introduces about 0.7 microseconds of additional latency, which is significant at the smallest message sizes and less so for larger messages.

When using send/receive operations on the same hardware, ESXi latency overheads drop to about 0.4 microseconds and this disparity disappears for message sizes larger than 256 bytes. Again, the impact of these overheads on performance will depend entirely on the messaging characteristics of specific applications of interest. GPUs for computation, called **general-purpose GPUs (GPGPU)**, have promising results. Customers may be interested in Intel's offering in this area with their accelerator product, Intel Xeon Phi.

It is essential that the platform be tuned appropriately to support the required latency of these applications. We are being very transparent about what works well and what doesn't on our platform so that customers have an accurate understanding of the values and challenges of virtualizing HPC workloads and environments.

Summary

In this chapter, we discussed the specific features of virtualization that enhance the outcome of an HPC environment. We focused on unique features above and beyond a generic virtualization platform and looked at how virtualization addresses an improved scientific productivity. The impact of virtualization on the runtime of a particular simulation or calculation may have different results, but the overall performance of a compute deployment has optimum throughput.

This book will help you to align the operational goals of your customers with their business objectives. Readers will learn how IT organizations can achieve both operational and business goals by providing a secure and flexible digital foundation to their businesses by addressing the key business issues. They will learn how VMware products help customers to deliver consistent and stable IT performance to the business. VMware recommend leveraging hyper-converged, virtualized resources in a solution that works out of the box to speed the deployment of a fully-virtualized infrastructure.

Readers should now know how a fully-virtualized infrastructure allows them to accelerate deployments and unify and streamline operations, monitoring, and IT management, while also improving the ability to scale. A software-defined infrastructure enables us to unify and ease operations, monitoring, and IT management, while improving scalability. All the solutions mentioned in this book have taken a software-defined approach to building a private cloud, one that extends virtualization across the entire digital infrastructure (compute, storage, and networking) through common hardware, which is managed with common existing tools and skill sets.

Other Books You May Enjoy

If you enjoyed this book, you may be interested in these other books by Packt:

VMware Cross-Cloud Architecture
Ajit Pratap Kundan

ISBN: 978-1-78728-343-5

- Install and configure the Cloud foundation with Cross-Cloud services
- Configure vSphere high availability with the vCenter redundancy setup
- Architect and configure VMware with AWS Cloud
- Deploy VMware components in IBM Soft Layer
- Extend your DR setup with VMware to consume DRaaS
- Design and configure software-defined networking
- Implement compliance regulations to fix violations

VMware vSphere 6.5 Cookbook - Third Edition
Abhilash G B, Cedric Rajendran

ISBN: 978-1-78712-741-8

- Upgrade your existing vSphere environment or perform a fresh deployment
- Automate the deployment and management of large sets of ESXi hosts in your vSphere Environment
- Configure and manage FC, iSCSI, and NAS storage, and get more control over how storage resources are allocated and managed
- Configure vSphere networking by deploying host-wide and data center-wide switches in your vSphere environment
- Configure high availability on a host cluster and learn how to enable the fair distribution and utilization of compute resources
- Patch and upgrade the vSphere environment
- Handle certificate request generation and renew component certificates
- Monitor performance of a vSphere environment

Leave a review - let other readers know what you think

Please share your thoughts on this book with others by leaving a review on the site that you bought it from. If you purchased the book from Amazon, please leave us an honest review on this book's Amazon page. This is vital so that other potential readers can see and use your unbiased opinion to make purchasing decisions, we can understand what our customers think about our products, and our authors can see your feedback on the title that they have worked with Packt to create. It will only take a few minutes of your time, but is valuable to other potential customers, our authors, and Packt. Thank you!

Index

A

Access Policy Manager (APM) tool 129
Advanced Service Designer (ASD) forms 202
AMD I/O Virtualization (AMD-Vi or IOMMU) 13
App analytics
  for smart planning 59
AppDefense
  about 10, 113
  configuration plan 116
  deployment, environment preparation 117, 119, 120
  detailed implementation 116
  enhanced security 112
  globally expanding 108
application development life cycles 184
application scalability
  on vSAN 34
application security readiness
  transforming 110
application-centric alerting
  for SOC 109
application-specific integrated circuits (ASICs) 159
automation, with vRealize
  about 195
  infrastructure, deploying as code 197
  SDDC Content Life Cycle 196
Autoregressive Integrated Moving Average
  (ARIMA) 129

B

big data infrastructure
  about 264
  Hadoop, as service 264
big data virtualization
  on vSphere 263
BIG-IP DNS components

customizing 160
data center 160
DIG 161
listener 160
pool 161
server 160
virtual server 160
wide-IP 161
BIG-IP DNS high-level design 160
BIG-IP DNS load-balancing algorithm
  global availability 161
  ratio 161
  round robin 162
BIG-IP LTM objects
  node 162
  pool 162
  pool member 162
  virtual server 162
BMC Remedy IT Service Management (ITSM) 201
bring your own device (BYOD) 68
business and operations challenges
  overview 210, 211
  responsibilities, of service owner 212
  solutio, with service owners 212
Business Process Management (BPM) platform
  279

C

Canadian Institute For Advanced Research
  (CIFAR) 14
CapEx 278
CD pipeline
  about 185
  code 185
  commit 185
  plan 185
Challenge handshake authentication protocol

(CHAP) 277
CI pipeline
  about 185
  control stack 186
  feedback stack 186, 188
  planning 186
clarity 277
Cloud Pod Architecture (CPA) 75
Cloud Security Alliance (CSA) 190
Cloud Service Managers (CSMs) 214
cloud-native applications
  about 284
  automation, with containers 285
  characteristics 284
Code Stream
  about 198
  technical advantages 199
collective operations, MPI applications 311
command-line interface (CLI) 134
commercial off-the-shelf (COTS) software solution
  278
computational fluid dynamics (CFD) 311
container as a service (CaaS) 285
Container Networking Interface (CNI) 86
containerized ML applications
  in VM 16
containers
  about 285
  automation, performing with 285
  challenges 286
  use cases 286
content pack 134
Content-Based Read Cache (CRBC) 42
continuous deployment (CD) 16
continuous integration (CI) 16
Criminal Justice Information Services (CJIS) 190
cumulative functions 139
Custom data centers (CDCs) 129
Customer Experience Improvement Program
  (CEIP)
  about 40, 169, 179
  de-registration process 179

D

data loss prevention (DLP) 104
data movement
  across, Wavefront and Log Intelligence 127
destination NAT (DNAT) port forwarding 197
Device Service Clustering (DSC) 162
DevOps model
  capacity management 191, 192
  change management 189
  compliance management 190
  event management 191
  incident management 191
  release management 190
DirectPath I/O (DPIO) 14
Distributed Execution Manager (DEM) 231
distributed firewall (DFW) rules 181
Distributed Logical Router (DLR) 159
distributed resource manager (DRM) 300
Distributed Resource Scheduler (DRS) 133, 302

E

Elastic Container Service (ECS) 128
electronic design automation (EDA) chip designers
  306
Endpoint Detection and Response (EDR) 113
expanded Win32 app delivery 75

F

fault tolerance (FT) 39
Fault Tolerance Method 52
Federal Risk Authorization and Management
  Program (FedRAMP) 190
Foundational VMware NSX-T deployment 85
FTT policy
  with RAID configuration 52
Fully-Qualified Domain Name (FQDN) 160
functions as a service (FaaS) 285

G

General Data Protection Regulation (GDPR) 105,
  111, 190
General purpose Input Output (GPIO) 13
general-purpose GPUs (GPGPU) 312
Global Server Load Balancer (GSLB) 298

Google Cloud Platform (GCP) 82
GPU configuration
  equal share scheduler 17
  fixed share scheduler 17
GPU scalability
  in virtual environment 15
GPU usage, modes
  hardware-assisted I/O MMU virtualization 13
GPU usage
  modes 13

H

Hadoop architecture
  Hadoop File System (HDFS) 308
  Map 308
  Reduce 308
Hadoop Distributed File System (HDFS) 265
Hadoop journey
  categorizing 265
Hadoop virtualization
  automating application delivery for major media
    provider, use case 279
  benefits 278
  security and configuration isolation use case 279
hard disk drive (HDD) 37
hardware-accelerated graphics, configuration
  virtual machine settings, for vGPU 24
  Virtual Shared Graphics Acceleration 23
  vSGA settings, in virtual machine 24
Health Insurance Portability and Accountability Act
  (HIPPA) 190
high availability (HA)
  about 33
  configuration, in stretched clusters 45
  two-node clusters 46
High Performance Computing (HPC)
  about 146, 299
  technical requisites 299
high-performance computing cluster performances
  about 305, 306, 307
  HPC challenge benchmarks 311
  standard Hadoop architecture 308
  standard tests 309, 310
Horizon 18
Hortonworks Data Platform (HDP) 270

HPC applications
  high-performance computing cluster
    performances 305
  multi-tenancy, with guaranteed resources 301,
    302
  unification, critical use case 303, 305
  virtualizing 300
HPC benchmarks 311
HTTP Service 80
Hybrid Linked Mode (HLM) 96
hybrid run time (HRT) 312
hyperconverged infrastructure (HCI) 33, 105

I

I/O operations per second (IOPS) 34
IaaS solution, with vRealize Suite
  about 226
  business-level administration 227
  organizational grouping 228
  vRA deployment 230
Identity and Access Management (IAM) roles 228
identity service, executing
  VMware directory service 231
  VMware KDC service 232
  VMware Secure Token Service 232
InfiniBand (IB) 300
Infrastructure as a Service (IaaS) 285
infrastructure as code (IaC) 286
integrated deep insights 58
Intel Virtualization Technology for Directed I/O (VT-
  d) 13
intelligent automation driven
  conceptual designs 62, 63
  design requirements 61
intelligent log management, with vRealize Log
  Insight
  about 126
  Log Intelligence value propositions 126
intelligent monitoring 40
intelligent operational analytics
  about 78
  capacity planning 80
  critical success factors 81
  Kubernetes solution, from VMware 82
  vRealize Operations Manager architecture 79

International Organization for Standardization (ISO) 190
internet group management protocol (IGMP) 39
Internet of Things (IoT)
  about 237, 238
  use cases 238
internet small computer system interface (iSCSI) 39
IoT data center network security
  Hybrid cloud, for scale and distribution 260
  NSX distributed firewall 258
  prerequisites, to any automation 258, 259
IoT support
  enabling 246
  prerequisites, for configuration 245
  use cases, with VMware Pulse 253
  virtual machines, in OVA 245, 247, 248, 249, 250, 252, 253
IoT use cases, with VMware Pulse
  automotive industry 254
  entertainment 254
  financial industry 256
  internet of trains (transportation and logistics) 256
  parks 254
  resorts 254
  smart hospitals 254
  smart surveillance (higher education) 255
  smart warehouse (retail industry) 255
  smart weather forecasting 256
IP flow information export (IPFIX) 218
IT security
  innovating, Ops team 111
  innovating, with developers 110
  innovating, with security 110

J

Jenkins 200

K

key performance indicators (KPIs) 56
Knowledge Base (KB) 167, 213
Kubernetes as a service (KaaS) 82

L

Large Receive Offload (LRO) 304
Lattice Boltzmann Magneto-Hydrodynamics (LBMHD) 309
LBaaS design use cases
  LBaaS workflow 153
  load balancer, modifying 153
  multi-site load balancer, deploying 152
  single-site load balancer, deploying 152
  VM, de-provisioning 153
LBaaS LTM design
  BIG-IP LTM objects, configuring 162
  LTM virtual server, designing 164
  oad-balancing method, designing 163
LBaaS network design, with NSX 159
LBaaS workflow 154, 155
least privilege security
  for containerized applications 111
Lightweight Directory Access Protocol (LDAP) 135, 230
line of business (LOB) 73, 303
load balancer as a service (LBaaS)
  about 145
  design use cases 151
  overview 151
Local Traffic Manager (LTM) 152
Log Insight Interactive Analysis
  about 136
  events 137
  query, creating 137, 138
Log Insight user interface
  dashboard 133
  interactive analytics 133
Log Insight
  about 134
  indexing performance 135
  report export 135
  storage 135
  user experience 135
Log Intelligence (LInt)
  about 126
  audit log examples 130
  dashboard 130
  key benefits, for service providers 129

Log Intelligence metrics
  features 127
Log Intelligence value propositions 126

M

M10 28
machine learning (ML)
  about 9, 10
  virtualized GPUs, using with 11
machine learning as a service (MLaaS)
  about 145
  in private cloud 146
  technical requisites 145
  VMware approach 146
macOS adoption
  simplifying 75
massively-parallel processing (MPP) databases 265
Maximum transmission unit (MTU) 84
mean time between failures (MTBF) 81
mean time to repair (MTTR) 81
mean time to resolution (MTTR) 129
Message Passing Interface (MPI) 300, 311
Microsoft Office 365 (O365) applications
  security 75
ML workloads
  comparing, to GPU configurations 13
ML, with NVIDIA GPUs
  about 19
  pool and farm settings, in Horizon 19
ML-based data analysis 10
MLaaS, using vGPU 146
MLaaS, using vRealize Automation 146
MxGPU 28

N

NaaS operating model
  about 156, 157
  BIG-IP DNS high-level design 160
  BIG-IP DNS load-balancing algorithm 161
  LBaaS LTM design 162
  LBaaS network design, using NSX 159
NaaS service
  NaaS transformation discovery 158
  NaaS transformation envisioning 158

NAT topology 293
National Security Agency (NSA) 304
net promoter score (NPS) 168
network and security
  challenges 155
network as a service (NaaS)
  about 145
  used, for transforming traditional network 159
Network Filesystem Storage (NFS) 304
network functions virtualization (NFV) 277
network interface card (NIC) 37
Network time protocol (NTP) 84
network time protocol (NTP) 220
network transformation, with IoT
  technical requisites 238
NFS Storage 217
NO-NAT topology 293
non-uniform memory access (NUMA) 223, 301
non-volatile memory express (NVMe) 36
NSX 113
NSX Public Cloud Gateway (PCG) 228
NSX, for vSphere
  about 216
  ESXi hosts 216
NSX-T
  containerized workloads, deploying 85
  containerized workloads, executing 85
  deploying, for network virtualization on ESXi 84
  foundation, deploying 85
NVIDIA graphics cards 9
NVIDIA Grid 18
NVIDIA GRID Virtual Applications (vApp) 27
NVIDIA GRID Virtual PC (vPC) 27
NVIDIA GRID Virtual Workstation (vWS) 27
NVIDIA vGPU configuration
  on vSphere ESXi 147
NVIDIA VIB 18

O

open network automation platform (ONAP) 277
open source software
  about 276
  solutions, with CapEx 277
  solutions, with OpEx 277
open virtualization appliance (OVF) 173

open virtualization application (OVA) 86
Open vSwitch (OVS) 277
Operational Summary Report (OSR) 181, 213
OpEx 277

P

P2P messages 311
packets per second (pps) 128
Particle Mesh Ewald Molecular Dynamics
  (PMEMD) 309
Payment Card Industry (PCI) 190
PC lifecycle management (PCLM) 74
Peripheral Component Interconnect (PCI) 38
persistent volumes (PV) 296
Pivotal Application Service (PAS) 285
Pivotal Cloud Foundry (PCF) 285
Pivotal Container Service (PKS)
  about 82, 128, 217, 283
  deploying, for private cloud 84
PKS availability zone (AZ)
  about 289
  compute AZ 289
  management AZ 289
PKS component
  compute and storage requisites 288
PKS deployment, on vSphere
  CIDR, for nodes IP block 292
  about 287
  K8s master node 288
  PKS data plane 288
  PKS Management Plane 288
  PKS/NSX-T networks 291
  vSphere cluster configuration 290
  vSphere clusters 287
PKS design topologies 289
PKS/NSX-T logical topologies
  about 293
  datastores 297
  PKS and NSX-T communications 295
  PKS and NSX-T Edge Nodes and Edge Cluster
    294
  storage, for K8s cluster node VMs 296
  use cases, with different configurations 293
policies, IoT data center network security
  automate coherent perspective 258

automate remediation 258
Distributed firewall (DFW) 257
guest introspection 257
network introspection 258
pool and farm settings, in Horizon
  configuring 19, 21, 22
Portable Batch System (PBS) 300
prerequisites, Skyline Collector
  networking requirements 171, 172
  software requirements 170
proactive support technology, with Skyline
  about 166
  benefits 166
product-related data utilization
  about 180
  customer advocacy surveys, for new SDDC
    product releases 180
  customer profiles and advanced analytics 180
  customer support 180
  product deployment reports 180
  SDDC analysis 180
Pulse IoT Center infrastructure management
    blueprint
  about 241
  IoT data center network security 257
  IoT support, configuring 245
  OVA, configuring 242, 243, 244
  OVA, deploying 241

Q

quad data rate (QDR) 312
quality of service (QoS) 50, 133

R

remote direct memory access (RDMA) 299, 310
Representational State Transfer (REST) 139, 232
role-based access control (RBAC) 87
Ruby vSphere Console (RVC) 42
rugged devices
  extended management 76

S

SDDC Content Life Cycle
  configuration 196
  Production Tenant 196

vRO 196
    workflows 196
    Xenon 196
SDDC journey stages
    about 83
    business partner 83
    capabilities 83
    cost center 83
    service provider 83
    VMware container-based services 84
SDDC services
    about 215
    service catalog management 215
Secure Shell (SSH) 139
Secure Token Service (STS) 232
Security Operations Center (SOC) 190
security operations center (SOC) 101
securitySimple Object Access Protocol (SOAP) 76
Self-Service Portal (SSP) 152
Service Broker stage
    about 132
    capabilities 132
service catalog management
    cloud business management operations 215
    design 215
    development 215
    release 215
    service definition and automation 216
service foundation areas
    AR foundation 187
    CI foundation 187
    CM foundation 187
    COM foundation 188
    HC foundation 188
    release pipeline automation (CD) 187
    SCM foundation 186
    SDLC foundation 186
service level agreements (SLAs) 50
simple mail transfer protocol (SMTP) server 135
Simple Network Management Protocol (SNMP) 139
simple object access protocol (SOAP) 232
Single Root I/O Virtualization (SR-IOV) 299
Single Sign-On (SSO) 195
Site Recovery Manager (SRM) 219

Skyline Advisor 167
Skyline Collector
    about 167
    admin interface 174
    admin interface, configuring 177
    appliance 174
    auto-upgrade 178, 179
    client plugin, integrating 173
    downloading 169
    endpoints, managing 176
    linking, with My VMware account 176
    overview 170
    prerequisites 170
    user permissions 172, 173, 174
Skyline tool
    about 165
    proactive support technology 166
    release strategy 168
    viewer 168
Soft 3D 18
Software-Defined Data Center (SDDC) 77, 209, 237
solid state drives (SSDs) 37
Source Network Address Translation (SNAT) 197
Splunk Enterprise 134
standardize stage
    about 131
    capabilities 131
Storage Policy-Based Management (SPBM) 33
strategic partner stage 132, 133
Support Account Engineers (SAEs) 213
Support Account Managers (SAMs) 213
Support and Subscription Services (SnS) bookings 167
Support request (SR) deflection 166
System Center Configuration Manager (SCCM) 74

T

time to resolution (TTR) 213
total cost of ownership (TCO) 77, 133, 210
translation look-aside buffer (TLB) 305
transmission control protocol (TCP) 304
Transport Nodes (TN) 294
two-node clusters 46

U

unified end-to-end monitoring 78
unprecedented scale 128
User Account and Authentication (UAA) 86

V

vGPU 13
vGPU Manager 18
vGPU profile selection 17
vGPU profiles
  about 17
  knowledge and task user profiles 18
  power user and designer profiles 18
  vGPU hosts, adding to cluster with vGPU
    Manager 18
vGPU scheduling 17
virtual appliance (vApp) 79
Virtual Cloud Network (VCN) 216
Virtual Data Center Workstation (vDWS) 26
virtual data centers 224
Virtual data centers
  IaaS solution, with vRealize Suite 226
Virtual Dedicated Graphics Acceleration (vDGA)
  18
virtual desktop infrastructure (VDI) 233
Virtual Desktop Infrastructure (VDI) solution 12
Virtual Extensible LAN (VXLAN) 159
Virtual Function (VF) 31
virtual machine disk (VMDK) 52, 296
virtual machine settings, for vGPU
  configuring 24, 26
  GRID vApps capabilities 27
  GRID vPC capabilities 27
  GRID vWS, to Quadro vDWS 28
virtual machine
  configuring, with MxGPU and vDGA 28, 30
virtual machines (VMs) 241
virtual network interface cards (vNICs) 222
Virtual Private Clouds (VPCs) 27, 216
virtual reality as a service (vRAAS) 198
virtual resources
  configuration recommendations 224
Virtual Shared Graphics Acceleration (vSGA) 18
virtual storage area network (vSAN)

about 33, 75
  application scalability 34
  network assessment 34
  network design policy 37
  storage assessment 34
  storage design policy 35
virtualization technology (VT) 13
virtualization-based security (VBS) 114
virtualized GPUs
  using, with ML 11
VMKernel NIC (vmknic) 46
VMware 10
VMware Analytics Cloud (VAC) 167
VMware approach
  business outcome 105
VMware Boxer
  with Intelligent Workflows 75
VMware Certificate Authority (VMCA) 232
VMware Cloud (VMC) 190
VMware Cloud Foundation (VCF) 217
VMware Cloud operations stages
  about 131
  Service Broker 132
  standardize 131
  strategic partner 132
VMware Cloud
  configuring, on AWS 90
  hybrid-linked-mode testing functionality 95
  implementing, on AWS 89
  installing, on AWS 90
  on AWS 86
  on AWS differs from on-premises vSphere 87
  on AWS disaster recovery 87
  on AWS implementation plan 88
  operating procedures, on AWS 90
  support 97
  troubleshooting 97
VMware Health Analyzer (vHA) 35
VMware Hybrid Cloud Extension (HCX) 87
VMware Infrastructure Planner (VIP) 152
VMware innovation
  for application security 102
  intelligent government workflows, with
    automation 104
  network, transforming 105

security, transforming 105
transforming, into digital government 103
VMware Integrated OpenStack (VIO) 131
VMware Kubernetes Engine (VKE) 82, 183
VMware product technical data
    configuration data 179
    feature-related data 180
    performance data 180
    product log data 180
VMware Pulse IoT Center
    about 239
    queries 239, 240
VMware technical support operations
    NSX for vSphere 216
    recommendations with priority 219
    recommendations with priority 1 219
    recommendations with priority 2 221
    recommendations with priority 3 223
    SDDC services 215
    transforming 213
VMware Validated Designs (VVDs) 213
VMware VDI solution 12
VMware vRealize Network Insight
    data collecting ways 140
VMware VRealize Business (vRB) 130
VMware vRealize Code Stream (vRCS)
    about 183, 198
    Pipeline automation model 201
    technical requisites 184
VMware vRealize Network Insight
    about 139
    supported data sources 140
VMware vRealize Orchestrator (vRO) 151
VMware vSphere Big Data Extensions (BDE)
    about 264
    BDE appliance, deploying 266, 267
    BDE plugin 268, 270
    configuring 267
    distributions, configuring 270
    Hadoop plugin, in vRO 271, 273, 275
VMware, network design policy
    best practices recommendations 38
    Customer Experience Improvement
        Program/vSAN ReadyCare 39
VMware, storage design policy

best practices recommendations 35
vRA deployment
    complete solution, with desired result 233
    services, executing as part of identity service
        231
    vRA appliance communication 230
vRA provisioning
    base Linux image 197
    base Windows image 197
    Linux linked clone component 197
    multi-machine blueprint 197
    Windows linked clone component 197
vRCS deployment architecture
    about 201, 202
    system architecture 202, 203, 204
    vRCS, integrating with standalone vRA 205
vRealize Automation
    blueprint, customizing 147, 148, 149, 150
    catalog, for software provisioning 189
vRealize Network Insight (vRNI) 217
vRealize Operations Manager (vROP) 223
vRealize Operations Manager architecture
    about 79
    overview 80
vRealize Operations Manager monitoring
    about 42
    business benefits 43
    business outcomes, challenges affecting 43
    log intelligence advantages 44
    technical issues 44
    technical solution 44
vSAN cluster
    configuring 47
    witness appliance 46
vSAN environment monitoring
    general monitoring practices 41
    vRealize Operations Manager monitoring 42
    vSAN Health Check plugin 41
    vSAN Observer 42
vSAN Health Check plugin 41
vSAN Observer 42
vSAN policy design
    business objectives, policy defining 50
    with SPBM 50
vSphere cluster groups 287

vSphere DirectPath I/O 13
vSphere Distributed Switch (VDS) 38, 222, 224
vSphere high availability 17
vSphere Installation Bundle (VIB) 224
vSphere Integrated Containers
  Docker container hosts 16
  virtual container hosts 16
vSphere vMotion 17

W

Wavefront
  about 128, 193
  dashboard 193, 194
  people working, monitoring for insights 194
Windows Communication Foundation (WCF) 76
witness traffic separation (WTS) 46
Workspace 10
Workspace ONE Intelligence
  about 56
  adoption of productivity apps, tracking 72
  App analytics, for smart planning 59
  business objectives 57
  compliance, increasing across Windows 10

  devices 71
  device utilization, monitoring 70
  integrated deep insights 58
  intelligent automation driven, by decision engines 60
  internal mobile apps, adopting 72
  migration of productivity apps, tracking 72
  mobile app deployment visibility, comprehensive 71
  mobile OS vulnerabilities, identifying 68
  mobile OS vulnerabilities, mitigating 68
  OS upgrade progress, tracking 70
  unsupported OS platforms, identifying 69
  unsupported OS versions, identifying 69
  usage, monitoring 70
  use cases 68
  Windows 10 Dell battery failures, predicting 69
  Windows 10 OS patches, insights 69
  Windows 10 OS updates, insights 69
Workspace ONE platform updates 74
Workspace ONE Trust Network
  about 73
  Workspace ONE AirLift 74

www.ingramcontent.com/pod-product-compliance
Lightning Source LLC
Chambersburg PA
CBHW080620060326
40690CB00021B/4759